THE ARCHDUKE AND THE ASSASSIN

Also by Lavender Cassels:

The Struggle for the Ottoman Empire 1717–1740
Clash of Generations

THE ARCHDUKE

AND

THE

ASSASSIN

SARAJEVO, JUNE 28th 1914

Lavender Cassels

STEIN AND DAY/*Publishers*/New York

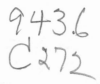

FOR ALL THE SOPHIES

First published in the United States of America in 1985
Copyright © 1984 by Lavender Cassels
All rights reserved, Stein and Day, Incorporated
Printed in the United States of America
STEIN AND DAY/*Publishers*
Scarborough House
Briarcliff Manor, N.Y. 10510

Library of Congress Cataloging in Publication Data

Cassels, Lavender, 1916-
  The archduke and the assassin.

Bibliography: p.
Includes index.
  1. Franz Ferdinand, Archduke of Austria, 1863-1914—
Assassination. 2. Princip, Gavrilo, 1894-1918.
3. Austria—Politics and government—1867-1918.
4. World War, 1914-1918—Causes. 5. Austria—Princes and
princesses—Biography. I. Title.
DB89.F7C37   1985   943.6′04′0924   84-40709
ISBN 0-8128-3021-0

Contents

Prologue: The House of Habsburg *1*

————————PART ONE————————
Archduke Franz Ferdinand

1 An Archduke of no interest *7*
2 Uncle and Nephew *18*
3 Illness *28*
4 Marriage *38*
5 Frustration *53*

————————PART TWO————————
The Monarchy and the South Slavs

6 The emergent South Slav threat *63*
7 Bosnia and Hercegovina: the world of Gavrilo Princip *70*
8 The Annexation of Bosnia and Hercegovina *79*
9 The Post-annexation Crisis *92*
10 A Man called Stefanović *101*
11 "The Smell of Blood" *110*
12 "History sometimes moves too slowly: it needs a push" *117*
13 South Slav imbroglio *131*

————————PART THREE————————
Encounter at Sarajevo

14 Decision making *143*
15 The Assassins and their Target *150*
16 On Stage in Sarajevo *165*
17 Sunday June 28th 1914 *172*

Epilogue: "The End of the Story" *181*

Sources *195*
Reference Notes *197*
Selected Bibliography *208*
Index *213*

Illustrations

Map (page 4): The Habsburg Monarchy in 1914.

Franz Ferdinand and Sophie shortly after their marriage. *Erzherzog Franz Ferdinand Museum, Artstetten*

Franz Ferdinand with his wife and children in the music room of the Belvedere, 1910. *Österreichische Nationalbibliothek, Bildarchiv*

Emperor Franz Joseph in 1910. *Österreichische Nationalbibliothek, Bildarchiv*

Janaczek in his House Steward's uniform. *Countess Nostitz, private collection*

Konopischt. *Countess Nostitz, private collection*

Alexander Brosch von Aarenau. *Österreichisches Staatsarchiv-Kriegsarchiv*

Franz Conrad von Hötzendorf. *Österreichische Nationalbibliothek, Bildarchiv*

Alois Aehrenthal. *Österreichische Nationalbibliothek, Bildarchiv*

Oskar Potiorek. *Österreichische Nationalbibliothek, Bildarchiv*

Kaiser Wilhelm II with Franz Ferdinand in the garden at Konopischt, June 1914. *Countess Nostitz, private collection*

Map: Franz Ferdinand and his assassins routes to Sarajevo.

Sarajevo: the Appel Quay is on the right bank of the river. *Österreichische Nationalbibliothek, Bildarchiv*

28th June 1914: Franz Ferdinand and Sophie leaving their train at Sarajevo. *Österreichische Nationalbibliothek, Bildarchiv*

28th June 1914: the departure of Franz Ferdinand and his wife from Sarajevo Town Hall, with Count Harrach standing on the running board of their car. *Österreichische Nationalbibliothek, Bildarchiv*

Map: Franz Ferdinand's route through Sarajevo and the location along it of Princip and his associates.

28th June 1914: Franz Ferdinand's car on the Appel Quay a few seconds before the assassination. *Österreichische Nationalbibliothek, Bildarchiv*

Left to right: Nedeljko Čabrinović, Milan Ciganović and Gavrilo Princip in a Belgrade park, spring 1914. *Österreichische Nationalbibliothek, Bildarchiv*

Gavrilo Princip after his arrest. *Österreichische Nationalbibliothek, Bildarchiv*

The trial in Sarajevo of those involved in Franz Ferdinand's assassination: *Front row, left to right,* Grabež, Čabrinović, Princip, Ilić, Veljko Čubrilović. *Second row,* Miško Jovanović, Jakov Milović. *Österreichisches Staatarchiv-Kriegsarchiv*

Foreword
and
Acknowledgements

THE assassination at Sarajevo on June 28th 1914 of Archduke Franz Ferdinand, the heir to the Habsburg throne, by Gavrilo Princip, a nineteen-year-old Bosnian student, triggered off a chain reaction amongst the Powers of Europe which resulted in the Great War of 1914-1918, and this in turn led to the Second World War of 1939-1945. No political assassination has affected the lives of more of the human race. This book describes the personalities of the Archduke and the student, the influences which shaped their characters, the sequence of events which culminated in their encounter at Sarajevo, and the circumstances of that encounter, the consequences of which are with us today.

*　　*　　*

Amongst the people in Austria who helped me, I am especially indebted to Countess Sophie Nostitz-Rieneck, Archduke Franz Ferdinand's daughter, for the care and patience with which she answered my many questions during our long discussions, for making available to me the typescript memoir by Baron von Morsey, a member of the Archduke's staff who was with him at Sarajevo, for all the support which she gave me. I owe her a very great deal.

I thank Fürst Albrecht Hohenberg for granting me access to the *Erzherzog Franz Ferdinand Nachlass*, the collection of the Archduke's papers in the Vienna Haus-Hof- und Staatsarchiv; Count Romée d'Harambure, for his assistance with illustrations and permission to reproduce a photograph of the Archduke and his wife which is in the Erzherzog Franz Ferdinand Museum at Artstetten, and Count Wladimir Aichelburg, the historical adviser to the Museum, who generously gave me the benefit of his knowledge.

The officials of the Austrian State Archives were – as always – unfailingly helpful. In particular I wish to thank Hofrat Dr Anna Benna of the Haus-Hof-und Staatsarchiv, and Dr Rainer Egger, Dr Peter Broucek, and Hofrat Dr Edith Wohlgemuth of the Kriegsarchiv, for the time which they devoted to dealing with my queries, and for directing my attention to documents which I would otherwise have overlooked.

In London I received assistance from the librarian of the Austrian Institute and the staff of the Institute of Historical Research for which I am most grateful. The only adequate way in which I can acknowledge my debt to the London Library is to say that without it, and the help given me by its staff, my task would have been immeasurably more difficult.

Finally I thank many friends, in Austria and in England, for their forbearance with the demands which research and writing made on my time, and their sustaining encouragement.

Prologue
The House of Habsburg

FOR over six hundred years most of the area which now comprises the Republic of Austria was ruled by one family, the Habsburgs. In the thirteenth century it was the eastern bastion of the Holy Roman Empire, wedged between two predatory neighbours, the Slav Kingdom of Bohemia and the Magyar Kingdom of Hungary. The Habsburgs established themselves there in 1282 after Rudolf von Habsburg, a minor German Count elected Holy Roman Emperor by the German Princes because they thought he was too weak to dominate them, defeated and killed the King of Bohemia who had usurped this Imperial fief.

The Habsburgs held on precariously in Austria for two hundred years, small fry amongst their contemporaries. Then they acquired great possessions – the Kingdoms of Spain and Naples, the Duchies of Burgundy and Milan, the Crowns of Hungary and Bohemia. By 1527 their empire was a power in Europe.

In 1882 by command of Franz Joseph I, ruler of this realm now entitled the Austro-Hungarian Monarchy, the six hundredth anniversary of the founding of the dynasty, the House of Austria, was celebrated. Its record was remarkable. The Habsburgs had maintained a special relationship with Germany for over four hundred and fifty years, from 1438 until 1806 except for a short interval in the eighteenth century, as Holy Roman Emperors of the German 'nation', then after Napoleon dissolved the Holy Roman Empire, as Presidents of the German Confederation, finally after the Confederation was destroyed by Prussia, by a close alliance with the new German Empire which replaced it. The Habsburg dynasty was the oldest in Europe. France, with whose Kings and Emperors they had waged a power struggle since the second half of the fifteenth century, was now a Republic; the Habsburgs had retained their throne. The Turkish Empire, whose armies had twice reached the gates of Vienna and for a hundred and fifty years occupied most of Hungary, was in decay; although the Habsburgs had gradually lost their possessions in Western Europe and Italy their realm was still vast, stretching from the Swiss frontier to beyond the Carpathians, inhabited by over thirty-six million people, and ranked as a Great Power.

It had never been an ethnic entity; Habsburg sovereignty was the only bond between the different nationalities which it contained (there were eleven in 1882). In the exercise of that sovereignty, generations of Emperors were sustained by the belief that God had entrusted their House with a mission to rule, and that this imposed on them two obligations. The first of these was to defend their multinational domain, which they regarded as their dynastic property, and when possible to enlarge it. The second was to bear the sole responsibility for the destiny and welfare of their subjects. They were convinced that in carrying out these obligations they were answerable only to their consciences before God. Imbued with this sense of mission, convinced that it set their dynasty above and apart from the rest of the world, Habsburg rulers did not attempt to play to the gallery. Their appearances on State occasions were surrounded by a ceremonial splendour, rooted in tradition, but they were never flamboyant. In Paris there is an equestrian statue of Louis XIV as a victorious Caesar. In Vienna on a monument which he commissioned in thanksgiving for the delivery of the city from the plague, Louis's contemporary and opponent Leopold I is shown kneeling before the Trinity.

Most of the Habsburg territories were acquired by marriage, inheritance or treaty settlements. Fear of hazarding the fortunes of their House by war more than was absolutely necessary was an outstanding family trait. They were professional rulers and political realists, few of whom went in for bold deeds or innovations. Their tendency was to weigh up carefully the consequence of each step and, if it failed, batten down and gather strength to recoup the loss. However dire that might be, their belief in their mission remained unshaken. In 1741 when the Austrians, attacked by the Prussians, the French and the Bavarians, lost Prague, their Sovereign Maria Theresa, who had only been on the throne for a year, wrote to Prince Kinsky her Bohemian Chancellor

> So Prague is lost and perhaps even worse will follow . . . only courage can save Bohemia and the Queen . . . .. My own resolve is taken: to stake everything, win or lose, on saving Bohemia . . . .. It may involve destructions and desolation which twenty years will be insufficient to restore; but I must hold the country and the soil, and for this all my armies, all the Hungarians, shall die before I surrender an inch of it . . . .. You will say that I am cruel; that is true. But I know that all the cruelties I commit today to hold the country I shall one day be in a position to make good a hundred-fold. And this I shall do.

Maria Theresa was then twenty-four. Her courage, tenacity, and belief in her high calling prevailed: two years later she was crowned Queen of Bohemia in Prague. These attributes ran in the family. Together with the built in capacity of the Habsburgs to survive, they enabled the dynasty to achieve its six hundredth anniversary in 1882.

The history of the Habsburgs is imprinted on the landscape of Austria –

fortified strongholds built to repel the Turks, baroque monasteries and churches glorifying the victory of their Catholic dynasty in the Counter Reformation, castles, great houses, hunting forests – palaces in Vienna, of the Imperial Family, of the nobility, some of them foreigners who entered the service of these supranational rulers and contributed to their greatest triumphs. By 1882 a boulevard, the Ringstrasse, had been laid out on the site of the old fortifications encircling the Inner City. Adjacent to it, completed or in the course of construction, were museums to house the art and other collections assembled by generations of Habsburgs, a new Court theatre, a vast extension to the Emperor's palace, the Hofburg. Imperial Vienna, the city which had grown out of the frontier town which the Habsburgs captured from the Slavs, was being restructured into a capital appropriate to a family which had ruled for six hundred years and now looked forward to the twentieth century.

But within four decades there was another encounter between Habsburg and Slav. It did not take place on the battlefield: its outcome was fatal to the dynasty. It involved two people – a Slav student aged nineteen, and Archduke Franz Ferdinand, the heir to the Imperial throne.

THE HABSBURG MONARCHY IN 1914

Key
Frontiers of the Monarchy in 1914
Boundary of the Hungarian half of the Monarchy

0   100   200 km
0   100 miles

RUSSIAN EMPIRE

GERMAN EMPIRE

BLACK SEA

OTTOMAN EMPIRE

Constantinople

AEGEAN SEA

GREECE

Salonica

ALBANIA

BULGARIA

ROUMANIA

BUKO-VINA

GALICIA

RUTHENIA

TRANSYLVANIA

KINGDOM OF HUNGARY

SLOVAKIA

R. Danube

Budapest

Belgrade

R. Danube

SERBIA

R. Drina

MONTE-NEGRO

Sarajevo

BOSNIA

HERCEGOVINA

Mostar

Ragusa

DALMATIA

Zara

R. Save

Krajina

CROATIA

Agram

R. Drave

Fiume

KRAIN

BOHEMIA

Prague

Königgrätz

Konopischt

Chlumetz

Artstetten

MORAVIA

Vienna

R. Danube

AUSTRIA

STYRIA

Graz

CARINTHIA

Salzburg

Innsbruck

TYROL

Trieste

ADRIATIC SEA

ITALY

Part One
Archduke Franz Ferdinand

An Archduke of no interest

FRANZ Joseph I, "by God's grace" Emperor of Austria, King of Jerusalem, Apostolic King of Hungary, King of Bohemia, Galicia, Lodomeria, Illyria and Croatia, Archduke of Austria, and Duke, Markgraf, Prince or Count of some thirty other places in his multinational empire, required members of his family to be present at important public ceremonies. When in 1888 he unveiled a statue beside the Ringstrasse in Vienna of his great ancestress Maria Theresa, sixty-seven of them turned out in what has been described as the last great dynastic parade. To the citizens of the capital who gathered to watch the ceremony, the Archdukes as they arrived in their carriages were enviable and privileged beings, but there were no cheers for them – cheers were reserved for the Emperor on whom the attention of every spectator was focused. Tall, still at the age of fifty-seven with the straight back of a fine horseman, his uniform, a white tunic and scarlet trousers, was sober by comparison with the splendour of his escort of Life Guards. But he carried himself with an air of effortless majesty, and beside him the younger Archdukes seemed to be uninteresting nonentities, notable only for the living proof which they provided that the continuation of the dynasty was assured.

One such apparently uninteresting young Archduke was Franz Ferdinand, the eldest son of the Emperor's brother Karl Ludwig. Born on December 18th 1863, his mother, a daughter of the Bourbon King of Sicily, died of tuberculosis when he was seven. Two years later his father married Maria Theresia of Braganza who, although only eighteen, by her warmth and understanding soon won the affection of her stepchildren. As everyone from the Emperor downwards came to agree, she was an exceptionally nice woman; Franz Ferdinand, who always addressed her as "Dearest Mama", was devoted to her. He was also fond of his father, of whom he saw a good deal, for Karl Ludwig avoided Court and public functions as much as possible. A devout Catholic, he was a man of conservative ideas but wide interests, an active supporter of the associations connected with the arts and learned societies of which he was patron. The family spent part of the winter in Vienna, and during the rest of the year

7

migrated between Schloss Persenbeug on the Danube, Artstetten set in rolling hills a few miles back from the river where, at a time when no such amenity existed in the Hofburg, Karl Ludwig installed a very large blue tiled bath, and Villa Wartholz, an unpretentious country house near Reichenau at the foot of the mountains about forty miles south of Vienna.

Franz Ferdinand, although somewhat serious and reserved as a child, got on well with his brothers and sisters, and they were a happy united family. Amusements included excursions in a donkey cart and amateur theatricals. He grew mushrooms, was allowed to keep rabbits and, while still a small boy, began to collect any objects which took his fancy. If he saw something which he liked, he wanted to possess it; acquisitiveness, of which he had a strong streak, was a Habsburg trait. He was taught to ride, about which he was not enthusiastic – he never became an outstanding horseman – but shooting he much enjoyed, for at this from an early age he excelled.

Lessons were not at all enjoyable. The standard education for Archdukes was instruction at home by private tutors, which no children of lesser birth could be imported to share. Franz Ferdinand was therefore boxed up with his brother Otto to work through a curriculum drawn up by their father. The principal subjects which Karl Ludwig thought important were history, the history of art, languages and, above all, religion. Later he added military studies, mathematics, and natural science. This programme was supervised by Count Degenfeld, an army officer to whom was also assigned the task of increasing the Archduke's knowledge of the world, how is a mystery in view of the segregated existence of his charge. Franz Ferdinand was backward for his age, had no power of concentration, no talent for languages, no aptitude for mathematics, and was uninterested in literature. His tutors complained that he was often sulky and inattentive. He later described his education as "a treadmill", one lesson succeeding another, hour after hour, from early morning until late evening.

In April 1878, when he was fourteen and a half, the prospect opened up of an eventual escape from this treadmill. Franz Ferdinand wrote a delighted letter about it to his stepmother

> . . . I had to write to the Emperor for as you will already know I have become a Lieutenant. I heard about it yesterday. I was to have been appointed Colonel in Regiment No 32, but Papa was against this and so I have been appointed to the regiment as a Lieutenant. It is a Hungarian regiment and its uniform is sky blue with yellow buttons . . .. Everything has already been ordered, uniform, coat, shako, gloves, sword etc. I am writing this letter to you wearing long trousers.

He signed himself proudly "Your most obedient son Franz, k.k. Lieutenant". But there was no question of sending him to an army cadet school. Tutorial instruction at home continued for over five years.

8

In November 1883, a month before his twentieth birthday, the Archduke's studies at last ended. By then it was apparent that, while he seemed to find difficulty in learning from books, he had exceptional powers of observation. Since natural history and the history of art and architecture related to objects which he could see for himself, his tutors in these subjects found it comparatively easy to arouse his interest in them; he retained it throughout his life. Gottfried Marschall, the Court chaplain, a clever ambitious priest appointed by Karl Ludwig to teach his son religion, also had an easy task. His pupil accepted without question that the Catholic faith, in the tenets of which he received a thorough grounding, provided the answer to all life's problems. The history which Franz Ferdinand learnt from Onno Klopp dovetailed with his religious instruction. Klopp, his history tutor, was a recent and ardent convert to Catholicism, to whom Protestant beliefs were detestable and any form of liberal thinking anathema. He dwelt on the divinely appointed mission of the Catholic House of Habsburg and its glorious past achievements, its defence of the eastern bastion of Christendom against the Turks, its triumphs in the Counter Reformation. Generally his teaching reflected his convert's bias, and the historical knowledge which the Archduke assimilated from him was therefore patchy.

No doubt Franz Ferdinand was told by his father as well as by his tutors of the disarray within the Monarchy when, in December 1848 at the age of eighteen, his uncle the Emperor succeeded to the throne and a conglomerate of an inheritance, which then included Lombardy and Venetia in northern Italy. During 1848 there had been popular uprisings throughout the Monarchy demanding political liberty and self determination and, in 1849, the Hungarian rebels led by Ludwig Kossuth followed up their declaration of independence by a proclamation deposing "the perjured House of Habsburg Lorraine . . . for ever". Troops had to be used to reassert Imperial authority and it took a year to restore order. No doubt too the Archduke heard grown ups discussing the battles of Solferino and Königgrätz; the former took place in 1859, and the latter in 1866 when he was three. At Solferino, Franz Joseph, in personal command of his army, was defeated by the French and Piedmontese, who had joined forces to liberate Lombardy and Venetia from Austrian rule. At Königgrätz the Imperial army was beaten by the Prussians, determined to end the primacy of the House of Habsburg amongst the German princes. As a result of these defeats Austria was ousted from the Italian peninsula – Lombardy, Venetia, and the Duchies of Tuscany, Parma and Modena, whose rulers were members of cadet branches of the Habsburgs, were incorporated in the new kingdom of Italy – and finally excluded from Germany.

Of the effect of Solferino and Königgrätz on the internal structure of the Monarchy, Franz Ferdinand began to learn at the age of nineteen, when Max Vladimir Beck, a young lawyer and civil servant, was appointed by his father to teach him constitutional law. Solferino compelled the Emperor, who until

9

then had ruled as an autocrat, to promulgate a constitution, because the exchequer was empty and no foreign loans could be raised without public control of the budget. Königgrätz forced him to concede a special status to the Hungarians, that section of the inhabitants of Hungary who spoke the Magyar language and who, although numerically in the minority, regarded all other races living within its frontiers as their vassals. They looked back to A.D. 1000 when their kingdom was founded by St Stephen, and acknowledged no King as legitimate unless he had been crowned in Budapest with St Stephen's holy crown. After their liberation by the Habsburgs from the Turks at the end of the seventeenth century, the Hungarians recognised the Habsburg Emperor as their King, and he in returned pledged himself to respect their rights, privileges and institutions. Thereafter they enjoyed and jealously guarded these, bitterly resented the loss of them after their revolt in 1848-49, and never ceased to demand them back. For several years before the outbreak of the war with Prussia in 1866, they had been refusing to send delegates to the central Parliament, or to pay taxes to Vienna. The *Ausgleich* – the Compromise – by which the Emperor reached a settlement with them in 1867, was a bilateral contract concluded directly between the Crown and the Hungarians. It established Hungary as a kingdom with internal autonomy, and left the remainder of the Habsburg lands as a loose federation nominally governed by a Parliament in Vienna. Outwardly, so far as foreign affairs, defence and finances were concerned Franz Joseph's domain, now renamed the Austro-Hungarian Monarchy (although still referred to for purposes of abbreviation as Austria) remained a unity; internally it was split in two.

At the age of nineteen as an aspiring officer, Franz Ferdinand was probably more interested in accounts of the performance of the army at Solferino and Königgrätz than in Beck's exposition of the legal complexities of the *Ausgleich*. The latter's verdict on his pupil was that he had taken in "at least something" of what he had been taught about constitutional law. The Archduke later said that Beck was the only tutor who had taught him anything, complaining that otherwise, because his education had been badly planned, he had "learnt everything and knew nothing". Unfortunately what he had not learnt was to think methodically or objectively.

When on December 18th 1883, his twentieth birthday, the Archduke was declared of age, he was given an attested copy of another law in which he had received no instruction from Beck. This was the Habsburg *Familien Statut* or Family Law codifying the Emperor's authority over the Imperial Family, which was defined in it as consisting of all the Archdukes (and their wives and widows), and Archduchesses, descended in the male line from Empress Maria Theresa. It had been promulgated in 1839 in the reign of Franz Joseph's predecessor Ferdinand I, its premise being that since the Crown was the only link between the nationalities in the Monarchy, and was vested in the House of Habsburg, it was imperative that all members of that House should present a united front in support of the Emperor, that he should have power over them to enforce this, and that they should be left in no doubt whatsoever of where they stood. Clause 3a, for example, stated that although they were entitled to all the public honours and privileges appropriate to members of the Imperial House, the Emperor could at any time command that these should be suspended. The rest of the Law was framed with the same object, to make it clear to all Archdukes and Archduchesses that they were dependent on his favour as head of the family, and that to enjoy it they must conform to his orders.

What the Emperor could decree was fully set out, and gave him more power over members of his family than the law of the land could exert over his subjects. Any of them who wished to marry had first to obtain his consent and, if they persisted in doing so without it, not only forfeited their rights and privileges for themselves and their children, but their marriage so far as the Emperor was concerned was "null and void". He could banish, place under police surveillance, or take such action as he saw fit against any member of the family whose behaviour he considered warranted it, and in all disciplinary matters his decision was final. Since he controlled the *Familien Fond* or family fortune of the House of Habsburg, and had the power to distribute up to two-thirds of the fund's substantial income amongst such members of the family as he might select, he was in a position to apply financial sanctions to any Archduke who misbehaved. The State had no power to interfere with the Family Law, which made the Emperor both judge and jury in all matters concerning his relations, who under it enjoyed no rights, only privileges conferred by his grace. None of them ever dared suggest to Franz Joseph that it should in any way be modified.

It is unlikely that any thought that the Family Law could or should be modified crossed Franz Ferdinand's mind when he was declared of age; he had been taught to accept without question that the Emperor's authority as head of the family was absolute. The Law stipulated that the wives of Archdukes must be of "equal birth", a restriction which meant that he could only marry a girl whose father was a member of a reigning dynasty, or of a short list of German princely houses. But marriage was of no immediate interest to him, nor did the knowledge that he was third in succession to the throne after Crown Prince Rudolf and his father Karl Ludwig weigh upon him. That he might one day become ruler of the Monarchy seemed improbable: the Emperor was only fifty-three and in excellent health, and Rudolf, married in 1881, already had a daughter and might well have a son. The Archduke was far more enthralled by the immediate prospect before him. He was about to join the 4th Dragoons and would no longer live at home, tutors were relegated to the past, the curtain was going up on the world.

Franz Ferdinand was now a tall lanky young man. His brown hair was parted in the centre and he had grown a moustache and side whiskers. He looked rather weedy and was not handsome, his best feature being his clear steel blue eyes. When he was presented by Karl Ludwig (who stressed that he wished his son to receive a "thorough military training") to the senior officers of the Dragoons, he did not give the impression of being either physically or mentally tough. The Archduke was in fact shy and unsure of himself, uncomfortably aware that he would be serving with officers even the most junior of whom knew a great deal more than he did, having started their military training at army cadet schools while in their early teens. But after joining the regiment, which was stationed at Enns not far from Artstetten, Franz Ferdinand's apprehensions soon vanished. His brother officers were easy going, cheerful and friendly, and his duties were interesting but not arduous. He later said that his time with the 4th Dragoons was the happiest of his life.

An annual report was made on every officer in the Austrian army, Archdukes included. The concoction of this presented a problem to any senior officer who had a member of the Imperial Family under his command for, if he valued his career, their shortcomings must be glossed over. At the end of 1884, after Franz Ferdinand had been with his regiment for a year, his Colonel reported that the Archduke was quick to grasp the essential of a situation and showed considerable military talent, an appraisal which his next commanding officer was to endorse. What he omitted to say, was that His Imperial Highness was rather too frequently absenting himself to shoot or to go to Vienna.

Franz Ferdinand was required to be in Vienna for Court ceremonial occasions, not because he was third in line to the succession to the throne, a fact to which Franz Joseph paid no apparent attention, but because the Emperor believed that *en masse* appearances of the Imperial Family contributed to the prestige of the dynasty. Every year at the Hofball, for example, all the Archdukes and Archduchesses who could be mustered had to form up, in strict order of seniority, to enter the Rittersaal of the Hofburg in procession at 8.30 p.m. precisely. The scene in the ballroom was dazzling. The uniforms of the officers of the best dressed army in Europe and the attire of the nobility of the Monarchy were a galaxy of colour – scarlet, black frogged with gold, purple, green, white, sky blue – the men glittering with orders and decorations, their wives bedizened with jewellery. But this did not compensate for the fact that many of the guests – members of the high aristocracy whose sixteen quarterings gave them the right of entrée at Court, diplomats, Privy Councillors and senior officials – were elderly and dull. The possibility of dancing offered some escape from the tedium of making conversation to them, but the dances were timed with military precision and, with the exception of the quadrille, short – seven minutes for a waltz, five minutes for a polka – and there was nowhere to sit out. At supper each Archduke had to preside over one of the small tables at which it was served, and rigid protocol demanded that the same people sat next to one another year after year. The food left a great deal to be desired – it was rumoured that the soup, which was disgusting, was brewed up from a three hundred year old recipe – and the heat was stifling.

Attendance at the Hofball or other Court ceremonies was a chore. So were the family dinner parties which the Emperor gave at intervals during the winter. The atmosphere at them was not convivial. Franz Joseph, no conversationalist at the best of times, tended to be more than usually monosyllabic. The number of subjects which could safely be discussed was limited and, since the Emperor was served first, ate rapidly, and all the plates were removed as soon as he had finished a course, young Archdukes such as Franz Ferdinand at the bottom of the table were liable to go hungry. They regarded family dinner parties with the same lack of enthusiasm as a visit to the dentist.

Attendance at Court and family dinner parties were not, however, the only reasons for Franz Ferdinand's visits to Vienna. One delighted foreigner wrote of that city "I doubt if one could enjoy oneself more in Paradise"; no other capital in Europe was so easy going and above all *gemütlich*. The adjective *gemütlich* is untranslatable. It is a compound of agreeable, cosy, tolerant, warm hearted and there is a hint of kindly laughter in it. It conjures up pictures of golden autumn days, light shining on a glass of wine, the comforting warmth of a tiled stove; it conveys an impression of live and let live and immediate pleasure in simple things. This sense of well being pervaded Vienna and was engendered by its citizens. To the Viennese, as they sang and danced to the music of Johann Strauss, their uncrowned king, only today mattered; the morrow would take care of itself, and as for the past, "happy is he who forgets what cannot be changed"; romance was the salt of life, but the end of a love affair no cause for a broken heart. Theirs was a world far removed from the Court and what Franz Ferdinand considered to be its "outworn ceremonial", about which there was nothing which could be remotely described as *gemütlich*. But, provided there was no scandal, the Emperor had no objection to an Archduke occasionally escaping into it, to spend an evening incognito with an attractive ballet dancer or actress.

It is likely that his brother Otto, extrovert, charming, the prototype of a dashing cavalry officer, had a hand in initiating Franz Ferdinand into this world. He found it delightful, and his visits to Vienna became more frequent. Inevitably there was some gossip about parties organised by Otto, which lasted until the early hours of the morning, and the girls at which were more entertaining than the young *Contessen* of impeccable lineage at the Hofball. But there was no hint that the Archduke's behaviour was in any way scandalous. He was, however, beginning to sail somewhat close to the wind, in that he was spending an increasing amount of time away from his regiment on visits to Vienna of which he did not inform the Emperor and, towards the end of 1884, Crown Prince Rudolf warned him that unless he was careful, he would be in trouble.

Rudolf, five years older than Franz Ferdinand, began to take a friendly interest in his younger cousin when the latter was a small boy, made a point of seeing something of him, invited him to shoot, and encouraged him to prepare himself for his army career, saying that to be an officer was the finest profession in the world. Towards the end of November 1884 he wrote to advise him on how to avoid getting into the Emperor's bad books:

If you are careful for a while, everything will be forgotten and you will avoid letting yourself in for a reprimand, which otherwise could well occur and lead to the ultimate disaster of your commanding officer being ordered to refuse you leave. In my view you must ensure that this does not happen; in life one has to learn to use ones wits. If the Emperor sees that you are coming less often (to Vienna) – and he will hear about this for he hears about everything – then he will certainly talk to me about it, and I shall be able to say that you had been coming because you had time to spare, but that now if there is any question of this being undesirable, you will of course be less away from Enns. This will certainly satisfy him for, as I well know, he dislikes having to be strict and issue reprimands . . ..

There was, Rudolf added, another reason for following his advice:

As regards Uncle Albrecht, if you do as I suggest you will deprive him of the opportunity of finding fault with you, and this will annoy him; he loves grumbling, picking quarrels, intriguing and making trouble, for he is malicious. If he discovers a mistake or weakness in someone it gives him pleasure . . .. If one has the honour of being in his presence one must . . . sit there in admiration like the angels around God.

Uncle Albrecht, born in 1817, was the Emperor's cousin, a Field-Marshal, since 1867 Inspector General of the armed forces, and much disliked by his younger relations. With his grey beard, protruding lower lip, and thick steel rimmed spectacles, he looked like a German professor. Austere, deeply religious, lacking in both humour and charm, he expected everyone to live up to his standards. No one was more insistent that the position of the Emperor and the honour of the House of Habsburg must be safeguarded. Habsburgs, he was never tired of preaching, were born into a position superior to that of all other mortals. And high above all Archdukes stood the Emperor whom he declared was their judge and Sovereign, whom they must honour and obey and be his most loyal servants, thereby setting an example to his subjects. He did not hesitate to report to Franz Joseph the peccadillos of any member of the younger generation who seemed to be getting out of step.

Albrecht decided in the second half of 1885 that Franz Ferdinand needed taking in hand, and began to admonish him about the necessity of applying himself to his military duties, and the importance of upholding the honour of the dynasty. In February 1887 he wrote at length to his young cousin warning him against "every kind of excess". He must not take risks with his health and therefore should not overdo his shooting expeditions; on no account must he allow shooting to dominate him. More time must be devoted to study, he had military talent and must develop this in order to fit himself for future high command. Franz Ferdinand tactfully thanked him for his good advice and encouragement. The Field-Marshal in the following August reminded him that God had called him to a unique position, that he must set an example to all as the Emperor's most loyal servant after the Crown Prince, and strive without ceasing to be an upright man and a devout Christian. He hoped the Archduke would marry before long. So did Karl Ludwig, who thought Maria Josepha, daughter of his old friend the King of Saxony, would be a suitable bride for his son. The Archduke went to Dresden to view the Princess, and announced on his return that she might be a tall blonde German girl, but she had neither grace nor charm: nothing would induce him to marry her. Marry eventually he knew he must, but in 1887 he had no intention of being tied down. He was enjoying himself far too much, and in any case at that time other aspects of his personal affairs were engaging his attention.

In theory Franz Ferdinand was a very rich young man. He was the last Duke of Modena Este's principal heir, and when the Duke died in 1875 had inherited from him the Villa d'Este in Rome, a castle in northern Italy, Chlumetz, a large country house and estate in Bohemia, and a great deal of money. But the Duke's will was five hundred pages long, there were debts, other legacies, and a mass of legal complications which in 1887 the lawyers were still endeavouring to disentangle. What the Este inheritance would amount to in terms of cash was uncertain, but undeterred by (or regardless of) this, the Archduke in 1887 bought another large castle and estate in Bohemia – Konopischt about thirty miles south of Prague. Chlumetz was an attractive baroque house; Konopischt, standing on a granite spur, was a *Burg*, a castle built to withstand a siege. In the seventeenth century it had belonged to Wallenstein, a complex, ambitious, devious military genius, one of the architects of the victories of that self appointed champion of the Catholic faith, Emperor Ferdinand II. It was very large – there were 82 rooms – and very dilapidated. Although it had the advantage of being within easy reach of Vienna by rail, nobody could quite understand why Franz Ferdinand had bought it. Possibly the fact that it had belonged to Wallenstein appealed to his sense of history. That it was virtually in ruins may also have attracted him, for this gave him an opportunity of exercising his creative instincts. He at once began to plan, regardless of expense, to restore Konopischt to its former grandeur.

In October 1888 the Archduke, now a Major (rapid promotion was automatic for members of the Imperial Family), was transferred to Infantry Regiment 102 in Prague. Most of the men in the regiment were Czech, a language in which he was not fluent, but he was fortunate in his commanding officer. Von Plönnies, an able soldier in the best tradition of the Imperial Army, got on well with his junior officers and had the gift of arousing and holding their interest. He recognised that His Imperial Highness had potential military ability and set himself to develop it. Franz Ferdinand learnt a great deal from von Plönnies whom he liked and respected. He lived in style in the royal palace on the Hradschin overlooking "golden Prague". At balls, shoots, and weekend house parties, he was in the midst of the landowning aristocracy of Bohemia with whom he felt at home. He was near Konopischt, and so able to supervise the beginning of its restoration. Life in Prague was enjoyable, he looked forward to being stationed there for some time, and at the end of 1888 there seemed to be not a cloud on the horizon.

In early October, shortly before he went to Prague, Franz Ferdinand was ordered by Franz Joseph to be in Vienna for the State Visit of the new German Kaiser, Wilhelm II. He obeyed this command with reluctance; Klopp his history tutor had drummed into him that, compared to the Habsburgs, the Hohenzollerns were an upstart dynasty. As an Austrian officer it was galling to have to listen to his uncle proposing a toast to the German army, "that perfect model of all military virtues". Moreover it meant missing a shoot. Rudolf commiserated with him about this, "I do pity you, fine stags are much better than a great German Kaiser".

A passion for shooting was perhaps the main bond between the two cousins, who, however, recently had seen rather less of one another. Like many people Franz Ferdinand may have noticed when they did meet that Rudolf, who at the time of Wilhelm II's visit admitted to feeling tired, looked ill, but he did not realise, neither did anyone else, the extent to which the Crown Prince was going to pieces. In fact Rudolf was in a state of black despair about the future of the Monarchy, communication between him and his father had practically ceased, his marriage had collapsed and he was seeking diversion elsewhere, slipping out of the Hofburg by a back entrance to go to some rendezvous, or to a tavern where he remained drinking until the early hours of the morning returning to be put to bed by his valet, engulfed in a world of private misery.

During the night of January 29th-30th 1889, at Mayerling, his shooting lodge in the Vienna woods, the Crown Prince shot his latest mistress, Mary Vetsera, and then himself. No information is available as to how Franz Ferdinand took the news of Rudolf's suicide but, judging from his reactions to another suicide many years later, it is likely that for religious reasons he was appalled that the Crown Prince had died without having received the last rites of the Church. On February 5th, as dusk was falling on a grey cold winter afternoon, he walked behind Rudolf's coffin as it was borne in solemn procession from the chapel of the Hofburg to the church of the Capuchins. There, one of the seven members of the Imperial Family selected by the Emperor to accompany him to the vault, he saw Franz Joseph break down and weep bitterly as his son was laid to rest amidst one hundred and twelve ancestors.

Franz Ferdinand was now no longer simply another junior Archduke of no particular interest. After his father he was next in line to the throne to which, since Karl Ludwig was only three years younger than the Emperor, it seemed he must eventually succeed. But at this time he was, as one diplomat and courtier said, "a blank sheet of paper". Very few people knew anything about him. All that could be said with certainty was that he was a Catholic, an officer, and a Habsburg. How he would develop remained to be seen. A great deal would depend on his relationship with his uncle Franz Joseph.

2
Uncle and Nephew

WHEN Rudolf killed himself in January 1889, Franz Joseph had reigned for forty arduous years. His conviction that there could be no abdication from the mission to rule entrusted to him by God and, no matter what happened, he must carry on, sustained him during the defeats and losses of the first two decades of his reign. It sustained him too when, on January 18th 1871, after France had also been defeated, "Old Wilhelm" as he privately called the King of Prussia, and whose "arrogance, vanity and sanctimoniousness" he found almost unendurable, was proclaimed Emperor of Germany, and dictated that, whatever his personal feelings, old enmities must be forgotten, if to do so was in the best interests of the Monarchy. Therefore, when in 1879 a proposal was made by Berlin for an alliance, he swallowed his pride and accepted it. Henceforward the German alliance was the pivot of his foreign policy, the direction of which he jealously guarded as his personal prerogative.

At home too the Emperor carried on, in the face of bitter criticism of his policies after Solferino, after Königgrätz when as he drove through the streets of his capital onlookers shouted for his abdication; after 1867 working ceaselessly to make the *Ausgleich* function. The overall political system set up by it was complicated. There were three Parliaments, one in Vienna, one in Budapest, and the Delegations, which consisted of twenty members of the Upper House and forty members of the Lower House of each Parliament, and met briefly twice a year alternately in the Austrian and Hungarian capitals. There were three joint subjects, Foreign Affairs, Defence, and Finance, the Ministers for which did not sit in either Parliament but reported to the Delegations. There were three military forces, a combined army, and an Austrian and a Hungarian militia – the Landwehr and the Honvéd. In this triune system Franz Joseph was Emperor of Austria, King of Hungary, joint Sovereign, and Commander-in-Chief of the joint army. He appointed and dismissed Ministers: if the Delegations could not agree, the point at issue was referred to him and his decision was final.

Although the powers vested in the Emperor by the *Ausgleich* were considerable, it increased the burden of ruling the Monarchy. The recurrent problems with which he had to contend were how to prevent the Hungarians from grabbing still more advantages for themselves; how to conciliate and gain the cooperation of the other nationalities, who considered they had been unfairly treated and in addition were at loggerheads with one another and, his overriding preoccupation, how to ensure that the internal splitting in two of his realm had no adverse effect on the joint army, the supranational praetorian guard of the throne. There were occasions when the *Ausgleich* was under considerable strain, but thanks to Franz Joseph's untiring efforts it had not collapsed. Shortly after succeeding to the throne he declared, "the man who holds the reins of government in his hands must be able to take responsibility; irresponsible sovereignty is for me a phrase without meaning". He never deviated from this belief and, a man of absolute integrity, held that an oath could not be broken. Therefore, having sworn in 1867 to rule in accordance with the terms of the *Ausgleich*, he would contemplate no alteration of it, whatever the difficulties with which he had to struggle.

The Emperor made full use of the powers reserved to him to appoint whom he wished to ministerial posts. He once said that his criterion in selecting them was that they were men whom he could trust. By this he meant men who thought as he did in terms of black and white, eschewing abstractions and theories, which he disliked because he found them incomprehensible, subscribing to his view that the maintenance of order took priority over the introduction of innovations however theoretically desirable. He treated his Ministers as junior officers, in discussion required them to confine themselves to matters within their own sphere, and if they attempted to raise other subjects would terminate the conversation abruptly. When they were no longer useful, he dismissed them out of hand.

Ministers came and went, Franz Joseph carried on, working harder than any of them. The young man, on his way home from a ball as dawn was breaking, who saw a lighted window in the Hofburg, knew that, as he was on his way to bed, the Emperor was already in his study and had started another day. During this he dealt methodically with a formidable amount of paper – memoranda from his Ministers, despatches from ambassadors, correspondence with foreign royalties, press summaries, police reports, recommendations for the promotion of middle and high ranking officers and civil servants. In addition he received up to one hundred and sixty people a week in audience, some of whom were neither important nor aristocratic. The humblest citizen, of whatever race or creed, knew that he could present a petition to his Sovereign and, if it was found worthy of consideration, would be summoned to him and his case heard with courteous attention. It was an experience of patriarchal benevolence never to be forgotten. But to everyone who saw him, whether face to face at a private audience or from a distance, inspecting troops, walking bareheaded through the streets of Vienna behind the Host in the Corpus Christi procession, on some other ceremonial or State occasion, Franz Joseph always contrived to convey the impression that there was a point beyond which none of them might trespass, and that he stood apart and above them all.

By the beginning of 1889 the Emperor's subjects, grumble though they did from time to time about aspects of his rule, could not conceive of existence without him, and accepted the dogma that he ran the Monarchy. As they read their morning papers they felt that, whatever the news, all would be well so long as the Emperor was there. And he was indeed there. He had managed to caulk the seams of the ship of state and steer her into what seemed to be relatively calm water. His preoccupation now was to keep her there, patching any further leaks she might spring as best he could. He had no intention of venturing out on to new and uncharted seas, and was determined to allow nobody on the bridge beside him. 'Nobody' meant not only his officials and ministers but also the entire Imperial Family.

Like all his relations, Franz Ferdinand knew that Franz Joseph would not tolerate comments by them on his policy; that Archduke Albrecht was the only member of the family from whom he sought advice, (but on military matters only), and that the only person to whose wishes he would defer was his wife, Empress Elisabeth. The Archduke had been brought up to revere the Emperor and invariably to address him as "Your Majesty" – even to refer to him as "my uncle" was unthinkable. He did not feel at ease in Franz Joseph's presence, nor did any of his contemporaries; there was a chilling air of Olympian detachment about the head of their House who seemed to be isolated from the range of ordinary human emotions. Because he allowed none of these to show, young Archdukes such as Franz Ferdinand did not realise that he was lonely because his conception of his position allowed him to make no close friends, nor the degree to which this loneliness was accentuated by the fact that Elisabeth, whom he loved deeply, unable to stand the formality of the Court was so often away. Franz Ferdinand's feelings when he saw Franz Joseph, whose self control seemed indestructible, break down and weep beside Rudolf's coffin can only be surmised. He may have been shocked, possibly embarrassed. Possibly too the realisation that his uncle was a vulnerable human being, led him to hope that in future he would be more approachable. However, within days of his son's funeral, the Emperor was back at his desk, working on punctiliously as if nothing had happened, remote as ever. He paid no special attention to his nephew, and the Archduke returned to his regiment in Prague.

Over six months passed. Then, in August 1889, when the Emperor went to Berlin on his first State Visit since Wilhelm II's accession, he took Franz Ferdinand with him. Wilhelm was determined to show off his army, and the Archduke watched with attention the succession of parades and manoeuvres which the Kaiser staged for his guests. He was impressed by them, but did not care for the overbearing attitude of the Prussian officers, commenting privately that as a good Austrian he could not forget Königgrätz. Neither no doubt could

Franz Joseph, but he did not say so to anyone, nor did he encourage Franz Ferdinand to express his views. Although by taking his nephew to Berlin he had implicitly recognised his status, he had no interest in hearing his impressions of the visit, and when it was over packed him off back to his regiment.

After returning to Vienna, the Emperor confided to a member of his entourage that he was exhausted and depressed. There had been much to endure since the Crown Prince's death. The Hungarians were being troublesome, so were the Czechs. The position of Count Taafe, the Minister President of the Austrian half of the Monarchy, who had managed to hold together a government for over ten years by a policy of inching along which suited Franz Joseph admirably, was shaky. It was noticed that although he worked on as usual, the heart seemed to have gone out of him. With Rudolf he had lost the future, and by the end of the summer of 1889 he was lonelier than ever. Elisabeth was no longer there or able to sustain him. At the time of the tragedy at Mayerling she was in Vienna, and broke the news of it to him with, the British Ambassador reported to Lord Salisbury, "fortitude and courage which surpassed the power of words to describe". But now she was in a state of semi-collapse. Franz Joseph seldom spoke of his son – Habsburg pride permitted no reference to private grief – but inwardly he was still haunted by "the whole tragic affair", unable to understand why it had happened.

As so often occurs, death had erased memories of past differences, and in his letters to Elisabeth Franz Joseph recalled sadly "our dear Rudolf", "our dear one whom we shall never forget". He wished to have no more contact with his nephew than was unavoidably necessary. He found him unprepossessing, gauche, not apparently particularly intelligent, did not care for him, and had no intention of allowing him any insight into affairs of State. By continuing his army career Franz Ferdinand, while stationed in different parts of the Monarchy would learn about its nationalities, be removed from the temptations of the bright lights of Vienna, and generally kept out of the way. The Emperor lent him a large sum of money to pay off the debts which he had incurred by pre-empting his Este inheritance, but otherwise during the autumn and winter following the Berlin visit ignored him. Archduke Albrecht did not. In August 1889, having heard that Franz Ferdinand had been involved in some escapade in Vienna, he wrote urging him to take warning from the lamentable example of "poor Rudolf", whose wild behaviour and disreputable death had done so much damage to the reputation of the dynasty. Now that he was de facto heir to the throne he must devote himself to serious study, appropriate reading, and the development of contacts with wise statesmen

> When you were younger and there was no prospect of your succeeding to the throne, you of course did not make an intensive study of subjects such as constitutional law and the history of the State. It is going to take you a long time to remedy this.

No similar exhortations were forthcoming from the Emperor, who took no further action about his nephew until the spring of 1890. He then decided that Franz Ferdinand should know something about the Czechs after the better part of eighteen months service in Bohemia, must now learn about Hungary, promoted him colonel, and told him that he was to command the Ninth Hussars who were stationed in Ödenburg (Sopron), a small Hungarian garrison town about fifty miles from Vienna.

Before leaving to take up his command the Archduke was received by Franz Joseph, who made no attempt to draw on his long experience of the Hungarians to brief him, but confined himself to delivering a homily on how he should behave. He must make a thorough study of conditions in Hungary, but refrain from making any kind of public comment about them; he must try to make himself popular in the regiment, and pay attention to building up comradely relations with its officers. The Emperor then terminated the audience. Franz Ferdinand had been told what to do and it was up to him to get on with it.

Not long after this audience the Archduke is alleged to have said

> I shall never be told officially whether or not I am heir to the throne. I seem to be regarded as though I am to blame for the stupidity of Mayerling. Formerly I was not treated so coldly; the sight of me seems to evoke painful memories.

There seemed to be no prospect of this depressing situation improving in the foreseeable future, and this was not conducive to building up Franz Ferdinand's self confidence. He was not yet twenty-seven, and knew that he lacked the military experience to command a regiment. He was also uncomfortably aware that his education had left him with a great many gaps in his knowledge of the Monarchy. But he had one rigid conviction about its eleven nationalities. They were all to be judged on one criterion – their attitude to the dynasty. Were they or were they not *schwarz-gelb*? (i.e. black-yellow which were the colours of the House of Habsburg). If they were *schwarz-gelb*, which meant their first loyalty was to the Crown and everything it stood for, they should be encouraged and rewarded; if they were not, they must be brought into line. As their attempts to exploit the *Ausgleich* in the interests of Budapest demonstrated, many Hungarian politicians were not *schwarz-gelb*, and this did not predispose Franz Ferdinand to view their countrymen with favour. He probably left for Ödenburg with mixed feelings. He would be stationed in a town where half the population was Hungarian, and he would have Hungarian troops under his command.

The Ninth Hussars, who considered themselves to be one of the crack cavalry regiments in the Imperial army, looked magnificent on parade. The saddle-cloths of their horses were red piped with black, white and yellow; the men wore green jackets and cloaks, scarlet shakoes, and red breeches with yellow stripes; the officers' tunics were royal blue frogged with gold. But when he took command of them the Archduke found much which displeased him. The majority of the other ranks and most of the officers were Hungarian. The latter prided themselves on their dash and their intrepid horsemanship. In the mess drinking and gambling parties lasted until dawn. Popularity depended on being a daredevil rider and a gambler prepared to wager a month's pay, and sometimes a good deal more, on a single throw. Franz Ferdinand was an indifferent horseman, a moderate drinker, and did not approve of gambling on this scale. He thought the Ninth Hussar officers flashy, affected, and all too inclined to put their amusements before their military duties. In addition, and this was far worse, the regiment was 'magyarised'. The officers flaunted their nationalistic views, and in the mess ostentatiously spoke Hungarian in front of him. On the parade ground orders were often given by the N.C.O.s in Hungarian, although it had been laid down that German was the official language of command throughout the army. On training courses words such as "patrol", which were used in every army in Europe, were translated into Hungarian.

Franz Ferdinand noted "in short in the entire regiment not a word of German, the language which the Hussars hate, is used". Faced with a regiment which must be disciplined and pulled into shape, a task in which he was severely handicapped by his minimal knowledge of Hungarian, the Archduke summoned the senior officers and told them that he would not tolerate the existing state of affairs. The only kind of cavalry officer he recognised was neither a Hungarian, a Bohemian, nor a Pole, but an Imperial cavalry officer, *schwarz-gelb* from the crown of his head to the soles of his feet, who spoke German, the universal language of the army and its supreme commander the Emperor. This reprimand was not well received. Later, when he sacked an idle and useless lieutenant, he found that virtually the entire regiment had turned against him. He took no notice, determined that it was his duty to eliminate slackness and inculcate a supranational spirit, even if this could only be done by repeated threats of punishment. At the end of 1891 his annual report stated that he had appreciably raised the standard of the Ninth Hussars, and Albrecht congratulated him on this.

Those who had known Franz Ferdinand when he was a carefree junior officer, noticed a considerable change in him during his first year as a regimental C.O. He was hypersensitive both to people and situations. Amongst those by whom he felt liked and appreciated, and when he felt sure of his ground, he was relaxed and charming. In Ödenburg he sensed an atmosphere of hostility emanating from men who were temperamentally antipathetic to him, and whom he did not know how to handle. He concealed his lack of confidence by displaying a determination which often amounted to obstinacy, became suspicious, and at times irritable. Inexperienced in his judgement of people, inclined to be impetuous and to take action on rumours without having ascertained the true facts of a case, he sometimes ordered unjust punishments. If he later discovered he had made a mistake he did not hesitate to acknowledge it, but this did not always repair the damage. The comradely relationships which the Emperor enjoined him to develop with his officers were non-existent.

Life in Ödenburg was not enjoyable, but mercifully Franz Ferdinand's "dearly loved" Vienna was within easy reach, and he escaped there whenever he could, to go to the theatre, for a ball, or to amuse himself at one of Otto's parties. (Otto had dutifully married the Saxon Princess Maria Josepha whom his elder brother had turned down, but not abandoned his bachelor habits. He read to his wife after she had gone to bed, and after she fell asleep went out for a night on the town.)

Another break came in the winter of 1891-92, when the Archduke was sent to Russia with a letter of friendship from Franz Joseph to Alexander III. When he arrived in St Petersburg he was met at the station by the Czar and a bevy of Grand Dukes, with an escort furnished by the Ismailowsky Guards. Military parades were staged, there was a court ball, the programme included several excellent shoots. Everything in Russia was on a vast scale. The splendour of the Winter Palace, which was over half a mile long, made the Hofburg seem like a modest dwelling. There were a thousand guests at the ball where the jewellery worn by the women was staggering. When the Czar, the ruler of a hundred million people, arrived to review his troops, he was surrounded by scores of generals, and the magnificence and size of the parade surpassed anything Franz Ferdinand had seen in Berlin. Invested by Alexander with the Order of St Andrew, he left for Vienna much impressed, and determined that it was essential for the Monarchy to draw closer to Russia.

After his return from St Petersburg, the Archduke decided that since it was evident that nobody, least of all the Emperor, was going to do much to help him to fill the gaps in his knowledge, he must continue his efforts to educate himself. An earlier attempt to do this had been abortive, "it is difficult for an independently minded pupil to come to an understanding with elderly teachers", and he therefore asked Max Vladimir Beck, his former tutor who was only nine years his senior, to come to Ödenburg and give him a refresher course in constitutional law. They got on well together; Beck's tuition probably took the form of discussions rather than lectures. But, whatever he taught Franz Ferdinand about the constitutional position of Hungary in the Monarchy, nothing altered the latter's dislike of many aspects of it. Nor – an added exasperation, in spite of every effort – was he making any progress in learning Hungarian.

The Archduke obeyed the Emperor's orders in so far as he refrained from making any public statement about his views on Hungary, but he was uninhibited about expressing them in private conversation. Inevitably they became known and, this made him very angry, in the summer of 1892 he was attacked in the Budapest press. By then he was convinced that neither the officers nor the men of the Ninth Hussars were to be relied on, and maintained that in no part of the Monarchy was the Emperor, the dynasty and the army spoken of so disrespectfully as in Hungary.

In addition, during the summer of 1892 Franz Ferdinand began to feel ill. He tired easily, had no appetite, lost weight and was running a slight temperature. The possibility that he might have inherited tuberculosis from his mother could not be ignored. The doctors suggested that he should leave Ödenburg before the winter and spend six months in a warmer climate, such as Egypt. The Archduke, however, announced that he wished to travel round the world. Nothing, he argued, would do him more good than a long sea voyage; moreover this would give him a chance of visiting foreign countries which would broaden his mind. He persuaded his father to seek permission for this project from the Emperor. Franz Joseph turned it down flat, telling Karl Ludwig he suspected that his nephew's real reason for proposing this journey was that it would give him unique opportunities to shoot. He could recover his health at some resort on the Adriatic within the Monarchy, no Habsburg had ever been round the world, the expedition would be far too expensive. Franz Ferdinand reacted violently to this veto, declaring that he was far iller than anyone realised, and that he must do what he wanted otherwise he would never get fit. His family had never known him so difficult nor so obstinate, and finally in despair his sister Margarethe appealed for help to Elisabeth. The Empress, horrified by the thought of more trouble in the family, interceded with the Emperor. Franz Joseph gave in and, having done so, treated his nephew generously, promoting him and arranging for him to travel as far as Japan in the cruiser *Kaiserin Elisabeth*.

On December 15th 1892 Franz Ferdinand sailed from Trieste. Christmas was celebrated "in true Austrian fashion" in the Red Sea on the way to Ceylon and Bombay. Although the Archduke was travelling incognito as Count Hohenberg, his tour of India was arranged in minute detail with the Viceroy, Lord Lansdowne; Maharajas entertained him, and big game shoots were laid on. At Calcutta he rejoined the *Kaiserin Elisabeth* and sailed via Singapore and Indonesia to Australia, from where he went on to Borneo, Hong Kong and Japan. In Japan he left the cruiser and crossed the Pacific in a passenger liner en route for America. With over half his journey behind him he was now beginning to think about the future, and wrote to his former tutor's namesake, Feldzeugmeister Beck the Chief of the General Staff, saying he had a request to make. Would Beck use his influence to get him appointed to the command of the Budweis brigade in Bohemia?

> I would like your Excellency to know, in strict confidence, why I am asking for this. I am thinking of getting married after my return, but before that I would like at least a year to get my affairs in order, particularly on my until now neglected properties in Bohemia. I can only do this without neglecting my military duties if I am stationed in Budweis, which has the added advantage of not being far from Vienna, so that I can be there quickly if His Majesty or my father want me for anything.

It would be impossible for me to take up another command in Hungary. I can no longer serve there, for if I do my duty as a senior officer I shall damage too much for the future. Your Excellency is perhaps aware of the resentment which I encountered when I was C.O. in Ödenburg, because I insisted that my officers spoke German in the mess, and that the N.C.O.s made their reports to me in German, and of the infamous articles in the Hungarian press . . .. Hungary is impossible for me and so I request Budweis.

When he wrote this letter Franz Ferdinand was feeling homesick. He hurried across America and by October 10th 1893 was back in Vienna, bringing with him a large number of crates of shooting trophies, assorted Orientalia, ethnological objects and natural history specimens. The two former were sent to Konopischt and Chlumetz; most of the ethnological and natural history collections were given to various museums. There remained the problem of the diary which the Archduke had kept during his journey, and which he wanted to publish. In this he made no mention of his illness. It contained accounts of his shooting experiences, detailed notes on everything which caught his attention – plants, animals, the Taj Mahal, "a dream in marble, a perfect harmony", the turn out of foreign troops, the "unforgettable majesty" of the Himalayas – and comments about people whom he had met and the reception he had received. There was much of interest, but it needed editing before publication, a task for which Franz Ferdinand enlisted Max Vladimir Beck's help, and which took some time to complete.

Before the diary was ready for publication the Archduke, determined to make a success of his new job, had assumed command of the Budweis brigade. Always himself impeccably dressed, he insisted on his troops being correctly turned out, demanded a high standard of drill and discipline, made unheralded inspections, and was forthright in his condemnation of anything of which he disapproved. It did not make him popular, but to this he seemed to be indifferent. On the whole life was agreeable. His command gave him some scope and a good deal of interest. If he was stationed in a dull garrison town, the climate of which he complained gave him rheumatism, there were plenty of opportunities to get out of it to shoot and visit his friends amongst the aristocratic landowners of Bohemia, who were far more congenial to him than their counterparts in Hungary. He was able to supervise the administration and improvement of Chlumetz and Konopischt, and the Emperor had generously made over to him the Imperial game preserve at Eckartsau on the Danube to the east of Vienna which contained some of the finest stags in the Monarchy.

While at Budweis Franz Ferdinand began to make a collection of newspaper cuttings which included all references to himself, whether favourably critical or hostile. He did not resume his discussions of constitutional law with Beck, but he was devoting serious thought to the future of the Monarchy, about aspects of the problems of which he talked to his brigade staff officer, Baron Margutti. The Baron, who came from Fiume, agreed with the Archduke about the importance of building up not only the navy, but also the merchant fleet. Franz Ferdinand had returned from his travels convinced that the latter must be expanded; in the ports which he visited there were few ships flying the Austrian flag. As a corollary to this Trieste and Fiume, the only important harbours which the Monarchy possessed, must be developed, and the entrance to the Adriatic, its only outlet to the oceans of the world, must be kept open. About His Imperial Highness's ideas for internal reform Margutti was, however, apprehensive. Franz Ferdinand likened the Monarchy to a body, one limb of which (Hungary) had become overdeveloped, and if this was not corrected by medication or an operation, the whole body would sicken and die. Searching for a remedy, it seemed to him that the Habsburg domain must be transformed into a federation of smaller national units, each with the maximum amount of local autonomy, all bound together under the Crown by a strong central government, with a common foreign policy and a common army. The official language of this Monarchical federation must be German.

The Archduke envisaged dividing Hungary into four or five national units, and Bohemia and Galicia into two each and said, which alarmed Margutti, that if they could not be established by legislation, force must be used. But, as Franz Ferdinand knew, these were merely ideas, and there was no question of discussing them with the Emperor, who still showed no signs of wishing to see more of him.

3
Illness

IN the spring of 1895 the Chief of Staff inspected Franz Ferdinand's brigade. He thought His Imperial Highness looked pale and unwell; so did a number of other people, and eventually the Emperor was informed. Blessed himself with exceptionally good health, Franz Joseph found illness difficult to understand but sent Widerhofer, his own doctor, to examine the Archduke. Widerhofer found that he was losing weight, had a high fever, and called in a lung specialist. Tests left no doubt that he had tuberculosis, the only known cure for which at that time was complete rest, preferably in a mild climate. Franz Ferdinand, who did not want to give up his command, refused to believe that he was seriously ill, and declared that he would not go abroad. Finally on August 2nd the Emperor wrote to him

> I must stress that you now have only one duty, and that is to get well. As soon as possible you must go to a peaceful mountain resort, stay there absolutely quietly, and then move on to a southern climate (not Tunis because it is too dusty) where you must remain and rest for the entire winter, obeying your doctor's instructions. I know this will be extremely boring, but I hope that for my sake you will patiently persevere with it.

Franz Joseph signed himself "In true friendship, your most affectionate uncle", but there was no doubt that this was an Imperial order which must be obeyed. The Archduke prepared to do so, with the inward hope that it might not be necessary to prolong the cure into the winter.

Dr Victor Eisenmenger, the young physician chosen to accompany Franz Ferdinand, went to see him at Chlumetz and found a tall man who looked "droopy", with a thin face and feverish eyes. He told him that he would have to undergo treatment for at least a year. This would involve a diet, spending as much time as possible in the sun and fresh air somewhere free of dust, keeping absolutely quiet both mentally and physically, and continuing the cure until there was a complete recovery. The Archduke refused to enter a sanatorium and, after turning down a list of suggested health resorts, reluctantly agreed to go to the Mendel plateau above Bozen in the South Tirol.

At the hotel on the Mendel, Franz Ferdinand was made to spend most of the day lying out of doors on a camp bed. No member of his family was with him; his only immediate companions were his Chamberlain, whom he disliked, Eisenmenger, who with his insistence on immobility was a mixture of doctor and gaoler, and Janaczek his valet who had been in his service since 1889, was totally devoted to him and acted as nurse, sleeping in his room. His only link with the outside world was the post, for which he waited anxiously every morning. The rest of the day was passed in reading light novels, shooting small twigs off a larch tree thirty yards away with a pistol, and writing letters. In one of these he said a few days after arriving in the Mendel

> As far as my illness is concerned I am sorry to be unable to send you a good report. I have a severe catarrh of the lungs with malignant complications and am feeling so weak and wretched that I am barely able to walk a hundred steps . . . . I am broken down physically and in terribly low spirits. A soldier, body and soul, I had to give up my brigade just before the manoeuvres and to renounce for a long time all the joys of life. I have to forego the pleasures of shooting, of riding, of every occupation and to live as a pining cripple. Here I am lying all day long on a veranda in a reclining chair, living on milk and medicines and coughing continually. You can imagine the frame of mind I am in, and that I am already suffering from black melancholia . . .

Franz Ferdinand ended this letter with an adjuration to himself, "but now! no more whining". Eisenmenger found that he had "iron will power and moral determination". At first he obeyed orders, but when his temperature began to go down became restless, insisting that he must get away from the Mendel, "it is unendurable. I am being shut up as though I am a wild beast". His father and stepmother were sent for, and succeeded in making him realise that he must continue the cure. A plan was hammered out whereby the Archduke agreed to make a journey up the Nile in one of the houseboats rented out to tourists by Thos. Cook and, since the weather would not be suitable for him to go to Egypt until December, to fill in the time until then on Lussin-Piccolo, an Adriatic island near the naval base at Pola. Having accepted that it was impossible to tell when he would be fit to return to the army, he wrote to the Emperor saying that he must continue for some time to be by the sea or in the mountains and therefore asked, "with a bleeding heart", to be relieved of his command because he was too ill to carry on.

At Lussin naval officers came to call, and a few friends turned up bringing news of the outside world, but his cough remained, he was still obliged to lie down for most of the day, and Eisenmenger said he must continue to avoid any kind of physical exertion or mental agitation. The latter Franz Ferdinand found difficult at the best of times, the former meant that he had little to do but think, and his thoughts revolved round one subject – the damage which the exploitation of the *Ausgleich* by the Hungarians was doing to the Monarchy. Writing in October to a close friend, Prince Karl Schwarzenberg, he epitomised the *Ausgleich* as the "ultimate catastrophe", Dualism as "the ruin of the Monarchy", and lamented that unfortunately the Emperor was dominated by the idea that "a so-called constitutional ruler must have no will of his own, and must comply with what is 'wished' and what the Ministers propose."

When he wrote to Schwarzenberg, the Archduke was finding it next to impossible to think calmly about the Hungarians. Any endeavour which he may have been making to do so ceased when he received a cutting of an article which had appeared in *Magyar Hirlap*, a newspaper which had close ties with the Budapest government. The gist of it was that His Imperial Highness would not recover, it only remained to pray for his soul, and there would be no mourning in Hungary when he died. It would not have been surprising if it had plunged Franz Ferdinand into an even deeper state of "black melancholia", but in fact it had the opposite effect. According to one account he turned "grey with rage" when he read it, and exclaimed that he was now determined to do anything to get well in order to deprive the Hungarians of the pleasure of his demise. He forwarded the article to the Emperor under cover of a letter in which he described it as "infamous", requesting that "if possible" he should be protected against such attacks. He had become used to them for

> These people know very well what I think about them . . . I know I am not loved in Hungary and I am in a sense proud of this, for I do not want to be honoured by such a people. But that such things can be written in a country which belongs to the Monarchy, such infamous things every line of which rejoices at my illness and possible death, is something which I did not believe could occur.

Franz Ferdinand, feeling wretchedly ill when he wrote this letter to Franz Joseph, was in a state conducive neither to the exercise of self control nor to the retention of a sense of perspective. Its implication that, since they had written him off, he had written off the entire Hungarian race, was not entirely true. He had some Hungarian friends, to one of whom, Count Nikolaus Szécsen, he also wrote about the *Magyar Hirlap* article, and while he began by saying

> Between ourselves, I think it is incomprehensible and possible only in Hungary, that one of the most widely read newspapers in a State which, up to now, is still monarchical is permitted to print such a degrading infamy about a member of the ruling house

then apologised if his letter was "somewhat caustic" and told the Count

If death does not overtake me this winter . . . it will be a great pleasure, as soon as I am back in the Monarchy, to talk about these matters with your Excellency, a Hungarian whom I esteem and admire and to whose judgement I defer.

There was now the winter to be got through. The Archduke became difficult about the whole question of Egypt, arguing that to hire a houseboat for the Nile journey would be too expensive, saying he would on no account take his Chamberlain with him, that the Austrian Ambassador in Cairo was useless, vain and only interested in "dinners and decorations . . .. He will want to take me out and drag me around everywhere in order to emphasise his importance. I need quiet, and quiet I shall have." When his cousin Archduke Eugen, of whom he was fond, said he would accompany him as far as Assuan, he agreed to carry on with the Egyptian expedition. Bored and restless, Franz Ferdinand then insisted on putting forward his departure from Lussin, decided to have a second medical opinion, and telegraphed the Khedive's private doctor von Becker, a Viennese, saying he wished to see him as soon as he arrived in Alexandria, and alone. He was closeted with von Becker for over an hour, after which the latter told Eisenmenger that he had informed his patient only that his stay in Egypt should bring him "some relief"; his personal opinion was that the Archduke would die.

In Cairo the visit got off to a bad start. Franz Ferdinand ignored the Ambassador who was waiting to greet him, and took advantage of the fact that Eisenmenger was ill to spend the day in the bazaar and the evening sampling the night life of the Egyptian capital. On the following morning he told the doctor that he had inspected the houseboat, locally called a *dahabiya*, and nothing on earth would induce him to board it, "I will not be locked up in such a cage". He deliberately disobeyed Eisenmenger's instructions "to show that nobody can force me to do anything I do not want to do." There seemed to be an impasse which the arrival of Eugen did not resolve. However, then the Archduke's cough got worse, the fever returned and, thoroughly alarmed, his attitude changed from "Is that really necessary" to "Do you think I must die?" Convinced that he was gravely ill, he agreed to start the journey up the Nile.

On December 6th, before leaving Cairo, Franz Ferdinand sent an S.O.S. to his stepmother. After Eugen left for home in January he would once again be "desperate" and need a nurse; he implored her therefore to "cut the stupid Hofball" and come out to him.

The journey to Assuan was monotonous. Day after day the flat landscape looked much the same, there was nothing to shoot except a few water fowl and pigeons, quarters were cramped on board the houseboat, tempers became frayed. After Eugen's departure, describing himself as "suffering acutely from homesickness" in the "land of crocodiles, Pharaohs and camels", the Archduke was very low

Owing to a cold, I am feeling quite miserable and there is, in addition, a bad complication of the larynx. So my doctor has even forbidden me to speak, and I am now actually forced to lead the life of an anchorite.

When a sandstorm blew he had to remain below deck. The prospect of spending another month on the *dahabiya* was becoming nearly intolerable when, on January 21st, a letter arrived from Maria Theresia to say that she, Karl Ludwig, and some of the family were on their way to join him. He replied at once

Only two lines, for, thank God, I shall be able to embrace you within a few days. I cannot tell you how much I have been longing for you, or what I have been suffering during the last month in this 19th century instrument of torture the *dahabiya*. I shall not await you at Assuan, but at Luxor, for, as I must not remain on the Nile beyond February because of the very injurious *khamsin* winds which start about that time, I must begin to proceed slowly downstream . . .. Your dear presence will make a pleasure of the deadly tedium of the voyage.

When the party got back to Cairo, Franz Ferdinand's relations went on to Palestine. His health had improved, but he was still far from well, continuing to worry about the state of the Monarchy and, as he told Beck, depressed about the effect of the length of his illness, "it is not very pleasant to be regarded on all sides as written off and pushed into the background". Promising Eisenmenger to behave "very hygienically", he moved on to Monte Carlo and continued the weary routine of lying in the sun, complaining yet again about being "locked up". Eisenmenger tried to cheer him by promising that he would recover if he exercised "patience and good will". Otto arrived, and together they visited Spain and Majorca. The Archduke then announced that he could stand the Mediterranean no longer, and was going to Konopischt. When told that he must wait until the weather there was warmer, he left Monte Carlo for Territet to see Elisabeth from where, on May 17th shortly after his arrival, he was summoned urgently to Vienna because his father was dangerously ill. He left at once, but arrived too late. After the funeral, his doctors at last allowed him to go to Bohemia.

At Konopischt Franz Ferdinand, still accompanied by Eisenmenger, was compelled to continue to rest for several hours a day, carrying on with a regime which had now lasted for the better part of a year and was monotonous to the point of being nearly unendurable. But at least he had the interest of directing the renovation of the castle and planning the landscaping of the park. He insisted on supervising every detail of this, driving round in a trap, designating where each new tree was to be planted, only agreeing to the felling of existing trees with the utmost reluctance, "I can rebuild houses and roads, but trees cannot be replaced". There was the interest too of dealing with wagon loads of the contents of the Villa d'Este and the castle which he had inherited from the Duke of Modena as they arrived from Italy and, helped by Janaczek, he personally decided where every picture and item of furniture should go. At the end of July, when Konopischt was thought to be too hot for him, he moved to a shoot at Lölling in Kärnten where, in order that he should avoid exertion, game was driven to him, and in mid September, when the rutting season began, was allowed to go to Eckartsau, where the stags were also driven to him.

Since his return from abroad, although the Archduke had been able, if to a limited extent, to do a number of things which he liked, his spirits did not improve. Eisenmenger noticed that by the time he got to Eckartsau, he was becoming more easily annoyed, sarcastic, embittered. The trouble was that there had been some developments which he had not taken at all well.

When Karl Ludwig died the Emperor did not issue a proclamation stating that Franz Ferdinand was now his direct heir. As a result of this, and as his illness kept him out of Vienna, many people began to assume that his brother Otto would be their future ruler, particularly when it became known that, at the suggestion of Count Goluchowski, the Foreign Minister and Minister of the Imperial and Royal House, Otto had been given the Augarten Palace and a Household of the size appropriate to a Crown Prince. Franz Ferdinand, increasingly aware that people were engaged in currying favour with Otto, and bitterly resentful of this, poured out his feelings to Beck. The latter wrote assuring him that the time was not far off when his health would be fully restored, and that it would come all the sooner if he exercised patience and ignored slights and insults, both of which he could afford to do for "Your Imperial Highness is the man of the future and will remain so". Another person also made it clear that they were in no doubt he would succeed to the throne. Elisabeth sent him her will for his approval, saying that she commended to his care "when the day comes when the Emperor and I are no longer there", her favourite daughter Valerie and her husband and children.

Expressions of faith in the future did not, however, mitigate the present. Franz Ferdinand appreciated Beck's exhortations to be philosophical "you understand so well how to rise above the unexpected in life", but found this quality extremely difficult to exercise. In September 1896 his reaction to what he took to be yet another sign that he was written off contained no shred of philosophy. It was occasioned by the State Visit to Vienna of Czar Nicholas II. His visit to Nicholas's predecessor in 1891 had been welcomed in the Russian press, one official newspaper stressing that he had established "a bond of friendly sympathy between the two countries." Since then he had not deviated from the conviction that the Monarchy must draw closer to Russia, and felt sure he could contribute to this by establishing friendly personal relations with the new Czar. He was therefore infuriated when there was no suggestion that he should be present in Vienna during Nicholas's State Visit, turned up there unannounced, and subsequently was caustic about every aspect of it, describing it as a "fiasco" for which Goluchowski was entirely to blame.

After what had occurred during the summer, Franz Ferdinand was in no mood to spend another winter abroad cosseting his health, and only agreed to this when his doctors were emphatic that he must do so, because although his illness was arrested, a relapse was still to be feared. The problem was where to go; a return to Egypt was not to be contemplated. *Faute de mieux* the choice fell on Corsica, and proved to be unfortunate. The hotel in Ajaccio was uncomfortable, the food indifferent, there was nothing to shoot except blackbirds, nothing to do. Shortly before Christmas he wrote to a friend in Vienna saying that although he was feeling better and had put on weight, "this terrible hole, Ajaccio, is again driving me to black melancholia". The arrival of his stepmother and other members of the family cheered him up momentarily, and Eisenmenger found that at times the Archduke was "even hilarious". But then Maria Theresia's admonitions about the care of his health – he must avoid getting his feet wet, put on his overcoat if he went out in a wind, not go out in the evening if it was cold – got on his nerves. He complained to Beck that to command seven Army Corps was simple compared to having to deal with the seven women who were hanging round his neck, and became extremely bad tempered. After his stepmother's departure he declared that he could stand Ajaccio no longer, and agreed to Eisenmenger's suggestion that they should move on to Algiers.

In Algiers Franz Ferdinand's principal occupation was bargaining for rugs, which were displayed to him in his hotel in order that he should avoid the dust of the bazaar. There was still too much time to think. Now convinced that almost every man's hand was against him, and that the only real friends he possessed were Eisenmenger and Janaczek, he worked himself up into a state about Goluchowski.

Franz Joseph was going on a State Visit to Russia in April, and the Archduke had hoped, since his health was improving, that he would be designated to accompany him. When, therefore, it was announced that Otto would go to St Petersburg, the Press implied that this indicated that he would be passed over for the succession in favour of his brother, and no official denial of this was issued, he wrote an enraged letter to Goluchowski. The Foreign Minister replied blandly that he should take no notice of articles in obscure newspapers; legally his position and rights were "crystal clear".

This was too much. Franz Ferdinand now saw in Goluchowski the arch villain in a conspiracy to push him into the background, and blasted off to a friend about that "deceitful and contemptible Pole". He had planned to return to Vienna in the latter part of May but

> In view of the manner, however, in which I am treated, I shall probably abandon this project and, when everybody is away, come quite stealthily to Vienna for a few days at the end of June . . .. You will understand that, in view of the sad and ridiculous position which has been forced on me, I

do not care to show myself in Vienna, and have no business to be there as "Successor to the Throne on leave with half-pay".

The things which this – in his opinion – God-like Goluchowski and his gang invent to humble me, to affront me and *actually to kill me morally*, are unbelievable . . . . At Goluchowski's instigation, Otto is now thoroughly informed of everything . . . he has to act the part of the Successor to the Throne, while I am not considered any more, but simply ignored. If they would at least be decent enough to ask me, whether this or that could not perhaps be entrusted to my brother so that I should not be over-taxed during my illness; but no – they simply continue to issue decrees behind my back and over my dead body, as it were . . . .

A fortnight later, having evidently been advised to calm down, Franz Ferdinand wrote rather more coherently

You are absolutely right and I quite agree with you. But it is very difficult to swallow some things. You know with what love and reverence I am attached to my Emperor and it is this very love which prompts me to have my own views on politics, in home as well as in foreign affairs, for I hope thereby to be of service to my Emperor and to my country.

If the policies of the day were the policies of my Emperor, I should, as a matter of course, submit to everything and make them entirely my own. I know, however, that the advisers of His Majesty are the ones who create these policies, and that they bother and torment him, until, in order to be left in peace, he gives in to them. I, therefore, consider it my duty . . . to avert as much as possible of the dangerous consequences of this.

In early March, when it was considered that Algiers was becoming unhealthily hot for him, the Archduke moved to Cannes. When the Emperor came to the Riviera towards the end of the month to visit Elisabeth at Cap Martin, Franz Ferdinand called on him with the intention of stressing the importance of improving relations with Russia, but when he broached this Franz Joseph refused to listen and changed the subject. Undeterred by this rebuff, he wrote to his uncle after the latter had returned to Vienna saying that various occurrences, in particular his exclusion from the visit to St Petersburg, made him feel that as heir to the throne he was being overlooked and – the perennial complaint – pushed into the background. The Emperor replied by return of post that his complaints were unfounded: as soon as he was passed fit his position would of course be recognised, and he would then have to undertake the duties which this entailed

I too have long felt the need of discussing with you all the points which you have raised in your letters, and much else besides. I have only refrained from doing so because I have been afraid that, since you are still unwell, this might damage your health, for the discussion will be serious and not entirely agreeable. But hopefully it will lead to an understanding and convince you that I only want to do what is best for you, although I must always bear in mind my duty to the Monarchy and the welfare of our family.

With this guarded statement Franz Ferdinand had to be content; whether the "duties" to which the Emperor referred would be more than, as hitherto, military and representational, remained to be seen. He returned to the Monarchy in May feeling better and having put on weight. The doctors allowed him to represent Franz Joseph at Queen Victoria's Diamond Jubilee celebrations in July, but no other official engagements were assigned to him during the summer, most of which he spent at Chlumetz and Konopischt. In the autumn he was told that, although still not cured, he need not again go abroad for the winter, and wrote cheerfully to Eisenmenger

> My health, thank God, is very good. I am feeling very well both physically and mentally, planting millions of trees in Konopischt . . . and shooting diligently, but with moderation . . .. I shall soon come to Vienna where I have to hold countless conferences in connection with the jubilee of His Majesty . . . after they are over, we will go to Meran and dig in for the winter like badgers.

In March 1898 Franz Ferdinand was at last pronounced clear of tuberculosis. He had won his fight to regain his health, but physically his illness left him with lifelong handicaps: he was compelled to avoid harsh climates, prolonged sojourns in cities, excessive exertion, and from time to time suffered from asthma. Psychologically it had sharpened, hardened and embittered him. Determined to assert himself and confound his detractors, his hope was that, as over nine years had passed since Rudolf's death, his uncle would now begin to take him into his confidence, and welcome his help and support in dealing with the many problems of the Monarchy. Franz Joseph still had no intention of doing anything of the sort. Faced with the problem of what to do with his heir, he decided that a military appointment must be found which insulated him from political controversy.

The Emperor consulted Bolfras, the head of his Military Chancellery, who suggested that His Imperial Highness should be placed under His Majesty's direct orders, and given an appointment approximating to that of an Inspecting General, which would enable him to learn at a high level about all aspects of the army and the navy. Franz Joseph agreed to this proposal, and on March 29th wrote to Franz Ferdinand informing him of his decision. In an accompanying letter Bolfras explained to the Archduke that, in addition to carrying out such inspections as the Emperor ordered, he would be required to put up memoranda on designated subjects, and could also make suggestions for improving the efficiency of the armed forces. At important manoeuvres he would command an army corps. The Ministries of War and Defence would send him papers on measures which had received Imperial approval. To assist him he would be given a military staff, consisting of a General Staff officer as his A.D.C., and a captain as his orderly officer.

To Franz Joseph this seemed to be a most satisfactory arrangement. It defined the scope of his nephew's activity, kept him under control, and gave him the chance of pursuing a career in which he was interested and for which he seemed to have talent. As a further recognition of Franz Ferdinand's status he allocated to him the Belvedere Palace as his official residence in Vienna. All that now remained was for him to marry suitably and settle down.

4
Marriage

WHEN pronounced fit for military duties in March 1898 Franz Ferdinand was thirty-four. He had never commanded any unit larger than a brigade and illness had kept him away from the army for over two and a half years. He knew he had much to learn and was keen to do so, but immediately much of his time was taken up by the celebrations of the fiftieth anniversary of the Emperor's accession in which, as heir to the throne, he was required to play a prominent part. A summer of celebration then ended in tragedy. On September 10th the Empress was assassinated in Switzerland by an Italian anarchist. When the news of her death was broken to Franz Joseph he said "nothing has been spared me in this world . . . nobody knows how much we loved each other", as at the time of Rudolf's suicide he sought refuge from his sorrow by burying himself in work.

Franz Ferdinand's reaction to "this terrible calamity" was "I must now redouble my efforts to be of help to His Majesty, our dearly beloved Emperor". He was also confronted by a personal problem – marriage. For over ten years after he came of age he had refused to consider a succession of 'suitable' brides who were suggested to him. Then he fell ill and all thoughts of marriage had to be deferred indefinitely. Eisenmenger noticed that when he was on the Mendel, he waited impatiently for letters and, because of the effect on his morale when they arrived, suspected they were from a woman whom he assumed must be of inappropriate rank, because one day Franz Ferdinand commented bitterly

> If some member of our family is attracted to someone, there is always some slight blemish in her ancestry which rules out marriage. So we constantly marry our relatives and the result is that of the children of these unions half are cretins or epileptics.

He wrote to Beck when the latter got engaged

> It must be wonderful to marry a woman whom one loves and has chosen for oneself. . . . . If I get well again, perhaps I will follow your good example,

but later said that he still had no desire to be tied down.

Shortly after Elisabeth was assassinated, Franz Ferdinand confided the essence of his predicament to a married woman whom he had known for some years

> You too urge me to marry and I am gradually coming to see that I should do so. I long for peace, a home, a family. But the question is, whom am I to marry? There simply is nobody available. You say I should have a loving, clever, beautiful and good wife, but where is such a woman to be found? Unfortunately there is absolutely nobody amongst the eligible princesses, they are all seventeen and eighteen year old ugly under-developed ducklings. I am too old for them and have neither the time nor the inclination to attend to the education of a wife. I can indeed picture to myself the ideal wife whom I should like to have and with whom I could be happy. She should be not too young and her character and views should be fully developed. Such a princess does not exist, and therefore I think it is better to remain single rather than make myself unhappy for the rest of my days.

By the spring of 1899, however, two members of the Imperial Family were beginning to entertain high hopes that the heir to the throne would soon become their son-in-law. After he was passed fit he started to visit his cousin Archduke Friedrich who was commanding an army corps in Pressburg (Bratislava) not far from Vienna. He was now turning up more frequently, and Friedrich and his wife Isabella concluded from this that Franz Ferdinand was courting their eighteen year old daughter, Maria Christina. Isabella, who was extremely am-bitious, encouraged these visits of the most eligible bachelor in the Monarchy, and no doubt dropped hints to her friends of her hopes of their outcome. But in the early summer of 1899 they were dashed. It is said that Franz Ferdinand, when changing after a tennis party left his watch behind, and a servant brought it to the Archduchess. She saw there was a locket attached to it, and confident it would provide confirmation of all she wished, opened it – to find that it con-tained a portrait of her lady-in-waiting, Countess Sophie Chotek. Whether this account of the circumstances of Isabella's discovery that her daughter was not the object of the Archduke's expeditions to Pressburg is correct cannot be determined, but there is no doubt that when she made it there was a row of spectacular dimensions. Sophie was told to leave the house immediately. Isabella told her husband that she was going to demand an immediate audience of the Emperor to inform him of Franz Ferdinand's outrageous deceit and abuse of their hospitality.

Sophie Chotek was thirty-one, tall, not an outstanding beauty, her best feature being her large dark intelligent eyes. Invariably kind and cheerful, she radiated warmth and charm and was the favourite aunt of all her younger relatives. Her father, a career diplomat, was not well off and she took the post of lady-in-waiting to Archduchess Isabella after his death in 1896. Franz Ferdinand had known her family for some time. Her elder sister married his friend Count Jaroslav Thun-Hohenstein in 1887, but she was then only nineteen and possibly he did not take much notice of her. Thereafter they saw one another at balls and country house parties, and it is generally believed that he fell in love with her in about 1894. When he became ill there seems to be little doubt that she was the writer of the letters for the arrival of which he waited so eagerly. But they managed to keep their feelings for one another secret, and although in Vienna society gossiped more than in any other capital in Europe, no rumours linking them together circulated.

The Emperor first heard of what was occurring from Archduchess Isabella. Franz Joseph, now nearing seventy, like many elderly gentlemen disliked scenes. Nor, in common with a good many other people, did he care for the Archduchess; she was short, squat (irreverent young officers nicknamed her 'Busabella'), and inclined to be strident. When he received her she was in a black rage, held forth at length about Franz Ferdinand's misdemeanours, and seemed to the Emperor to be somewhat over dramatic. She could produce no proof that the Archduke had done anything more improper than carry Sophie's portrait with him. Nor could he be considered to have insulted her eldest daughter since he had never proposed to her. The whole affair seemed to be one more case of a member of the Imperial House forming an unsuitable attachment. In one or two instances the Archduke in question had insisted on contracting a morganatic marriage and was expelled from the Imperial Family. Because Franz Ferdinand was heir to the throne this was unthinkable, and although the Choteks were one of the oldest aristocratic families in Bohemia, so far as the Habsburgs were concerned they were commoners, marriage with whom was not admissible under the terms of the Family Law. Therefore he must break off all contact with Sophie. Franz Joseph told Isabella that he would order his nephew to stop seeing her former lady-in-waiting, and had no doubt this would put an end to the matter.

When the Emperor summoned the Archduke, he did not anticipate that the audience would be difficult. While he personally did not care for him, he was certain that their dynastic beliefs were identical, nor had he any reason to doubt his heir's obedience to his orders. He accordingly simply told Franz Ferdinand that his behaviour was regrettable because it had caused a rift with his cousins which he must now repair, and that he must break off all contact with Isabella's former lady-in-waiting. He then indicated that the audience was terminated and waited for his nephew to leave the room. Franz Ferdinand stood his ground and formally asked for permission to marry Countess Sophie Chotek. The temperature dropped to a good many degrees below zero. Franz Joseph said he forbade the marriage. Franz Ferdinand said he must and would marry Sophie. The Emperor, icily, gave him a week to think it over.

After leaving the Imperial presence, the Archduke sent an urgent message to

Eisenmenger summoning him to dine in a private room at Sacher's. When the doctor arrived at the hotel he found his host alone and in a sombre mood. Franz Ferdinand opened the conversation by complaining bitterly about the rigidity of the Habsburg Family Law, saying he had at last found a woman whom he loved and with whom he could be happy, and now "they" (he did not mention the Emperor) were putting every conceivable obstacle in his way because of a trifling defect in her family tree. He would overcome this, provided Eisenmenger could reassure him about something which was worrying him a great deal – would the fact that he had had tuberculosis in any way endanger his wife and future children? Were the children likely to inherit it? The doctor replied that the disease was rarely inherited; it was only passed on by infection and at present there was no danger of this, for the last two years tests had revealed no trace of active bacillus. Should His Imperial Highness have a relapse, which was most unlikely, measures could be taken to protect his family. Eisenmenger added that he was certain that the Archduke's health would benefit in every way from a happy marriage.

Franz Ferdinand's omission to consult his doctor earlier about this all-important point suggests that Isabella's complaint to Franz Joseph may have forced him into announcing his wish to marry Sophie sooner than he intended. He may have planned to wait, in the hope that he might succeed in building up a relationship with the Emperor which would make it easier to gain his permission for this marriage, or because he felt that time was necessary for them both to be sure of their feelings for one another. But, now that he was faced with the prospect of never seeing her again, he became certain that life without her would be intolerable, returned to the Emperor and repeated that he was determined to marry Countess Chotek. Franz Joseph said that then he must renounce the succession to the throne. Franz Ferdinand declared he could not do this for it had been conferred on him by God. He would have the throne and he would marry Sophie. His uncle told him he must choose between one or the other, gave him a year to make up his mind and dismissed him.

The Chotek affair blew up within a year of Elisabeth's death. Franz Joseph unhappy, more lonely than ever, was in no mood to attempt to understand his heir, and extremely angry with him for his apparent total lack of any sense of dynastic responsibility. He would not contemplate making an exception to the Habsburg Family Law. If Franz Ferdinand insisted both on retaining the succession and on this marriage, to ensure that Sophie could not become Empress of Austria and her children could not succeed to that throne, it must be morganatic. But Hungarian internal law, which he had sworn in his *Ausgleich* oath to uphold, did not recognise the existence of morganatic marriage: it would therefore theoretically be possible for Sophie as Franz Ferdinand's wife to become Queen of Hungary and for her children to inherit the Hungarian crown, thus establishing another reigning branch of the House of Habsburg and finally splitting the Monarchy in two. This could not be contemplated, and the Emperor let it be known that all available means must be deployed to prevent this disastrous marriage.

Franz Ferdinand discovered that, with the exception of his stepmother Maria Theresia, the entire Imperial Family were ranged against him. That Friedrich and Isabella could find nothing too bad to say about him was to be expected; there were others from whom he hoped for more understanding, but it was not forthcoming. The reaction of his brother Otto was particularly wounding. Otto had married 'suitably', but it was a loveless match and Franz Ferdinand thought that he of all people would support his bid for happiness. Otto refused to do so, delivering a lecture on the dynastic impossibility of his marrying Sophie, which he said the Emperor was right to forbid. The Archduke's other brother, Ferdinand Karl, took the same line, so did the rest of his relations. The heir to the throne could not marry a jumped-up lady-in-waiting for this would hazard the future of the dynasty, which meant the future of them all. Only Maria Theresia pleaded with the Emperor for him. Franz Joseph, who was fond of her, listened courteously to what she had to say, and at the end of the audience bowed and kissed her hand, but repeated that he forbade the marriage.

Meanwhile, pressure from other quarters was brought to bear on the Archduke. Two Ministers were sent to try and induce him to change his mind, Koerber the Austrian Minister of the Interior, and Goluchowski. Koerber got short shrift. Goluchowski, high on Franz Ferdinand's personal black list for trying to push him on one side when he was ill, got no shrift at all. The Church too was invoked in the person of Marschall, the Archduke's former religious instructor, and now a bishop. Franz Ferdinand and Sophie were both devout Catholics; he was told to appeal to their consciences and try to drive a wedge between them. Marschall, who had set his sights on becoming Cardinal Archbishop of Vienna, was not enthusiastic about his mission, saying frankly "If I do not succeed, with which Emperor shall I be out of favour? The present or the future one or both?" He had three talks with Franz Ferdinand, to whom he represented it was his sacred duty to give up Countess Chotek, and got nowhere. Hopeful of more success with Sophie, he told her that she should give up the Archduke because she loved him. He could be a great Emperor, she would never forgive herself if their marriage forced him to abandon the Crown. She should go into a convent, and console herself with the thought of the contribution which she had made to the Monarchy by her sacrifice. Sophie's reply to this specious reasoning was that she trusted in God, and would do whatever Franz Ferdinand wanted; she seemed to be prepared to wait for him for ever.

The Archduke was enraged by Marschall's attempt to drive a wedge between himself and Sophie, and vowed that he would ensure (which he did) that the prelate had no further advancement in the church. He could not protect her from the pressure to which she was subjected, and in despair turned to Max Vladimir Beck for advice. Beck told him that the affair could not be allowed to drag on indefinitely. His Imperial Highness must before long name the date by which he felt he must marry, meanwhile do all that he could to state his case, and then abide by the Emperor's final decision. Franz Ferdinand havered; the impasse continued. At the Family Dinner on New Year's Day 1900 the Emperor raised his glass in a silent toast to Otto's twelve year old son Karl, as if to say "the future will be yours". Franz Joseph's daughter noted in her diary that Franz Ferdinand looked very grave. Later in the day he said that if need be he would wait for Sophie until the Emperor died, when nothing could stop him from marrying her.

Sophie had gone to Dresden to stay with her sister. Franz Ferdinand, left alone to fight for their marriage, after some while decided to follow Beck's advice, and with the latter's help drafted a letter to the Emperor appealing for his understanding. It was dignified, honest, and could have left his uncle in no doubt of his loyalty

> I have once again summoned up courage to approach Your Majesty, and to lay before you the reasons which impel me to make this plea to you. I can only repeat that my wish to marry the Countess is not a caprice, but springs from the deepest affection, maintained through years of trial and suffering . . ..
>
> My behaviour to date provides Your Majesty with an absolute guarantee of my future attitude, for I have always striven to act loyally and to do nothing either openly or secretly contrary to Your Majesty's will, as many another might have done in my despairing situation . . .. Marriage to the Countess would make me for the rest of my life true to the position to which I have been called, and happy. Without this marriage I shall continue to lead my present anguished existence which must result in my premature uselessness . . . to be eternally alone is unbearable, the need of someone who will care for me, who will unwaveringly share joy and sorrow with me is unfortunately for a person of my temperament something which I cannot overcome. I never can nor will marry anyone else, for the idea repels me, and I will not enter into a union with someone whom I do not love, making her and myself unhappy because my heart belongs to the Countess now and for all eternity . . ..
>
> Last time Your Majesty told me you thought that my marriage could harm the Monarchy. I venture most humbly to say that this marriage, because it will make me happy and give me strength to bear my responsibilities, will enable me to do my duty to the Monarchy far better than if I have to spend the rest of my life consumed with unfulfilled longing, unhappy, lonely . . .. I ask Your Majesty to believe that in my difficult position I am determined to do the best I can, but I must also be able to feel happy, and so I plead with Your Majesty for this, for permission to make this marriage for which I long.

The Emperor did not reply, but when Maria Theresia, fearful that his silence would lead to an irrevocable breach between him and her stepson, again asked for an audience, he agreed to receive her. He may have realised from Franz Ferdinand's letter that, for all his protestations of obedience, he might in desperation marry the Countess without his permission. If this occurred there would be no alternative but to expel him from the Imperial Family and then Otto would become the heir, which in view of Otto's love affairs, now an open scandal, was out of the question. He may also have heard that Franz Ferdinand had declared he was prepared to wait for Sophie until he succeeded to the throne, when nobody could stop him marrying her. This meant that a child of hers would inherit the Habsburg Crown, which must not be allowed to happen. It is impossible to be certain how much these considerations influenced Franz Joseph, and there is no record of what he said to Maria Theresia, but after he had seen her, Beck on April 8th 1900 noted in his diary, "Important developments, His Imperial Highness has talked to the Emperor and as good as got his approval." Beck also noted that Franz Joseph had stipulated that the constitutional problems posed by the marriage must be resolved before he would finally consent to it. He did not record the Emperor's decree that the marriage must be morganatic, and before it took place his nephew must solemnly renounce all rights to the throne for any future children, nor that he had given even this conditional consent with the utmost reluctance.

The responsibility for ironing out the constitutional position devolved mainly on Koerber, now Minister President of Austria. Beck, described by Sieghart, Koerber's *chef de cabinet*, as the Archduke's confidant, was faced with the task of trying to explain to His Imperial Highness the nature of the problems, and shuttled to and fro between him and Koerber. Neither he nor the Minister President found Franz Ferdinand easy to deal with; in spite of "hours" of explanation he seemed to be incapable of grasping what was involved, and was tense and impatient. During the next four weeks he told Koerber successively that he could not renounce the throne because that would be contrary to the law of God; if he did not marry Sophie he would go mad and shoot himself; he had reached the limit of his psychological strength; marriage to Sophie was "a question of my life, my existence my future". On May 20th, unable to understand the procedural difficulties, he exploded to Beck

> Please exert your skill to help me by making this disastrous Koerber stop making further difficulties so that I can marry at the beginning of June . . ..
> Please try and frighten him into action by letting him know that I am despairing (which indeed I am), and that I am not the sort of person who can be led up the garden path or is either impressed or alarmed by Parliament and its Ministers . . .. Normally if Parliament is being uncooperative it is ignored . . . but when it is a question of the happiness and existence of the Heir to the Throne then the bugbear of constitutionalism rears its head. So make Koerber very well aware that I am not going to put up with

44

this nonsense, and that I simply will not wait longer than the beginning of June.

The first of June came and went, but a fortnight later a formula was evolved enabling both the Vienna and Budapest parliaments to recognise the morganatic marriage. All that remained was for the Emperor to give his final permission. Beck made an entry in his diary

> This fraught episode is now over. From now onwards the Archduke must carry on alone and with God's help.

On June 23rd Franz Ferdinand was received by the Emperor. He affirmed that he agreed to marry morganatically, and would sign and swear an act of renunciation debarring his possible children from succeeding to the throne. Franz Joseph said he would confer on Countess Chotek the title of Princess on her wedding day. The solemn renunciation ceremony would take place in the Hofburg at noon on June 28th. That was the end of the audience.

Beck was among the crowd which gathered outside the Hofburg on the 28th to watch the arrival of the Imperial Family and other dignitaries, who had been summoned to witness this act of state for which there was no precedent in Habsburg history. He saw Franz Ferdinand in full uniform drive into the courtyard in a closed carriage, its spokes gilded to denote his rank, looking straight ahead of him and very pale. The ceremony took place in the Privy Council Chamber, in which were assembled all Archdukes of age, the principal Ministers, senior court officials, the Cardinal Archbishop of Vienna, and the Cardinal Prince Primate of Hungary. The Emperor stood on a dais, the Archdukes grouped on his left, Franz Ferdinand alone on his right, and explained coldly that the act which they were summoned to witness was necessary to ensure an orderly succession to the throne. The Minister of the Imperial and Royal House then read out the German text of the act

> We, Archduke Franz Ferdinand Karl Ludwig Joseph Maria of Österreich-Este declare it to be our firm and considered resolve to unite in marriage with the high-born Countess Sophie Maria Josefina Albina Chotek von Chotkowa und Wognin . . ..
>
> We feel it incumbent on us to declare that our marriage with Countess Chotek . . . is a morganatic marriage to be considered as such now and for all time; therefore neither Our wife nor the children to be hoped for with God's blessing from this Our marriage, nor their descendants will possess or be entitled to claim the rights, honours, titles, armorial bearings, privileges etc., which accrue to the eligible wives of Archdukes and the issue of their marriages.
>
> In particular We again emphatically recognise and declare that the children of Our aforesaid marriage and their descendants, since they are

45

not members of the most high Arch House, possess no right to succeed to the throne . . ..

We pledge Our Word that We acknowledge this declaration of the meaning and significance of which we are fully aware, as binding for all time on Ourself, Our Wife and Our children of this marriage and their descendants.

In the silence which followed Franz Ferdinand walked forward to a small table flanked by the cardinals, on which, between two lighted candles, lay the crucifix of that most Catholic Habsburg, Emperor Ferdinand II. He took off his right glove and placed two fingers on the German text of the act of renunciation, touching the Hungarian version of it with his left hand. The Cardinal Archbishop of Vienna raised the crucifix before his eyes and recited the oath which the Archduke repeated after him. Then he signed both documents. The Emperor left the room without a further word. The ceremony had taken under half an hour. During it Franz Ferdinand had been compelled to acknowledge that, in the eyes of the Habsburgs, he was marrying a second-class citizen.

Later in the day the Archduke asked Beck to come and see him at the Belvedere, the palace built in 1714 by Prince Eugen of Savoy, that great servant of the dynasty, the wise adviser of three Emperors, who thrashed the armies of France, drive the Turks back deep into the Balkans, and captured Belgrade. From the Belvedere, a masterpiece of triumphant baroque, there is a superb view of Vienna. Looking across the city, the capital of the Monarchy over which he would rule, Franz Ferdinand may have thought on that afternoon of June 28th, that in Beck he too had someone who, when he came to the throne, would serve him well. He had to leave at 6.15 p.m. to attend an advance celebration of the Emperor's seventieth birthday at which all the Imperial Family would be present – notwithstanding what had occurred earlier in the day the Habsburg show of a united front must go on. Beck later recalled that, as they said goodbye in the courtyard the Archduke was

> deeply moved, flushed and with tears in his eyes. I too had tears in my eyes and could hardly speak. We shook hands long and warmly; he assured me of his lifelong trust and friendship. I confess that I finally became so moved that I forgot myself so far as to kiss his hand, which was quite incorrect, but he made no attempt to stop me, and I had the impression that he really understood what I was feeling and was pleased by this expression of it – then we parted.

Three days later, on July 1st, Franz Ferdinand and Sophie were married in the chapel of Schloss Reichstadt in Bohemia, a castle given to his stepmother Maria Theresia by the Emperor. She made the wedding arrangements, and she and her two daughters were the only Habsburgs who attended it – to Franz Ferdinand's sorrow his brothers refused to come. He wore the full dress uniform of a cavalry general with the Order of the Golden Fleece and the Grand Cross of the Order of St Stephen. Sophie, in white with a train seven feet long, a diamond necklace and earrings, carried a bouquet of myrtle and lilies of the valley. The ceremony was performed by the village priest assisted by two Capuchin monks; at the Archduke's request there was no address. There was no reception, after the service Maria Theresia gave a simple wedding breakfast for the immediate family. A telegram arrived from the Emperor's adjutant announcing that "His Imperial and Royal Apostolic Majesty" had conferred on "His Imperial and Royal Highness the Most Serene Archduke Franz Ferdinand of Österreich-Este's morganatic consort, Sophie née Countess Chotek, the rank of Princess under the name Hohenberg."

The cold formality of this telegram must have left Franz Ferdinand and Sophie in no doubt of the Emperor's continued displeasure, but it did not cloud their happiness. Before leaving for their honeymoon at Konopischt the Archduke telegraphed Beck

> On the most beautiful day of our lives my wife and I express to the co-founder of our happiness our warmest and most heartfelt thanks for all you have done and achieved for us in this long time.

From Konopischt on July 9th Franz Ferdinand wrote to the other and principal founder of their happiness, Maria Theresia

> Dearest Mama,
> There is at last a little peace, in which the first thing I want to do is to send you a few lines and to thank you myself and on behalf of Sophie in writing with all our hearts for all the indescribable love and kindness which you showed to us in Reichstadt. We shall be grateful to you until the end of our days for everything which you have done for us . . ..
> We are both more happy than I can begin to say, and this happiness we owe to you. Where would we be now if you had not so steadfastly stood by us.
> Soph will *not* be reading this letter . . .. So I can tell you dearest Mama that Soph is a *treasure* and that I am indescribably happy. She is looking after me so well that I feel splendid, I am so well and much less nervy. I feel as if I had been reborn. She adores you and talks of nothing but your love and kindness. I am certain in my inmost being that we shall both be indescribably happy until the end of our lives.
> Dear good Mama, you were so entirely right when you helped me.

By the autumn of 1904 Franz Ferdinand and Sophie had three children, a daughter Sophie, known in the family as 'Pinki', and two sons, Max and Ernst. Writing to his "dearest Mama" about them, the Archduke said that Pinki was a darling, Max a splendid intelligent boy, and Ernst a good and beautiful baby. He adored them, "You have no idea dearest Mama how happy I am with my

47

family" and spent all the time he could spare with them

> because I love them so much . . . in the evenings, when I smoke a cigar
> and read the newspapers, Sophie knits, and the children play and pull
> everything off the tables, it is so deliciously cosy.

An early riser, whenever possible he started the day by having breakfast in the nursery. At tea time the children came down to the drawing room where a special corner was set aside for them to play. After they were tucked up in bed he went up with Sophie to say goodnight to them.

This pattern of family happiness continued. As the children grew older Franz Ferdinand took a keen interest in their education, would come up to the schoolroom and question them about what they had learnt, and made a point of getting to know their teachers. Except on very formal occasions they appeared for lunch, were allowed to stay up for dinner, and were always introduced to whomever their parents had invited. If they were in Vienna when Franz Ferdinand and Sophie gave an evening reception, they were allowed to stay up in their dressing gowns to watch from the upper windows of the Belvedere the arrival of the glittering array of guests. Their father often took them with him when he went out shooting, and Sophie had no difficulty in persuading him to find time when in Vienna to go with them to the theatre, or at Konopischt to the circus. Konopischt was their principal home, but during the summer the family also spent some time at Chlumetz and at Blühnbach near Salzburg, where the Archduke had acquired another shoot. After Christmas they went for several weeks to Switzerland, and in the early spring to Brioni or Miramar on the Adriatic. Many years later, talking about her childhood, his daughter said "We always travelled as a family".

The bond between parents and children was very close, and to Pinki, Max, and Ernst, Franz Ferdinand was a delightful and loving father. When he disapproved of something which one of them had done, the resulting explosion only lasted for a few minutes, and once it was over he never referred to the incident again. When speaking of the Emperor to his children, the Archduke always referred to him with the utmost respect. He never talked about Rudolf. Neither did he mention Elisabeth: his daughter only learnt years later from her aunt that, when her father was a young man, the Empress was one of the few people who understood and sympathised with his determination only to marry someone whom he loved. As soon as they were old enough to understand, Franz Ferdinand explained to his children very simply the effect of the renunciation oath which he had sworn when he married their mother, telling them that they were ordinary people who had nothing to do with the Court. His daughter remembers him saying that he hoped her future husband would be a Bohemian Count. The aim of the curriculum which he drew up for his sons' education was to fit them to run Konopischt and Chlumetz. He wanted them to be aristocratic landowners – and no more – free to marry whom they chose.

48

The children did not see a great deal of their relations, for their father did not encourage large family gatherings. Of his Chotek in-laws, only Sophie's youngest sister was invited for long visits and addressed by Franz Ferdinand by the familiar second person singular "*Du*". His marriage had estranged him from most of his own family, and the breach caused by his brother Otto's opposition to it remained unhealed. But when Otto died in 1906 after a horrible illness, he was deeply distressed, "in the past we were very close", and took on the guardianship of Otto's sons, "I will do everything in my power to bring them up as good Christians, Austrians and Habsburgs". To Karl, the eldest, who after him would succeed to the throne, he paid special attention, talking to him about the problems of the Monarchy, making a point of getting to know him, concerned that Karl should not suffer from the handicap of ignorance with which he struggled.

Except on special occasions such as his children's First Communion, in honour of which he appeared in uniform, when in the country or travelling with his family Franz Ferdinand always wore civilian clothes. He supervised every detail of the renovation of Konopischt and the development of his estates and, a man who always wanted to see for himself what was being done, spent hours going round them. When he was away, daily weather reports were telegraphed to him, together with requests from gardeners and builders for instructions, for nothing major could be undertaken without his approval. His pride and joy at Konopischt was the rose garden. Guests who displayed an interest in it might, to their astonishment, be conducted by their Archducal host to the window of one of the upstairs lavatories in the castle, because this was the vantage point from which they could best appreciate the additions to it which he was planning. At Konopischt there was a complete absence of pomp and court ceremonial, both of which Franz Ferdinand detested. When surrounded by his family he was a charming host, a good conversationalist, relaxed and lighthearted. On one evening he and his guests danced a conga through the castle. As they entered one of the guest rooms there was a squawk of dismay from its owner the reason for which was immediately apparent. An article of her underwear which had been washed by her maid was dangling from the chandelier where it had been hung up to dry. Nobody laughed more heartily than the Archduke.

Sophie was the mainspring of Franz Ferdinand's life. He told his "dearest Mama" in 1904 that the best thing he had ever done was to marry her. She was everything to him, "my wife, my adviser, my doctor . . . in a word my entire happiness. After four years we still love one another as we did on the first day of our marriage". Five years later he said that she was the greatest gift that God had bestowed on him, that since he had married her he had been utterly happy, and found in his home consolation for all the trials of life.

After Marschall failed to persuade Sophie to give up Franz Ferdinand, the disgruntled prelate spread a story round Vienna that she was devoured by ambition. This smear persisted after her marriage, and the gossip amongst people who did not know her was that she was cold, haughty, determined to assert herself and to dominate her husband. But people who met her found her charming, intelligent, natural and easy to talk to, apparently taking no notice of the protocol slights inflicted on her because of her morganatic status. Sophie confided to her sister that she minded these only because they upset and hurt Franzi, not for herself; her daughter is emphatic that she never tried to push herself forward. Deeply religious, she undoubtedly prayed constantly that she might be a channel of God's grace to help and support her husband. As in any exceptional marriage, she knew better than anyone else what was in his mind, but she never attempted to influence him. He would listen to her, but if he did not agree with what she was saying, would smilingly and courteously appear to ignore it, and she in her turn would smile and fall silent, accepting this without argument or criticism. She had a quality of repose which, combined with her skill in dealing with him, made a very great contribution to the happiness of their marriage.

If Sophie was worried about Franz Ferdinand's health, she neither showed it nor fussed. Occasionally the children might be told "Papa has a cold" or "Papa has catarrh", but never that they must keep quiet because he was feeling ill again – they remembered him as someone of boundless energy. But she no doubt knew that her husband, understandably in view of the nature of the illness which he had survived, was from time to time worried that it might recur. Although in July 1901 he wrote to Eisenmenger "I am doing splendidly, I feel like a fish in water and marriage is working wonders with me", later he had moments of alarm. Eisenmenger repeatedly had to reassure him "although not always with an entirely clear conscience" that his fears of a relapse were unfounded. Finally the Archduke himself thought of an expedient – perhaps Sophie suggested it – and asked his doctor to

> write on a slip of paper that I am completely cured and that I shall never again have anything to do with the disease. This paper I shall always carry with me and read whenever I have an attack of hypochondria.

In fact after his marriage Franz Ferdinand had no serious illness. Its happiness strengthened his determination to keep fit. In addition, because it was morganatic, if anything happened to him, Sophie and the children would receive nothing from the Habsburg Family Fund and, since his sons were debarred from taking the title "Österreich-Este", under the terms of the Duke of Modena's will, everything which he had inherited from the Duke would pass to Otto's son Karl. To provide for the future of his family it was vital to find a way round this problem, and to do so the Archduke yet again turned to Max Vladimir Beck. A solution which saved part of the Modena inheritance for the children took four years to evolve and it was not until then that he was able to make a will, the drafting of which he also entrusted to Beck.

The only reward which Beck received for a great deal of work was an invitation once a year to shoot – he was paid no fee. This sort of behaviour, of which there were other instances over the years, led to much adverse comment about what was described as Franz Ferdinand's stinginess. On the whole it would be more accurate to say that he was not munificent, and that his sense of money could be erratic. On the one hand he insisted on petty household economies – Eisenmenger once heard him berating the cook for serving up too many strawberries – on the other if he wished to acquire or do something, he did not always stop to consider how it was going to be paid for. Financial acumen is not invariably an attribute of royalty, and it was lacking in many of the Habsburgs, who tended to assume that money would always be found for whatever they wished. When Empress Maria Theresa ran short of funds while building Schönbrunn, her new palace on the outskirts of Vienna, she did not contemplate reducing its planned size (fourteen hundred rooms), but simply borrowed from the Jews. Franz Ferdinand's extravagances were modest compared with those of his ancestress but, the future of his family regardless, he spent a great deal of money on improvements to his various castles, on the park and garden at Konopischt which ate up the profits of the estate, on the purchase of antiques and *objets d'art*, and on shooting.

Franz Ferdinand's love of shooting continued throughout his life, and his total bag, over a quarter of a million head of game of various kinds, included six thousand stags. To the present day mind slaughter on this scale is sickening, and the Archduke's indulgence in it has been condemned as one of his most unattractive traits. It must, however, be considered in the context of the age in which he lived, when the idea of the preservation of wild life did not exist, and shooting was thought of in terms not of the destruction of living creatures, but as marksmanship, the exercise of a skill, the greater the opportunities for which the more enjoyable and successful the shoot. The British aristocracy, led by the Prince of Wales, took this view of the sport. Lord Ripon too shot more than a quarter of a million head of various kinds of game. Lord Walsingham once had every grouse on his Yorkshire moor driven over him and brought down 1,070 in under eight hours.

One of the reasons for the astronomical number of entries in the Archduke's game book was his doctor's orders after his illness to avoid undue exertion, and indeed he was not up to it; on one occasion when walking up a slope he showed signs of distress, and said ruefully to his companion, "It's easy for you, you are not even getting hot". Therefore he could not stalk and game had to be driven to him. In addition to beats which he owned or rented, he had taken over some of the best State beats, and was also frequently invited to shoots, where he was always given the best stand and so every opportunity of doing well.

Franz Ferdinand was a phenomenal shot. He had amazing eyesight and could spot a chamois on a ledge which his companions had difficulty in seeing through field glasses. He never used a telescopic sight nor a repeater rifle, both of which he considered unsporting, always killed his game cleanly, and never boasted about his achievements. The walls of Konopischt and Chlumetz were festooned with antlers, but he never tired of his favourite sport. Possibly it provided some satisfaction for his deep seated psychological need to assert himself. Possibly too it gave him an opportunity to work off some of the adrenalin aroused by his frustration at his lack of power to arrest what he was convinced was an accelerating drift towards the disintegration of the Monarchy.

5
Frustration

THE Emperor received Franz Ferdinand and Sophie in September 1900, two months after their marriage. She seems to have got through this alarming ordeal successfully – Franz Joseph thought that "things went quite well". His verdict on her was that "she was natural and modest, but does not look quite young any more". Faced, much as he disliked it, with a *fait accompli*, henceforward when writing to the Archduke he sent greetings to Sophie. Nine years later he made her a Duchess which entitled her to be addressed as "Highness". But as the Archduke's morganatic wife, at Court she still ranked after the youngest Archduchess, could not drive in a court carriage with her husband, appear with him in the royal box at the Opera or any theatre, nor at official functions within the Monarchy. When Franz Ferdinand asked permission for her to accompany him on an official visit to the Tirol, although the Emperor replied "Your wife belongs to our family and I see her with much pleasure at intimate gatherings of our relations", he went on to say that he thought it better for her not to go with him to Innsbruck because this would transgress "the laid down ceremonial rules".

After their marriage the Archduke and his wife therefore withdrew increasingly from the Court and spent a great deal of time away from Vienna, either travelling or on their country estates. Franz Ferdinand came to the capital when summoned by the Emperor, in connection with his military duties or for some unavoidable official function, but frequently alone. Whether alone or with Sophie he rarely stayed for more than a week. There were a great many people in Vienna whom he disliked: his relations from whom he was estranged by his marriage, elderly members of the court hierarchy who disapproved of it and whom he referred to contemptuously as "paid officials", prominent personalities who had written him off during his illness. His limited circle of personal friends consisted of Bohemian landowners, many of whom he had known since he first entered the army, and he appeared to have no wish to enlarge it. Generally his withdrawn existence meant that for a number of years after his marriage he remained virtually unknown to the general public.

No human being is perfect: one of his closer associates described Franz Ferdinand as having a chiselled character with many rough corners and sharp edges, and some of them were very rough and sharp indeed. Many men endeavour to conceal their imperfections from the world at large, but make little or no attempt to do so when at home; the reverse was true of the Archduke. The accounts of those who saw him with his family are unanimous that when in their midst he was relaxed, charming, an excellent host. But in other surroundings, and particularly with people with whom he was not sure of his ground he could be, and often was, aloof, morose, sarcastic, impatient, unpredictable and prone to sudden outbursts of rage. He did not appear to care what people thought about him, and was not prepared to make any effort to court popularity.

An ideally happy marriage had not eradicated Franz Ferdinand's less attractive traits, nor had it altered his complex temperament. He had a great deal of Habsburg pride and acknowledged the superior authority of two beings only – God and the Emperor. While insisting on being told the truth, he could react badly to it if he felt it implied criticism of his convictions; was inclined only to accept advice if he had sought it, and almost never if it was proffered in the form of a lecture or contained any hint that he was being underestimated. In addition to pride the Archduke also had an inordinate amount of another family trait – mistrust. Much of this derived from his embitterment, which he never entirely lost, over the way in which he had been treated during his illness and his struggle to marry. It led him to suspect the motives of those with whom he came in contact

> For seven hundred years people have been coming to us Habsburgs and flattering us in order to gain something they want – promotions, honours, orders, money.

and, as he acknowledged, to expect the worst of people

> When I meet anyone for the first time, I assume he is a good for nothing, and only gradually change my opinion if he proves otherwise.

It took time to gain Franz Ferdinand's trust and this could easily be lost. He found it difficult to think objectively and his judgement could be faulty. If it was represented to him that someone was intriguing behind his back or engaged in some activity of which he disapproved, his reaction was to write them off without pausing to find out whether or not what he had been told was correct. Anyone whom he considered had let him down, or supported some action which might undermine the power of the Crown or the supranational position of the army, was finished so far as he was concerned. He would at times express himself violently without stopping to think whether what he said was likely to be repeated. As a result he made many enemies and acquired a reputation for having a vile temper and being "a good hater". That he could be charming to anyone who interested him or whom he wished to win round to his point of view; that he could apologise and endeavour to make amends when he realised he had been unjust, was not widely known. Only those closely associated with him realised that his violent language often stemmed from a need to relieve his feelings, and did not necessarily reflect his fundamental thinking.

Franz Ferdinand was also uninhibited in his condemnation of policies, above all those which resulted in what he stigmatised as "weakness" towards the Hungarians, which he saw as failures of government endangering the future of the Monarchy. He blamed for these failures those of the Emperor's Ministers and entourage whom he held – and he was not alone in this – were shutting off their Sovereign from reality, propagating the attitude that on account of his age he must neither be disturbed nor upset. To Franz Joseph himself the Archduke's loyalty was absolute, and he never failed to show the respect due to him both as ruler of the Monarchy and head of the family. They were at one in their conception of the mission conferred by God on the House of Habsburg. They were at one too about the necessity of preserving the supranational character of the army, the shield of the throne. In almost all other respects they were poles apart.

Franz Joseph was an elderly conservative who, after many disappointments, had lost belief in the efficacy of radical change, wished only to maintain the status quo, and plodded on in an unending struggle to make an imperfect system work. Franz Ferdinand, thirty-three years younger, was impatient, eager for action and convinced of the necessity of change, but without the experience fully to realise what this would entail. Franz Joseph ruled the Monarchy from behind his desk, working through files in accordance with a set routine with meticulous attention to detail, and saw no profit in wide ranging political discussions. He did not understand modern innovations and did not care for them, once describing the telephone as an invention of the devil. Franz Ferdinand disliked paperwork and any form of set routine. He learnt not by reading files but by seeing situations on the ground, and would discuss whatever political problem was uppermost in his mind regardless of whether this fell within the competence of his listener. He had not the insight to realise the degree to which the Emperor had become too old to be receptive to new ideas nor that, as with many old people, tact and patience were necessary when talking to him.

The Archduke's marriage put a further and severe strain on this difficult relationship. The Emperor could never bring himself to forgive his nephew for having insisted on it regardless of the interests of the dynasty. Franz Ferdinand sensed this and it did not help his self confidence. When summoned to an audience, at which he had to appear in uniform and, since Franz Joseph started work at 4 a.m., often at a dauntingly early hour, during the long drive to Schönbrunn he was, according to his secretary, as nervous as a schoolboy going to an examination for which he was ill prepared. Both when talking and on paper he had an unfortunate tendency to over hammer a point. The Emperor detested vehement outbursts and did not trust his nephew's judgement. Their meetings, which both disliked, sometimes ended in disagreement, or Franz Joseph said he would think over their discussion, but then took no further action. He required the Archduke to carry out his orders, not to put up ideas, reiterating that any major decision was for him and him alone to make – "*I* rule".

Shortly after his marriage Franz Ferdinand complained that the Emperor was excluding him from acquiring any insight into affairs of State. In view of Franz Joseph's age he might before long succeed to the throne, but how would he be able to undertake the "hard and thankless" task of ruling if his only knowledge of governmental proceedings and decisions was derived from what was reported in the newspapers? If he submitted a memorandum drawing the Emperor's attention to anything outside the military sphere, it was ill received, and he was left in no doubt that he was meddling in matters which did not concern him.

The Archduke then began to discover that even in the military sphere his scope was limited. No specific responsibilities had been allocated to him; his duties were confined to set piece appearances in attendance on the Emperor at parades and manoeuvres, and inspections of troops in different parts of the Monarchy, approval for which had to be obtained from his uncle. Franz Ferdinand carried out the latter meticulously, was prepared to spend all day in the pouring rain watching a field exercise, when visiting a regiment devoted hours to going round the barracks and talking to the men, and when dining with the officers encouraged them to express their opinions, listening with attention to what they had to say. Any recommendations which he subsequently made in his inspection reports were, however, generally ignored. The Emperor had grown accustomed to relying for advice on anything to do with the army on Feldzeugmeister Beck who, the same age as himself, had been the head of his Military Chancellery and his principal A.D.C. before becoming Chief of the General Staff in 1881. Beck, having known Franz Joseph well for over thirty years, was an adept at handling him and had a low opinion of Franz Ferdinand's military ability. So had the Emperor's other closest military adviser Bolfras, only eight years younger than Beck, and head of Franz Joseph's Military Chancellery since 1889. Count Paar, a year older than Bolfras and also very close to the Monarch having been his principal A.D.C. since 1887, did not care for the heir to the throne. None of this trio of ageing gentlemen were inclined to support Franz Ferdinand's recommendations, nor to suggest that he should take part in top level conferences about the organisation of the army or senior military appointments, nor be told of what occurred at them. In spite of Bolfras's assurance when he was passed fit for military duties in 1898, the Archduke received little information from the Emperor's Military Chancellery, and even less from the Ministry of War. The overall result was that he was ill informed and, until 1906, relegated to the sidelines during the internal crisis which threatened the cohesion of the Monarchy, the supranational spirit of the army, and the power of the Crown.

The root of the crisis was that the Monarchy's eleven nationalities were each becoming more determined to secure for themselves greater political and cultural autonomy. Therefore they were not good neighbours and their leaders were not prepared to work together in the spirit of "all for one and one for all". In the Austrian half, by 1801 all attempts by a succession of Minister Presidents to achieve some sort of lasting cooperation in the common interest between the nationalities there had failed. They were, as Max Vladimir Beck later said

> confronted with a problem without parallel in any other country in Europe. 8 nationalities, 17 provinces, 20 parliamentary bodies, 23 parliamentary parties, two different philosophies, a complicated relationship with Hungary, a variety of cultures, extending over an area of about $8\frac{1}{2}$ degrees latitude by a similar number of degrees longitude.

Beck maintained that "to govern effectively in Austria all this must be drawn together in one centre". This was not happening in the Vienna Parliament, which resembled a squabbling tribal assembly to which the representatives of each nationality came for the purpose of furthering their own cause.

There was no similar wrangling in the Budapest Parliament because it was dominated by one nationality, the Hungarians, that part of the population of the lands of the Hungarian Crown who spoke the Magyar language. This was the result of an astonishing franchise law whereby, although only 45% of the inhabitants of those lands were Hungarians, they occupied 405 of the 453 parliamentary seats. The core of the Hungarian oligarchy were the feudal landowners and the landed gentry. They were daring and ruthless, united in their determination to further their nationalist aspirations, passionate upholders of their traditions and, as one of their leaders wrote, if these were threatened

> the most cool-headed becomes ecstatic, the perspicacious stricken with blindness, and the fairest and most just ready to forget the first of the unalterable rules of eternal truth . . .. "Do unto no one what thou would'st not have done unto thee!"

Hungarian politicians dealt with the political aspirations of the other national groups in their half of the Monarchy by ignoring this "first of the unalterable rules of eternal truth". Assured of parliamentary support by 1901 they were demanding not only additional constitutional guarantees of the internal autonomy of Hungary, but also the transfer of all officers domiciled in Hungary to Hungarian regiments, in which Hungarian would replace German as the language of command, and the division of the officers corps of the Imperial army into nationalities. Politically they were determined to loosen the ties between Vienna and Budapest; militarily their ultimate goal was the establishment of a separate Hungarian army.

The only person who could cut the Hungarians down to size was the Emperor, but he seemed to be beginning to "let the reins fall"; many people in Vienna feared that eventually he might, out of sheer weariness, give in to them. When, at the beginning of 1903, Franz Ferdinand wrote to him saying that any military concessions to them would tempt other nationalities to make similar demands, he replied that he thought the army's supranational spirit was virtually intact, "even though there was a short sighted nationalist chauvinist element which was vehemently demanding an independent Hungarian army". Patience was necessary, long experience had taught him that one must edge along a middle way, but he could assure his nephew that the army would not be jeopardised by ill considered concessions to the Hungarians.

For the Hungarians the term "middle way" did not exist. The Budapest Parliament refused to agree a much needed increase in the annual quota of conscripts (it had not been raised since 1889), unless Hungarian became the language of command in regiments recruited mainly in Hungary. One of the deputies said that every opportunity must be seized to grab concessions "because of the advanced age of our King, which means that we must make the utmost use of his respect for the law and for his oath." Franz Joseph at last acted, and during the manoeuvres in the autumn of 1903, issued an Order of the Day stating curtly that he was the head of the army, that it was the army of the Monarchy as a whole, and undivided it would remain. It had no effect. The Hungarian government remained stubbornly uncooperative, pressing relentlessly for every kind of concession. The crisis dragged on.

In March 1905, in despair, Franz Ferdinand submitted to the Emperor a memorandum drafted by Max Vladimir Beck, de facto his principal political adviser, setting out their joint views on the state of the Monarchy. It urged that the Crown should use its constitutional powers and break the deadlock by dissolving the Budapest Parliament, and continuing to do so until it became more amenable, "experience has shown that in view of the attitude of the Hungarians, a policy of concession does not work. The most it achieves is a limited respite which collapses under the next wave of nationalist demands." Franz Joseph, who was in Budapest, replied that he agreed with Beck's memorandum. If, as he assumed, his nephew did so too this, and it pleased him, meant that their view of the situation was identical. The present crisis was one of the gravest he had ever faced, "I pray God my remaining strength may not fail me . . . . In view of the incredible disorder here and the lack of people with any sort of courage, to find a solution is a next to impossible task". That was all. The Emperor had no intention of allowing his heir any part in solving the crisis, did not dissolve the Hungarian Parliament, and continued, alone, to search for a "middle way". By the beginning of 1906, however, Franz Joseph was forced to admit that no negotiated settlement with the Hungarians was possible. He sent in troops and forcibly dissolved the Budapest Parliament. The Hungarian politicians promptly threatened a tax strike but then, faced with the prospect of being ruled by royal absolutism enforced by what amounted to martial law, climbed down. Two months later they reluctantly formed a coalition government and undertook to obey the Emperor's orders in return for measures "to preserve the constitutional rights of the Nation."

Some sort of *modus vivendi* had been established, and the acute phase of the crisis between the Crown and the Hungarians seemed to be over. During it Franz Ferdinand referred to the Budapest politicians as "rabble" and "traitors", and at one point in a black rage lashed out not only at them but at all their compatriots, "the so-called 'decent Hungarian' simply does not exist . . .. Every one of them thinks precisely what the most infamous deputy says." There has been a tendency to assume from outbursts such as this, and the repetitive violence of some of his comments about the Hungarians in years to come, that the Archduke had no use for any of them. This is not entirely correct. Soon after his marriage he appointed a Hungarian priest as chaplain to his household, and a Hungarian naval officer as one of his personal A.D.C.s, telling the latter that this was to demonstrate to his countrymen that his attitude towards them was not that of an ogre. They would converse in Hungarian, "I must somehow learn this infernal language which I find so frightfully difficult". He retained some friends amongst the aristocracy, is said once to have declared that he liked the peasants, and maintained that he did not hate all Hungarians indiscriminately, only those chauvinist elements in the nation which were "anti-dynastic and traitorous".

Since Franz Ferdinand considered that, with a very few exceptions, all Hungarian politicians were "anti-dynastic and traitorous", he did not believe that the new government in Budapest would honour its undertakings. But, in view of the Emperor's refusal to consult him, all he could do was to continue to assert that no more concessions must be made, for they would be "the beginning of the end" of the Monarchy, and to stress that any Minister in Vienna who was "weak with the Hungarians" would, so far as he was concerned, be committing a cardinal sin.

Part Two
The Monarchy and the South Slavs

6

The emergent South Slav threat

FROM the turn of the century until 1906, the threat posed to the unity of the Monarchy and the army by the demands of the Hungarians absorbed the attention and energies of most leading personalities in Vienna from the Emperor and Franz Ferdinand downwards to whom, by comparison with this, dissatisfaction amongst the other nationalities appeared to be a cloud on the horizon no bigger than a man's hand. Very few people realised the significance of certain developments amongst the ethnic South Slavs – Slovenes, Croats, and Serbs – who by 1900 totalled nearly four and a half million of Franz Joseph's subjects. Of these, the million Slovenes lived in the southern provinces of the Austrian half of the Monarchy, and seven hundred thousand Croats and Serbs in Dalmatia on the eastern shore of the Adriatic which was also administered by Vienna. The majority of the remainder of the Croats and Serbs (about one and a half million of the former and a million of the latter) were in the lands of the Hungarian Crown, principally Croatia and southern Hungary, where they were so intermingled that no territorial demarcation line could be drawn between them.

Although they were ethnic kinsmen, there were profound dissimilarities between the three national groups. The Slovenes and Croats were converted to Christianity from the west during the eighth and ninth centuries A.D. and remained staunch Catholics; their cultural heritage was Roman and Central European. The Serbs, converted from Constantinople, were Greek Orthodox, and their cultural heritage has been well described as Turkish-Byzantine.

The Slovenes, who had been ruled by the Habsburgs since the fourteenth century, had an ancient culture but no independent national history. The Croats had over a thousand years of such history dating from 924 when, over three hundred years before the Habsburgs established themselves in Austria, the kingdom of Croatia was founded. It lasted until 1094 when, their national dynasty having died out, the Croats entered into a personal union with the Kings of Hungary, of whose lands they became a dependency but retained their own national assembly, the *Sabor*, and continued to do so after 1527 when the Habsburgs inherited the Hungarian crown. Assigned by successive Emperors to guard the Military Frontier, the outer bastion of their realm against invaders from the south-east, the Croats also provided the Imperial army with some of its toughest soldiers, who for the next three hundred years fought and died for the Habsburgs in their wars against the Turks, the Kings of France, the Prussians, Napoleon. In 1848–49 when the Hungarians revolted they remained loyal to the dynasty.

The Serbs also had a long national history, but it had taken a very different course. In the first half of the fourteenth century the kingdom of Serbia extended across most of the western part of the Balkan peninsula. It was destroyed on June 28th 1389 when Tsar Lazar's army was wiped out by the Ottoman Turks at Kosovo, the Field of the Blackbirds. For over four hundred years Serbia was a Turkish pashalik and the principal battlefield in the wars between the Habsburgs and the Ottoman Sultans. Many Serbs in the Monarchy were descended from refugees who had fled there to escape from the Turks. They too served the Habsburgs and remained loyal to the dynasty in the 1848–49 revolt but, unlike the Croats, had no national assembly of their own.

Members of the three South Slav national groups who lived in provinces administered by Vienna were not affected by the 1867 *Ausgleich*. The Slovenes continued to send deputies to the Vienna Parliament, so did the Croats and Serbs of Dalmatia. For the Croats and Serbs in the Hungarian half of the Monarchy, however, the *Ausgleich* meant a severance of direct political links with the Imperial capital.

Under the terms of an additional *Ausgleich* agreement concluded between the Crown, Croatia and Hungary in 1868, Croatia was recognised as "a political nation possessing a special territory, and a country which in its internal affairs possesses a legislature and government of its own". The Croats kept their *Sabor*, which sat in Agram (Zagreb), and it was laid down that Croat should be the language of their bureaucracy. They were represented in the Budapest Parliament by forty of the *Sabor* deputies. But the authority of the *Sabor* was confined to the internal administration of the province and its educational and judicial affairs. A wide range of subjects considered to be of joint interest to Hungary and Croatia such as taxation, laws relating to recruiting and military service, customs and trade, postal and telegraph services, the railways, were decided by the Hungarian Parliament in which the Croatian deputies could always be outvoted. In subjects common to both Austria and Hungary – foreign affairs, defence and finance – the Croats had no voice. Their only constitutional link with Vienna was the Governor of Croatia who was appointed by Franz Joseph, but always on the advice of the Hungarian Minister President. He therefore represented Hungarian interests and, although responsible to the *Sabor*, could evade its control by the simple device of suspending or dissolving it.

64

Although de facto the Croats were handed over to the Hungarians, at least within Croatia after the *Ausgleich* they retained the possibility of some limited national self expression. The Serbs by then had none. A minority in Croatia, for a time they had enjoyed a measure of political and religious autonomy within Hungary, and as a reward for their part in putting down the Hungarian revolt of 1848-49, the Imperial government set up an autonomous Serb province. It lasted for barely ten years; Vienna abolished it in 1860 to placate the Hungarians. Thereafter the Serbs began to look elsewhere for the fulfilment of their national aspirations.

Towards the end of the nineteenth century a cultural renaissance in all three South Slav groups was gathering momentum. Amongst the Slovenes, who had little in the way of a historic past to look back to, it was primarily linguistic. Amongst the Serbs, endeavours to update their language was leading to the development of a Serb literary nationalism, much of it expressed in poetry glorifying and romanticising the spirit of Serbia and the deeds of bygone heroes. Croat writers and scholars were engaged in rediscovering the historic past of their nation, and extolling the epic deeds of South Slavs of former times in the defence of Christianity. A South Slav Academy was founded in Agram, born of the concept of the ethnic, linguistic and cultural relationship of all South Slavs and of their common historic destiny. But the Croats and Serbs disagreed as to how that destiny should be fulfilled. The former's vision was of the establishment of an autonomous South Slav kingdom within the Habsburg Monarchy under Croat leadership; the latter's of the creation of a Serbian-led South Slav state outside the Monarchy. In Croatia the Serbs set up their own party and contested the Croatian assumption that theirs was the only nationality which counted there. By the early 1890s the local political scene in Agram resembled a kaleidoscope: parties were formed, broke up, regrouped, Serb and Croat politicians quarrelled. Ill feeling between them suited the Hungarians admirably, and on the principle of divide and rule they lost no opportunity of exacerbating it.

The first significant move towards South Slav unity was initiated in the Austrian half of the Monarchy. It began after a row in the Vienna Parliament in 1894 over the grammar school in Cilli, a small town in an area of the south Steiermark largely inhabited by Slovenes. The Slovene deputies demanded the introduction of classes in their language in the school, and were bitterly opposed by their non-Slav counterparts. The wrangle over this apparently trivial matter was won by the Slovenes, after it had dominated parliamentary proceedings for the rest of the year and ended in the fall of the government. They realised, however, that to exploit this victory, they must make common cause with their South Slav kinsmen – it was a case of "united we stand, divided we fall" – and began to draw closer to the Croats, their neighbours over the border in the Hungarian half of the Monarchy.

A few years later the Croats and Serbs within the Monarchy also began to draw closer together. The younger generation of Serbs realised that the cause of South Slav unity transcended their differences. So did many of the Croats, "With the Serbs we can do a great deal, without them little, in opposition to them nothing." In May 1903, the Governor of Krain, a province in the Austrian half of the Monarchy bordering on the Adriatic where the majority of the inhabitants were Slovenes, sent a disturbing report to the Minister of the Interior in Vienna

> What is occurring in Croatia . . . threatens to give rise to a united South Slav movement in Austria. Many demonstrations in favour of this are being reported from Dalmatia, it is supported by propaganda by Slav journalists in the coastal areas, and is now making headway here.

The Governor thought it not improbable that a carefully planned campaign would develop for the realisation of the "constitutional Utopia of the South Slavs." The possibility could not be ruled out that if the "revolutionary movement" in Croatia was not rapidly suppressed, and if there were clashes with troops stationed there, "fanatics" from Dalmatia and the Slovene areas might move in to help the Croats. There was solid Slovene support for the "oppressed" Croats in Hungary, and ties between the two national groups were "very close".

There was another development of which the Governor made no mention. This was the increasing effect on South Slavs in the Monarchy (particularly the Serbs) of propaganda emanating from their kinsmen across the frontier in the kingdom of Serbia. It had been reborn because during centuries of Turkish rule the Serbs had never lost their sense of national identity. Stories of the days when they had a great kingdom were handed down from generation to generation, evolving into a legendary folklore, episodes from which were the themes of ballads sung by the minstrels, *guslas*, who wandered from village to village. Of these none was more deeply embedded in the national consciousness than the battle of Kosovo, and above all, the deed on the evening of that St Vitus Day – Vivodan – June 28th 1389 when, after the battle was lost, a Serbian nobleman, Miloš Obilić, crept into the victorious Sultan's tent, stabbed him to death, and was then hacked to pieces by the Sultan's guards. Down the years the legend of Kosovo grew in the imagination of the Serbs. In 1870 an English traveller found that

> there is not a name in that heroic muster roll which is not a household word wherever the Serbian tongue is spoken. Epic lays of the fatal days of Kosovo are still sung every day to throngs of peasant listeners by minstrels of the people . . . .. Tragic and romantic as were the central incidents of that great contest, they stand out against the disastrous twilight which succeeded it, in fantastic and supernatural relief.

Miloš Obilić became the epitome of the heroic warrior who sacrificed his life to kill the cruel oppressor; the defeat of Kosovo was portrayed as a national

66

martyrdom which would be followed by resurrection, and so as an inspiration for the overthrow of foreign tyrants. In 1804, when it was evident that the Ottoman Empire was decaying, it seemed that the day for this was at hand. As a Serbian priest said, his countrymen having prayed to God to deliver them from their oppressors for centuries without avail, took their guns to do the job themselves and rose against the Turks. By 1830, after a series of insurrections, they succeeded in establishing an autonomous state ruled over by a Prince elected from amongst them, the existence of which was acknowledged by the Powers in 1856. Serbia once again appeared as a name on the map of Europe, but the new state was small compared to the fourteenth-century kingdom of Tsar Lazar, landlocked, and its total population of about two million comprised only a proportion – less than a half – of the ethnic Serbs in Central Europe and the Balkan peninsula. The majority of the rest were either subjects of the Habsburgs or still ruled by Constantinople.

Some Serbs within this new state therefore envisaged its establishment merely as the first step upon the road to their ultimate goal, defined by one of them in a secret memorandum written for the reigning Prince in 1844, as a Greater Serbia which would include not only all Serbs, but also their South Slav kinsmen, the Croats and the Slovenes. In 1871 Svetozar Marković, a Serbian journalist, enlarged on this theme

> The conception of Serbian unity is rooted in revolution . . . from Stambul to Vienna . . . it means the destruction of Turkey and Austria and a reorganisation of the whole political structure of the Serbian people . . . a new Serbian state will arise, united Serbia.

Nikola Pašić, who while studying in Switzerland was influenced by Russian revolutionary writers, founded the Radical Party in 1878. Its programme included propaganda in the Serbian inhabited provinces of the Turkish and Habsburg Empires, aimed at promoting national feeling and preparing for the day when a war of liberation would join them to a Greater Serbia. Societies and associations, ostensibly cultural or educational, crusading for a Greater Serbia, began to multiply.

Although raised to the status of a kingdom by the Powers in 1882, at the turn of the century Serbia was in no position to follow up this crusading rhetoric by action. Its administration was still primitive by the standards of most European countries; since there was no aristocracy and no middle class, Government officials had to be recruited from amongst the peasants. In the officers' corps the Praetorian Guard spirit of the Janissaries, which assumed that the simplest way of solving political problems was by murder, lived on. For decades after its emergence as an independent state the country had been rent by the power struggle of the two rival families of Karadjordjević and Obrenović; there had been several palace revolutions resulting in changes of dynasty as one or other of them gained the upper hand, and the feud between them continued to smoulder. The current occupant of the throne, Alexander Obrenović, had abolished the constitution and assumed absolute power.

Belgrade was still a Balkan town rather than a capital city. Alexander Musulin, seconded from the Austrian Embassy in St Petersburg to act as Chargé d'Affaires there for a few months in 1901, found it dull. There were no theatres, museums nor picture galleries. The diplomatic corps spent their time entertaining one another. Contact between the Austrian Legation and Serbian officials was restricted to what was necessary for the transaction of a limited amount of official business. The Court was primitive by western standards. In 1900 the King had married his mistress Draga Mašin, one of his mother's ladies in waiting, and seven years older than himself. Musulin, who was received by them both, thought Alexander, although not unintelligent, was unattractive and a bundle of nerves. He described Draga as "overblown, over made up, plump, stupid, and middle class". It was widely known that she used her influence over the King to further the interests of her relations and interfere in army appointments. She was, as Musulin said, abused and hated in Belgrade.

Alexander was attempting, and this was much resented, to rule as a despot. His marriage added to his unpopularity. On June 11th 1903, a group of army officers forced their way into the palace, murdered the King and his wife, and threw their mutilated bodies out of the window. Petar Karadjordjević, grandson of the founder of the rival dynasty, was installed on the throne. The new King had spent years in exile in Russia. His wife was a daughter of Nicholas of Montenegro, the ruler of the other independent South Slav state, a poor mountainous principality about half the size of Wales, and his two Montenegrin sisters-in-law were married to Russian Grand Dukes. He was reputed to be a fanatical protagonist of a Greater Serbia, and after his accession Pašić's Radical Party came to power. Petar, no longer young, was content to leave the direction of politics to Pašić.

Across the frontier in the Monarchy, during the next two years the rapprochement between Franz Joseph's Croat and Serb subjects continued. It culminated in October 1905, when Croat deputies from Agram and Dalmatia met in Fiume and issued a declaration calling for the incorporation of Dalmatia into Croatia, an extension of autonomy there, and the introduction of a democratic electoral law in the lands of the Hungarian Crown. Twelve days later the Serbian deputies of Dalmatia met at Zara (Zadar), the capital of the province, and announced their support for the Fiume declaration on condition that the principle of equality between Serbs and Croats be recognised. This was followed on November 18th by a conference at Zara of Serb and Croat political leaders, who declared that "the Serbs and the Croats are one nation" and agreed a joint policy, the goal of which was the union of all the Monarchy's South Slav peoples. A coalition was formed between the main Croat and Serb political parties in Dalmatia, and in the Agram *Sabor*.

Meanwhile in Serbia a new organisation, Slovenski Jug, had been founded;

as one of its leading members openly stated, Serbia must have scope for expansion, and must develop its contacts with the rest of the Serbo-Croat world. When in the summer of 1906, Serb and Croat signatories of the Fiume and Zara declarations went to Serbia for discussions, they were therefore warmly welcomed in Belgrade.

7
Bosnia and Hercegovina:
the world of Gavrilo Princip

IN addition to the South Slavs within the Monarchy, much attention was focused in Belgrade on the Serb and Croat inhabitants of Bosnia and Hercegovina, legally Turkish citizens, de facto under Habsburg rule, and a prime target for Greater Serbia propaganda.

These provinces extended over the greater part of the hinterland of Dalmatia. To the north the Bosnian frontier marched with Croatia, and on the south-east with Serbia; Hercegovina adjoined Montenegro. Their original inhabitants were Croats and Serbs, who first settled there during the seventh century A.D., and like their kinsmen elsewhere, were converted to Christianity by missionaries from the west and from Byzantium. After 1463, when the kingdom of Bosnia and the Duchy of Hercegovina were overrun by the Ottoman Turks, some of them went over to Islam and were rewarded with grants of land by their Turkish overlords.

During the nineteenth century, as the Sultan's hold upon his European provinces became tenuous, the Christians in Bosnia and Hercegovina followed the example of members of their faith in other parts of the Balkans and rose against the Turks, but by 1870, in spite of seven insurrections, they were still under the direct rule of Constantinople. Unrest continued, and in July 1875 yet another revolt broke out. Franz Joseph, who in the previous spring had for the first time visited Dalmatia, a tour which filled him with enthusiasm for "this primitive but loyal province", was alarmed and told one of his senior diplomats after the revolt had been in progress for the better part of a year

If for example Bosnia becomes independent we shall lose Croatia and Dalmatia. We can never agree to this, we have already lost enough territory ... the western provinces of Turkey are my direct concern.

How to implement that concern was another matter. Constantinople failed to put down the insurrection in Bosnia and Hercegovina, there was an uprising in Bulgaria, Serbia and Montenegro declared war on the Porte. All the indications were that Turkey might collapse. In this event the probability had to be faced that the Russians, the self-appointed champions of the Sultan's Christian Slav subjects since the reign of Peter the Great, would attempt to set up a large satellite Slav state, wholly under their influence, and possibly extending across the Balkan peninsula. This would prevent the Monarchy from expanding south-eastwards towards the Aegean (the only direction after its loss of Italy and exclusion from Germany in which expansion was possible) and jeopardise Dalmatia. Andrassy, the Imperial Foreign Minister, agreed with his sovereign that the "oriental confusion" of which the Monarchy had a "stage box view" was a "depressing spectacle".

Four years earlier the German Emperor, the Czar and Franz Joseph had banded themselves together in the *Dreikaiserbund* or Three Emperors' League, announcing that they were united in their desire for peace. It could now only be hoped that the Czar would continue to adhere to the spirit of this declaration. Franz Joseph neither liked nor trusted him. Alexander II was moody and unpredictable, and appeared to be either unwilling or unable to control the growing Pan-Slavist movement in Russia, members of which were vociferously demanding action to liberate their fellow Slavs. The openly proclaimed aims of this movement had never been reassuring. The assertion by one of its founders that

> Our most helpful and powerful allies in Europe are the Slavs, our kinsmen by blood, tongue, heart, history and faith, and there are ten million in Turkey and twenty million in Austria

was not agreeable reading in Vienna and still less in Budapest. It was all very well for Disraeli to advise Queen Victoria to take no notice of the Czar. England was an island. Part of the frontier of the Monarchy marched with Russia and, except in the Crimea, Russia had never been defeated in a war. Franz Joseph was advised by his generals that an armed confrontation with the Czar must at all costs be avoided. Therefore, when in April 1877 Alexander announced that he must come to the aid of the oppressed Slavs in the Balkans, and for the ninth time the Russian army took the field against Turkey, the Monarchy continued to sit passively in its stage box, its attitude reminiscent of a timid early Christian contemplating the lions in the Circus, with a fixed resolution to do nothing to cause an encounter with them, for it would undoubtedly be fatal.

When the Czar was asked about the objective of his campaign, he replied laconically "Constantinople". Ten months later the Russians were within sight of the walls of the Ottoman capital. They dictated the peace of San Stefano to the Porte which set up a large new state, Bulgaria, stretching across the Balkan peninsula and bordering on the Aegean. Since it would undoubtedly be a Russian puppet, it would provide the Czar with a base from which to foment more trouble in the Balkans and mount a further attack on Turkey which could jeopardise the sea route to India. It therefore posed a threat to the balance of power which the European governments were not prepared to tolerate. Diplomatic pressure was brought to bear on Russia from all sides, and finally St Petersburg reluctantly agreed that those clauses of the peace of San Stefano which were of general interest – which in effect meant most of them – should be discussed at a Congress in Berlin presided over by Bismarck.

The Congress met in June 1878 and was attended by a galaxy of leading statesmen. Its outcome was a treaty aimed at containing Russia, bolstering up Turkey and – hopefully – stabilising the Balkans. The greater Bulgaria of San Stefano was trisected into an autonomous principality under a Christian prince to be elected by the Bulgarian people, East Rumelia, a semi-autonomous province under Turkish administration, and Macedonia, which was returned to Turkey. A new independent principality, Roumania, was set up. Bosnia and Hercegovina remained nominally under the Sultan's suzerainty, but the Monarchy was awarded a mandate to occupy and administer them for an unspecified time, and to garrison the Sanjak of Novi Bazar, a tongue of territory between Serbia and Montenegro. Franz Joseph was delighted. Crown Prince Rudolf wrote to his former tutor

> The joining of the two provinces to the Monarchy has as we all knew it would overjoyed Papa . . . . I believe that in Bosnia and Hercegovina he is aiming at compensation for Lombardy and Venetia.

All the Habsburgs were convinced that more acres meant more power, and throughout their history acquired them whenever the opportunity offered, regardless of the problems of administering them. In terms of acreage it could be said that the Emperor had compensated himself for Lombardy and Venetia, but that was all. Bosnia and Hercegovina in no way resembled the two lost Italian provinces. They were remote, isolated from the main Balkan trade routes and thinly inhabited by about one and a half million people, of whom approximately 320,000 were Croats, 650,000 Serbs and 530,000 Muslims. Most of the population were illiterate and miserably poor. Sarajevo, which with its minarets, bazaars and veiled women, seemed to one western visitor to be more oriental than Cairo, was the only town of any size. Much of Bosnia consisted of mountains covered with thick forests and split up by deep gorges. Hercegovina was an arid plateau, large areas of which were devoid of vegetation, hemmed in by mountain ranges. Communications were primitive. Apart from about three hundred and fifty miles of indifferent road, there were only tracks which were impassable in bad weather. The Christian peasants, the *kmets*, were oppressed by the Muslim landowners. An English traveller in Hercegovina in 1875 thought that the *kmet* there "is worse off than many a serf in our darkest ages, and lies as completely at the mercy of the Mahometan owner of the soil as if he were a slave". With the possible exception of Albania, the area was generally considered to be the most backward of all the Sultan's European territories.

A number of memoranda were submitted to the Congress of Berlin by various national groups. Amongst them was one from "Mr Widowitch and several other inhabitants of Bosnia" "asking for the reunion of Bosnia with the Principality of Serbia, or the introduction of an autonomous status under the sovereignty of the Porte". "Mr Widowitch" was Vaso Vidović, a leading Bosnian insurgent who, ill at ease in a western suit acquired specially for the occasion, came to Berlin to present his memorandum in person. No attention was paid to him. It did not occur to any of the statesmen there that some of the inhabitants of Bosnia had their own views about their future, and disliked the prospect of an indefinite Austrian occupation. Andrassy is alleged to have maintained that the entry of the Habsburg troops into the mandated provinces would be merely a "parade march" which could be carried out by "a company of Hussars and a band". But when the Austrians crossed the frontier on July 29th 1878, although they brought with them a proclamation informing the local inhabitants that they had come to restore order, peace, and prosperity and (with doubtful veracity) that "the Sultan had entrusted the Emperor, his friend with their protection", within a few days they found themselves involved in a campaign against guerillas who sniped from the hillside, threatened their supply lines, and could not be brought to battle. It lasted for three months. When resistance finally ended more than 150,000 Austrian troops had been engaged, had suffered over 5,000 casualties, the operation had cost 85 million gulden and by no stretch of imagination could be described as a parade march.

In view of the constitution established by the 1867 *Ausgleich*, it was decided that Bosnia and Hercegovina must be administered as a condominium of Austria and Hungary. Supreme authority for this was therefore vested in the Joint Minister of Finance, a post held from 1882 until his death in 1903 by a Hungarian, Count Kalláy. The head of the administration in the occupied provinces was the military governor, the General in command of the large number of troops stationed there, who worked in conjunction with a civilian adviser, the latter being the Minister's representative and responsible for carrying out his orders. Since these on occasion conflicted with the views of the General, relations between them were not invariably harmonious. The task to be undertaken was formidable. Law and order had to be restored. Communications – roads and narrow gauge railway lines – had to be developed, for military purposes, and as part of the infrastructure of an economic programme devoted to exploiting the natural resources of the provinces for the benefit of the Monarchy. State schools had to be established – under the Turks there had only been confessional schools. A bureaucracy had to be built up, and senior officials for it imported from other parts of the Monarchy – twenty-five years after the beginning of the occupation there were only about thirty Bosnians and Hercegovinians who had completed their education at a recognised university.

Altogether there was a great deal to be done if the Monarchy was to carry out what Kalláy described as its "civilising work" in Bosnia and Hercegovina but, as Josef Baernreither, a member of the Upper House of the Austrian parlia-

73

ment said, few of his parliamentary colleagues took "a serious interest" in what was going on there. In October 1892 Baernreither went to see for himself. His first stop was in Sarajevo, which he described as

> Perfectly charming: the general view of the town as beautiful as anything of the kind in Europe. Set in the centre of a great bowl, it is surrounded by range upon range of mountains, the lower slopes being wooded, the higher ones heath-clad. Everywhere one sees the new Sarajevo, with its European buildings and modern streets pushing through the bright confusion of the old Oriental city . . .. Mosques with their minarets rising up on all sides give the characteristic decorative note.

He called on some of the senior civil servants, by whom he was much impressed. Thanks to their "disinterested work" the "disorder and disregard of authority" which was rampant when Bosnia was under the Turks had been done away with, "today there is complete security of life and property".

When he got outside Sarajevo, however, Baernreither began to realise how much still needed to be done. He went on by train over the mountains to Mostar the capital of Hercegovina, "a stony treeless country",

> this journey made clear to me that railway development would be a big step on the way to economic advance. On one side of the stretch of narrow gauge line, right up to the Serbian and Montenegrin frontier, there is no connection at all; nor is there on the other side, that towards Dalmatia and the sea.

After a few days in Hercegovina he returned to Bosnia, travelling round the countryside by train and carriage, which gave him a chance of "seeing the smaller towns and villages, and especially the agriculture and the way the peasants lived and worked". Having learnt from a Government official that "the Bosnian peasant is a *kmet* – that is to say, he has the usufruct of his ground and in general, hands over one-third of the yield to the superior owner . . . as a rule, a Muslim", he noted in his diary

> it does not require much insight into social conditions on the land to perceive that this system of gross deduction is a major obstacle to full production and agricultural development in the occupied regions.

Shortly after his return to the Monarchy, Baernreither made a speech to the Delegations about Bosnia and Hercegovina. He laid particular stress on the necessity of abolishing the "intolerable" *kmet* system – "nobody will work for somebody else's benefit" – and of providing more schools – "a thoughtful schoolmaster told me that the children are like ducks, so eagerly do they drink up the knowledge and education offered to them". Kalláy's reply to both points was negative. The Muslim landowners would not agree to any programme of agrarian reform, and to emancipate the *kmets* would ruin them economically.

74

Education was a question of money, and there was none to spare.

Since Baernreither was in Bosnia and Hercegovina for under three weeks, he did not have time to visit the remoter mountainous areas inhabited by the poorest *kmets*. One of these, Krajina in north-west Bosnia, the scene of bitter fighting during the insurrection of 1875-77, was the subject of a Serb folksong:

> Krajina's like a blood-soaked rag;
> Blood is our fare at noon, blood still at evening,
> On every lip is the taste of blood,
> With never a peaceful day or any rest.

Bordered on the west by the Dinaric Alps which, rising to a height of over 6,000 feet, separate Bosnia from Dalmatia and the Adriatic, it consists of highlands split up by valleys a few miles long by a couple of miles broad, covered with fertile red earth irrigated by melting snow at the end of the long and bitterly cold winter, oases in a harsh landscape in which in the last decade of the nineteenth century the population of this sparsely inhabited area huddled together in small villages, their habits and customs unchanged over hundreds of years.

Life was hard for the Serb *kmets* of Krajina, of whom the Princips in the Grahovo valley were a typical example. Petar Princip and his wife Nana lived in a house which had belonged to his family for generations. It was built of wood with a steeply pitched roof; the doors were small and low, and the only light came through a hole in the roof which let out the smoke from the open hearth – there were no windows. It consisted of one large room, the only furniture in which was a low table, some wooden chests, cooking utensils, earthenware pots, a barrel of water, and a small room leading off it containing a bed. Of the nine children born there to Petar and his wife, six died in infancy. He had about four acres of land on which it was impossible to grow enough grain to feed his family, and had to pay annually in cash the customary tribute of one-third of the value of all his produce to his Muslim landlord. To supplement his income he carried mail and passengers on his wagon over the mountains to Dalmatia; while he was away his wife looked after the children and worked on their land. A photograph of them both shows Petar as a short stocky man wearing a fez, baggy breeches, a shirt with broad sleeves gathered at the wrists and over it a loose waistcoat. Nana, in a long black skirt with a white apron over it and a black scarf over her head tied under her chin, looks older than her husband. In fact she was fourteen years younger, but prematurely aged by child bearing and ceaseless toil.

On July 13th 1894, after working all day although she was nine months pregnant, Nana Princip gave birth to a boy. Relatives arrived and agreed that the baby was sickly and probably would not live long. A priest was hurriedly summoned to baptise him, and insisted that he be called Gavrilo because he was born on St Gabriel's day. Contrary to expectation the child survived. He inherited his mother's curly hair, her pointed chin and large eyes, but neither of his parents' physiques. Never robust and always undersized for his age, he was quiet and withdrawn, preferring to watch the peasants working in the fields to playing with other children. When sent at the age of nine to the primary school two miles away, he proved to be one of the pupils who "drank up education" and became a voracious reader.

After school hours the only entertainment in the village was an occasional *selo*, when the peasants gathered together to drink plum brandy, exchange gossip, and tell stories and legends of the heroic past. As Princip said years later, the *selos* made a lasting impression on him

> The wet logs on the open fire gave the only light to the closely packed *kmets* and their wives, wrapped in thick smoke. If I tried to penetrate the curtain of smoke, the most I could see were the eyes of the human beings, numerous, sad, and glaring with some kind of fluid light coming from nowhere. Some kind of reproach, even threat, radiated from them, and many times since they have awakened me from my dreams.

This scene was a world away from the triumphant baroque and Imperial splendour of the Austro-Hungarian capital. To the *kmet* families like his, huddled round the fire at a *selo* at the turn of the century when he was a child, the Emperor in Vienna was as remote as the Sultan in Constantinople, and as disinterested in their plight.

Growing resentment in Serbia at the award to the Austrians of the mandate to occupy Bosnia and Hercegovina was apparent in a brochure entitled "La Bosnie et l'Hercegovine", sponsored by Pašić's Radical Party, which appeared in Paris in 1899. This stated that the purest section of the Serb race was in these provinces, and Serbia must have them. It argued that either Austria had carried out the terms of the mandate – in which case there was no longer any reason for her to remain there – or she had not, in which case it should be withdrawn from her. The "weeping brethren in chains across the frontier", from 1900 onwards a recurrent phrase in articles in the Belgrade press, referred to Serbs not only in Turkey and the Monarchy, but also in Bosnia and Hercegovina.

The aim of Greater Serbia propaganda was to make clear to every Serb "in chains" where his only hope of liberation lay

> Serbia knows of its great mission to fulfil its destiny . . .. Serbian nationalist mythology stems from the immortal deeds of Serbian heroes . . .. Our mythology is unique, it has nothing to do with the mythology of antiquity. The history of the rights of the Serb race is not written down, it is told in the songs of the *guslas*.

The Serbian Orthodox church had no validity unless it identified itself with "the Serbian soul". Christianity was equated with the nationalist theme, a conception eventually summarised in a newspaper article, which declared that Good Friday was the Golgotha of the Serbian nation; Easter Saturday stood for the resurrection of Greater Serbia; Christmas was the birth of the nation, and at Whitsun the "Serbian God" strengthened the spirit of revenge. There was barely a day in the church calendar which was not related by the propagandists to some nationalist sentiment, and at an early stage the sum total of their thesis was that, as Christ had redeemed the world by shedding his blood, so the "Serbian mission" could only be realised through blood, "either we shall make Serbia one vast graveyard or we shall build a greater Serbia."

In Bosnia and Hercegovina the impact of Greater Serbia propaganda steadily increased. *Srpska Riječ*, the largest newspaper in Sarajevo, was stridently pro-Serbian and found fault with everything the Austrian administration did. Prosvjeta, ostensibly only a cultural society and therefore permitted by the Austrians, founded in 1902 in the Bosnian capital, took its orders from Belgrade, and gave grants to poor but talented students to enable them to continue their studies there or elsewhere abroad. In the countryside, where 80% of the population was illiterate, the flame of Serbian nationalism was fanned by the *guslas*, their songs plugging again and again three main themes – Serbian heroes, hatred of the Turks, hatred of Austria. By 1907 articles were appearing in newspapers in both provinces referring to the Austrians as "vampires and oppressors", and proclaiming it to be the duty of Serbs there

> to identify themselves with the fate of Serbia, their country and their brethren . . . if the call to arms rings out we have many reasons to respond to it, and to join those who are fighting to defend their freedom and their country . . .. Our people have been deprived of national self-expression for thirty years.

This rhetoric was founded on a stratum of truth. The Austrians banned political organisations, and permitted the inhabitants of Bosnia and Hercegovina no say in the administration of the provinces. Faced with the alternative of winning over the *kmets* by emancipating them, or retaining the existing feudal system and so the support of the Muslim landowners, they chose the latter. They spent practically nothing on dams, irrigation or other measures to increase agricultural output, but a great deal on building roads and railways for strategic purposes, a large army barracks in Sarajevo, and two hundred police stations in various parts of the countryside.

But for some the Austrian occupation was by no means intolerable. There were, for example, jobs to be had on their construction projects, or with the private firms (many of them Hungarian) who were engaged in exploiting the natural resources of Bosnia – timber and minerals. One young Bosnian who benefited from this was Petar Princip's elder son Jovo, who left home, settled in a village near Sarajevo, managed to acquire a couple of horses, and set himself up as a small entrepreneur hauling logs down from the forest to the railway.

Jovo kept in touch with his family and sent them money. In 1907 he wrote to his father saying that the Austrian military school in Sarajevo was accepting boys as cadets, and that tuition, food and uniform were free. This, he suggested, would provide an answer to the problem of what to do with his brother Gavrilo who, now aged thirteen, had finished primary school. Petar agreed, there was no prospect of the lad earning a living in the Grahovo valley. He took him down to Sarajevo – they had to ride for three days over the mountains to get to the nearest railway station – and handed him over to Jovo. A shopkeeper friend then pointed out to the latter that at the military school his brother would feel uprooted and fall under Austrian influence; it would be far better to send him to the commercial school, there was money to be made in the Sarajevo bazaar. Jovo acted on this advice, enrolled the boy at the commercial school, and found him a lodging with Stoja Ilić, a Serb cobbler's widow, who because her eighteen year old son Danilo was unable to stick to a job, supported him by letting a room to students and taking in washing.

Young Princip settled down at the commercial school and was rated a good pupil. He also began to learn much which was not on the curriculum. Throughout Bosnia and Hercegovina the Austrians forbade schoolboys and students to form any kind of organisation or association, however apparently innocuous and non-political. Many of them therefore met in secret to discuss literature, ethics and, above all, politics. In the evening Princip listened to such discussions between Ilić and his friends, one of whom, Vladimir Gaćinović aged seventeen, had organised a secret society in the Orthodox seminary near Sarajevo where he was ostensibly studying for the priesthood. Trotsky, who met Gaćinović some years later, described him as "one of those types who are born to provoke a feeling of uneasiness amongst orderly people". Someone who knew him well said that "he carried to extremes a tendency to feel the sufferings of the society in which he lived as though they were his own". He had a capacity for communicating this and made a profound impression on Princip.

In addition to listening to Ilić and his friends, Princip also began to read the socialist, nationalist and anarchist literature which they passed from hand to hand. This ranged from the works of western political philosophers to the writings of Russian populists and anarchists such as Chernishevsky, Kropotkin and Bakunin, and included accounts of the Italian Risorgimento and the part played in it by Mazzini. At the age of thirteen he no doubt understood little of what he read, but Mazzini's belief that a country must be liberated by its youth, self-denying crusaders prepared to sacrifice their lives for liberty and justice, also made a lasting impression on him, as it did upon them all – Gaćinović referred to himself as a "Garibaldino" as well as a Serb nationalist. Like many of their contemporaries, they were keenly interested in the Risorgimento and its origin in Piedmont. To them Serbia was the Piedmont of the South Slavs, and Belgrade its capital the focal point. Vienna they thought of as the capital of the Occupying Power, of "them" – the Emperor, his heir Archduke Franz Ferdinand, his Ministers and Generals – their oppressors.

8
The Annexation of Bosnia and Hercegovina

IN 1907 Franz Ferdinand knew nothing about the Princips and Ilićs of Bosnia and Hercegovina, submerged in the, to him, faceless mass of students and peasants there. When occasionally the former were insubordinate and threw ink at their teachers, or the latter demonstrated about their treatment by their landlords, the police and the army seemed to have no difficulty in restoring order. Generally the situation in the two mandated provinces, which he had never visited, appeared to be reasonably under control and therefore did not figure in his list of immediate preoccupations. The same could not be said about the internal state of the Monarchy, into the many problems of which, although still excluded by the Emperor from any significant role in dealing with them, the Archduke since appointing Alexander Brosch von Aarenau as his A.D.C. and head of his Military Chancellery in January 1906, was gaining more insight.

Brosch, seven years younger than Franz Ferdinand and unmarried, was a small animated man and highly intelligent. An officer in the 2nd Kaiserjäger, one of the best infantry regiments in the army, he had considerable staff experience, having worked for six years in the Ministry of War. The Archduke's Military Chancellery was situated in a small office in the Lower Belvedere; when he started work there he had one assistant, no telephone, and the filing system was primitive. As a trained staff officer he was accustomed to working methodically. Franz Ferdinand was not a methodical worker and Brosch had to adapt to this; he adapted. A dedicated professional officer, he soon recognised in the Archduke "a soldier through and through", for whom it was stimulating to work because he had a wide-ranging mind, a quick grasp of the subject under discussion, and did not get bogged down in detail. But, as Brosch also discovered, His Imperial Highness was not always easy to deal with. He stuck to his ideas with "a degree of tenacity which could almost be described as obstinacy". A great deal of diplomacy was necessary when putting up a new proposal to him

He is prepared to listen . . . and it is easy to convince him that an idea is good provided he is not mistrustful of its originator, but this must be done in the right way, for he will not tolerate direct contradiction. On the other hand he will accept the unvarnished truth better than most people, and demands to know it. Therefore if one knows how to put it to him without appearing to be contradictory, one can get practically anything accepted. Admittedly this takes a great deal of patience and skill and one must choose the right moment, so it is a laborious process.

Brosch had patience, tact, and a flair for sensing when it was best not to press a point but to wait for a more propitious time to raise it. He had a gift for calming down the Archduke; Franz Ferdinand once said to him with a laugh "I have to blow off steam sometimes, but then it is for you to apply the brakes", and was invariably polite, but never sycophantic, never afraid to express an opinion. Eighteen months after taking up his appointment he had won His Imperial Highness's trust, a feat achieved by very few people. The Archduke's letters to him, in which his comments on Ministers and senior officials were uninhibited, began "Dear Brosch", and were signed, as to a friend, "Yours sincerely" or "With best wishes".

The tasks with which Franz Ferdinand now entrusted Brosch were not confined to military matters, but concerned every aspect of his activities and interests – politics, economics, the preservation of old churches and buildings, his personal affairs – and included the representation of his views to Ministers, senior officers and officials. This meant that Brosch, a major, had to deal with members of a hierarchy who were extremely rank conscious, and there were times when he skated on very thin ice. He had also to deal with a daunting amount of paperwork. The Archduke, when away from Vienna, required up to date reports of all political and military developments, addressed a stream of letters and telegrams to the head of his Military Chancellery to which he expected a speedy reply and, at short notice, would summon him to Konopischt or wherever he happened to be, to discuss the problem currently uppermost in his mind. Since he was out of the capital for an average of two hundred days a year, and when there avoided giving routine audiences because they bored him, it also fell to Brosch to see many people on his behalf and write up a report of what they had said.

Totally loyal to a man whose convictions he shared and whose frustrations he understood, Brosch worked eighteen hours a day seven days a week, and in the teeth of opposition from the old guard surrounding the Emperor, began to expand the Military Chancellery. He sought out people whom he thought might be of interest or useful to His Imperial Highness, acted as a link between him and those whom it would be impolitic for him to receive personally and, always accessible, effectively Franz Ferdinand's man in Vienna, built up contacts with representatives of the smaller national groups who, denied a hearing at the Hofburg, turned to the Belvedere.

By the summer of 1907 Franz Ferdinand was therefore becoming better informed than the Emperor about the ground swell of opinion amongst the nationalities of the Monarchy, particularly in Croatia and Dalmatia. Clinging to the belief that the Croats would not succumb to South Slav propaganda and that their loyalty could be relied on, he had been shocked and astonished when at Zara in 1905 their most influential political leaders agreed to work with the Serbs for the union of all South Slavs, "we must do everything possible to retain the allegiance of these people". This meant, as he constantly reiterated, that in Croatia they must not be abandoned to the Hungarians, and in Dalmatia their allegiance must be fostered by economic measures to bring some degree of prosperity to the province which for decades had been neglected – as Baernreither with whom he was in touch said "we govern Dalmatia without any real affection". Nothing happened. Dalmatia was a small remote province on which the Austrian government, as always short of cash, was not prepared to incur additional expenditure. When a group of Croatian deputies from there asked for an audience of the Emperor to appeal for support for their kinsmen in Croatia, Franz Joseph refused to see them.

In May 1907 a crisis blew up in Croatia when Budapest decreed that henceforward Hungarian would be the official language on the Croatian railways. The Croats promptly responded to this flagrant interference in their internal affairs with strikes by officials and obstructive tactics in the Agram *Sabor* and the Budapest Parliament. On July 9th the *Sabor* was suspended by the Governor. Anguished appeals from loyalist elements reached Vienna. If support against the Hungarians was not forthcoming Croatia might be lost to the Crown; the outlook was very grave. The Emperor took no action. According to the *Ausgleich* which he had sworn to uphold, relations between Vienna and Agram must be conducted through Budapest, and the Crown was debarred from direct intervention in the internal administration of Croatia. In his attitude towards this oath he personified the classic definition of the property of inertia, "it keeps on doing what it is doing"; he was determined to stick to the letter of it come what may.

The situation in Croatia continued to fester. Greater Serbia propaganda there had been stepped up during the past year after a sharp deterioration in official relations between Vienna and Belgrade. Austria's attitude to Serbia resembled that of a governess towards her charge; good marks were awarded for good behaviour (which meant doing what the Monarchy wished), bad behaviour was punished. In 1906 Serbia fell from grace by placing a large order for arms in France instead of with Skoda in Bohemia. Vienna dealt out punishment by embarking on a tariff war, closed the frontier to imports of Serbian livestock, and assumed these economic sanctions would bring Serbia into line. The Serbs found other trading partners; propaganda emanating from Belgrade hammered into the Croats that it was from there that their salvation would come.

Exercised though Franz Ferdinand was about the deteriorating situation in Croatia and Dalmatia, in 1907 it was not his major preoccupation. Brosch said of the Archduke that he had a great deal of energy, but unfortunately manifested this in a series of explosive bursts. During 1907 most of these were concentrated on attempting to ensure that the negotiations for the long overdue decennial revision of the commercial and financial clauses of the *Ausgleich* were concluded without making any concessions whatsoever to the Hungarians. Max Vladimir Beck, his mentor and political adviser, nominated by the Emperor Minister President of Austria with a mandate to achieve this revision (always the subject of prolonged and acrimonious wrangling) got the full force of them. Franz Joseph appointed Beck without consulting his heir and (perhaps deliberately) while the latter was abroad. This embarrassed Beck and annoyed the Archduke who then, however, swung round to the view that at last there was a Minister President of Austria who would implement his ideas. He adjured Beck "not to give an inch and not to make any significant concessions". Unfortunately he could not understand that Beck felt his duty was to carry out the task with which the Emperor had entrusted him; nor could he understand that, as in most negotiations, some compromise was necessary. When in October the *Ausgleich* revision was agreed, but at the price of some concessions which were hailed as a national triumph to the Hungarian press, Franz Ferdinand decided that Beck had sold the pass to "the clique of arch traitors in Budapest". Apparently oblivious of how much he owed to this man, of all he had done to make his marriage possible, he settled down to conduct a vendetta, not only to oust him as Minister President, which could have been just understandable, but to ensure that he never again held public office, which was not. It was one of the most unbecoming actions of the Archduke's life.

By now there was beginning to be talk in Vienna of a "Hof" party and a "Belvedere" party, and the day would come when a leading politician would comment "We have not only two Parliaments, but two Emperors". This would never be strictly true. Ultimate power, of decision on important matters of policy, to appoint and dismiss Ministers, was always retained by Franz Joseph, and Franz Ferdinand realised that, so long as the Emperor was alive, the degree of influence which he could exercise on "important developments" was dependent to a large extent on whether there were men in high office who subscribed to his views. His expectations of Beck had not been fulfilled, but there were two other men recently appointed to leading positions through whom he believed much could be achieved. One was Conrad von Hötzendorf, the Chief of the General Staff, the other Baron Alois von Aehrenthal, the Minister of the Imperial and Royal House and of Foreign Affairs. The former's views on the army were, he was certain, identical with his own. The latter he knew to be a protagonist of that closer understanding with Russia which he had been advocating for years.

Conrad von Hötzendorf's appointment to succeed Feldzeugmeister Beck as

Chief of the General Staff was forced through by Franz Ferdinand convinced, as were the younger generation of officers, that while the Feldzeugmeister remained in situ, no progress could be made with the much needed reorganisation of the army. The Emperor was averse to parting with Beck, but when in 1906 it was evident that, now aged seventy-six, he was no longer physically able to take part in manoeuvres, reluctantly agreed with the Archduke that he must be dismissed, and gave in, also reluctantly, to his heir's insistence that Conrad must succeed him.

A portrait of Conrad shows a strikingly handsome man, looking straight at the onlooker with the air of someone accustomed to lead from in front and to bear full responsibility for his actions. Dedicated from the time when he was a cadet at the Military Academy, where he was always top of the class, to becoming a master of his profession, Conrad first came to Franz Ferdinand's notice in 1899. Thereafter he followed his career and rapid promotion with attention, and became convinced that he was an officer of outstanding ability, *schwarz-gelb* to the core.

In the autumn of 1906 Franz Ferdinand summoned Conrad, then commanding a division in the Tirol, to the Belvedere, and told him that he had proposed him to the Emperor as Chief of the General Staff. By temperament and inclination a front line fighting soldier, Conrad did not want the job and said so, protesting that he had little staff experience. The Archduke deployed all his powers of persuasion; he would not budge. Finally he was dismissed with the ominous comment, "Well, I have not taken the fortress at the first assault". A few weeks later he was again summoned by Franz Ferdinand who told him that his appointment had been approved by the Emperor, and it was his duty as an officer to accept it. He now had no alternative but to do so, much as he disliked the prospect before him.

Shortly after taking up his post, Conrad wrote to the new Minister of Foreign Affairs, Baron Aehrenthal, stressing that harmony between them was all important, and received "a formal, correct, courteous reply". Aehrenthal was a career diplomat. He had experience of the Balkans, having served as Minister in Bucharest, and before coming to the Ministry of Foreign Affairs (generally referred to as the Ballhausplatz), had been an outstandingly successful Ambassador in St Petersburg, the key post in the Austrian Diplomatic Service. In almost every way he was the antithesis of Conrad. The Chief of Staff resembled a wiry alert fox terrier; Aehrenthal was tall, ungainly, with what the son of his British colleague in St Petersburg described as "sad turbot eyes". Conrad never attempted to disguise his views and was often disastrously outspoken. The Foreign Minister tended to conceal what he was thinking, and Berchtold, who succeeded him as Ambassador in Russia, complained of his "frightful characteristic of overlooking facts which do not fit in with his political house of cards". Aehrenthal, who had no use for other people's opinions on foreign policy, preferred to play the cards with which he was constructing this edifice very close to his chest. He was in a stronger position than Conrad; the dominant figure in the Council of Ministers, over meetings of which he presided in the Emperor's absence, and unhampered by Parliament which neither in Vienna nor in Budapest was empowered to debate foreign policy. The Chief of Staff, whose political superior was the Minister of War, only attended the Council when his presence was required for the subject under discussion, and was handicapped by the fact that parliamentary agreement had to be obtained for the armed forces budget. Altogether he had less scope than Aehrenthal who in addition, skilled at managing the Emperor to whom he worked directly, enjoyed the old gentleman's full support.

Aehrenthal and Conrad were both determined that the prestige of the Monarchy, which had declined during the years of introverted wrangling between its politicians, must be restored. Both were convinced that high priority must be given to dealing with Serbia, the source of a great deal of trouble, not only amongst the Emperor's South Slav subjects, but also in the Monarchy's hostage to fortune in the Balkans – Bosnia and Hercegovina. But, agreed though they were on these aims, on the means of achieving them they differed profoundly.

When Conrad became Chief of Staff, because of Beck's inability to move with the times, the Emperor's non-comprehension of the necessity of doing so, the chronic parsimony of the Vienna and Budapest Parliaments and Hungarian obstruction, the army was below strength and ill-equipped compared with the armies of the other Powers, and the navy existed in little more than embryo. He made a long list of what must be done to improve this parlous state of affairs. The army must be radically reorganised and trained in modern methods of warfare. Top priority must be given to increasing the annual quota of conscripts. Three thousand guns of various kinds were needed for the artillery; machine-gun units, and technical troop units for signals, bridging and railways must be formed and equipped; strategic road and rail communications must be improved; there must be adequate supplies of all kinds of munitions; more strategic fortifications were needed; naval construction must be speeded up.

A very large sum of money was needed to make the armed forces of the Monarchy fit to meet the demands which Conrad envisaged might be made on them. In addition to Serbia and Russia, he was certain that Italy, although a member of the Austro-German alliance, must be regarded as a potential enemy. Her ambition to secure a foothold on the eastern shore of Adriatic, and the virulence and persistence of irredentism, supported by Rome, amongst the Italian minority in Trieste and in the South Tirol, left no room for doubt that if the opportunity offered she would stab the Monarchy in the back. The Chief of Staff was also uncertain about Roumania, a member of the Triple Alliance of Germany-Austria-Italy since 1883, although King Carol was a staunch friend of the Monarchy. The treaty binding Roumania to the Alliance was secret, its existence known only to the King and a few of his advisers. Carol was unpopular with his subjects amongst whom, because of Budapest's treatment

84

of over two and a half million Roumanians in Hungary, hostility to the Monarchy was increasing. It was possible that if Roumania was called upon to honour her Treaty obligations, he might be unable to carry his people with him.

Conrad's overall assessment of the situation was accordingly that the Monarchy had only one reasonably firm ally, Germany (who, however, had made it plain that she had no intention of becoming involved in military operations in the Balkans), and was encircled by enemies, two or more of whom could not be fought at once with any hope of success. Therefore she must not wait to be attacked, and act to forestall this by knocking out her weaker potential assailants. From the military point of view there was no doubt that Serbia and Italy should be dealt with. He was convinced that a pre-emptive strike should be launched against Serbia as soon as possible, and lost no opportunity of saying so.

"The relationship of Serbia to the Monarchy fundamentally depends on Russia." It is unlikely that Aehrenthal would have disputed this comment made by Musulin when he returned to the St Petersburg Embassy after acting as Chargé d'Affaires in Belgrade in 1901, nor that he would have been surprised to hear from Musulin that the Russian Minister in Belgrade was constantly in the company of the Serbian Foreign Minister. But, although the Pan Slav press was as vociferous as ever about Russia's mission in the Balkans, the government, engaged in a drive for expansion eastwards through Central Asia to Manchuria and the Pacific, was in his estimation not in a position to support Serbia if she became troublesome.

This was correct. Nicholas II had been advised by his Foreign Minister that until the Far Eastern venture was consolidated, the Balkan question, as far as official government policy was concerned, must remain in cold storage. When Aehrenthal prepared to leave St Petersburg in the autumn of 1906 it seemed likely to remain there for some time. In the Far East Russia had been defeated by Japan in a disastrous war, during which the Japanese captured Port Arthur, put the Pacific Fleet out of action, and sank the Baltic Fleet which had been sent half way round the world to replace it. At home strikes, riots and mounting unrest throughout the land as peasants and workers demanded better living conditions and civil liberties, had compelled the Czar to issue a manifesto proclaiming himself a constitutional monarch and setting up a constituent assembly. The Ambassador was therefore disconcerted when at a farewell dinner which the Czar gave for him in Tsarkoe Selo, Nicholas said he hoped that as Foreign Minister Aehrenthal would not forget that the Balkan Slavs were members of the Orthodox Church, like the Russians who for decades had followed a "traditional policy" towards them, and was evasive when asked if this was a notification of the resumption of an active Russian policy in the Balkans. In his instructions to Berchtold before the latter left for St Petersburg, Aehrenthal said that a rapid shift of Russian interest from the Far East to the

Balkans was from the Monarchy's point of view totally undesirable, but it must be assumed that if within "the next few years" Russia overcame her internal difficulties and reorganised her army, she would "immediately again concentrate her policy on the West and on the Balkan peninsula".

To make use of "the next few years" to strengthen the position of the Monarchy in the Balkans was imperative, but nothing could be done until the revision of the *Ausgleich* had been agreed, and this took until October 1907. Aehrenthal's first exposé of his objectives was therefore not made until 1908 when, on January 27th, he addressed the Delegations. He announced that he had negotiated an agreement with Turkey for an extension of the Bosnian railway network through the Sanjak of Novi Bazar, which would give Vienna a direct railway link with Salonica via Sarajevo bypassing Serbia. He also said that he hoped to see a commercial treaty concluded with Serbia, "our policy of making Serbia economically and politically dependent and treating it as a *quantité négligeable* has foundered. Only a third party would benefit by a conflict between Serbia and the Monarchy." With regard to the South Slav problem he begged "urgently, for such a conduct of Croatian, Dalmatian and Bosnian affairs as would place the centre of gravity for the Serbo-Croat people within the Monarchy". After stressing that "it is not to Austria-Hungary's interest to have the Balkan waters troubled", and that "good relations between the Monarchy and Russia will bear fruit", he made a sombre prophecy

> There is much agitation throughout the world. The stage is set, the actors are ready. Only the costumes are lacking for the play to begin. The second decade of the twentieth century may witness very grave events. In view of the combustible material about they may come soon.

The Foreign Minister assured his audience, "the Monarchy will act so as to avoid conflict". The Sanjak railway agreement with Turkey did exactly the reverse. It was ill-received in Serbia, where the government promptly riposted by demanding the construction of a railway linking Belgrade with the Adriatic. There was a howl of protest in the Pan Slav press stigmatising the Sanjak project as a move by Austria to push forward into the Balkans. On February 3rd a secret Ministerial conference was held in St Petersburg at which Izvolsky the Foreign Minister urged that Russia must resume an "active aggressive policy" in the Balkans, otherwise she risked being rated as a second-class power. This was not, however, received with enthusiasm by his colleagues. The Minister of War said reorganisation of the army after the disasters in the Far East would take years. The Minister of Marine said the Black Sea Fleet (which was all that remained of the Russian navy) was unfit to fight. The Minister of Finance pointed out that to make good the deficiencies in the army and navy, huge sums of money were needed which he saw no means of raising. The Prime Minister feared any aggressive adventure abroad might lead to revolution at home, and ruled that Izvolsky must for the present achieve what he could by diplomacy.

The Czar approved this decision, commenting on the minutes of the meeting "God helps those who help themselves".

Within the Monarchy the situation in Croatia deteriorated. When elections for a new *Sabor* were held at the end of February, the Serbo-Croat coalition won 57 of the 88 seats. The Governor denounced the coalition as "anti-dynastic and treasonable", and a fortnight later again suspended it. The commanding General in Agram wrote to the Minister of War describing the position as "desperate" and warning that there might be an "explosion". He thought the province was wide open to Greater Serbia agitation.

The General's letter reached Vienna a few days after Conrad produced a memorandum on Bosnia and Hercegovina based on reports from the military authorities in Sarajevo. This was even more gloomy. The Chief of Staff began by saying

> During the past weeks Serbian agitation against the dynasty, Catholicism, and the authority of the State in the occupied territories has increased and reached the point where they give the impression of being riddled with irredentism.

He pointed out that one of the reasons for this was the Sanjak railway project, and quoted from an article in *Otacbina*, a newspaper published in Banjaluka in north-west Bosnia

> In the Balkan peninsula there is a strong smell of gunpowder in the air . . ..
> The Serbian government has categorically demanded permission to build the railway through Serbia from the Danube to the Adriatic. If this is refused, Serbia will oppose the building of the Austro-Hungarian railway through the Sanjak by force of arms. This will lead to a war between the Kingdom of Serbia and the Austro-Hungarian Monarchy . . . which will not simply be a war between two states with conflicting interests, but a war of the South Slavs against their oppressors. The people of Bosnia and Hercegovina must take part in it.

Conrad went on to say that at the beginning of February the Serbian government had instructed its Bosnian agents to seize every opportunity of organising nationalist demonstrations, because this would provoke the Austrians into taking repressive measures, and so inflame feeling to a degree where the people would be ready to revolt. Serb publications in the occupied territories were being financed by Belgrade, as were Orthodox churches and schools; there were instances of arms being smuggled over the frontier from Serbia into Bosnia.

The Chief of Staff stressed that an uprising in Bosnia and Hercegovina was likely to occur if Hungarian chauvinism caused another internal crisis in the Monarchy, and would undoubtedly occur if the Monarchy was forced to fight a war. This would have dire consequences

An uprising at some future date in Bosnia would certainly be actively supported by Serbia, to whom the Monarchy could then be forced to send an ultimatum which, if the reply to it was unacceptable would have to be followed up by force of arms. The question therefore is whether diplomatic action can guarantee that in this eventuality other countries (?Italy) will not attack the Monarchy, for if they do, as I have already pointed out in 1906 and 1907, we shall be confronted with the worst possible situation, namely outbreak of war against one of the powers at a time when our troops are heavily committed in the Balkans.

He concluded

I therefore urge, as so often before, that it is imperative to take vigorous action to counter Greater Serbia propaganda, and to restore order and the authority of the government in the occupied territories.

Conrad, as he said, had been pressing for "vigorous action" – preventative war against Italy, against Serbia, the annexation of Bosnia and Hercegovina – for over a year. The Foreign Minister, who held that any decision as to whether or not there should be a war rested with the Ministry of Foreign Affairs, found this extremely irritating. He did not share the Chief of Staff's mistrust of Italy and would not contemplate a preventative war against her. If all else failed it might be necessary to settle with Serbia by force of arms, but this should only be done as a last resort. The only point on which he agreed with Conrad was the desirability of annexing Bosnia and Hercegovina; in addition to frustrating Serbian ambitions there and safeguarding the hinterland to Dalmatia, it would demonstrate to the world that the Monarchy was a power to be reckoned with in the Balkans.

In July the question of the annexation was brought to a head by a political coup in Turkey, the perpetrators of which forced the Sultan to agree to a parliamentary constitution. This threatened to undermine the position of the Austrians in Bosnia and Hercegovina. The inhabitants of these provinces, still legally Turkish citizens, would be entitled to elect representatives to the parliament in Constantinople; the new regime there could demand that the signatories to the Treaty of Berlin should withdraw the occupation mandate from the Monarchy. Aehrenthal and Conrad now agreed that Bosnia and Hercegovina must be annexed forthwith. The former persuaded successively the Emperor and then the Council of Ministers that he could achieve this by diplomacy. Nobody would accept Conrad's contention that troops must be mobilised, and the annexation accompanied by an attack to knock out Serbia. At the age of seventy-eight Franz Joseph's one wish was to end his reign in peace; the Council thought the annexation "dangerous but necessary", and empowered the Foreign Minister to proceed with preparations for it.

Franz Ferdinand was adamant that until such time as the army was reorganised, equipped with modern weapons and brought up to strength war, for whatever reason, must be avoided. Therefore, although he shared the Chief of Staff's mistrust of Italy, and increasingly appreciated his anxiety about Serbia, he turned down flat all the latter's suggestions for a pre-emptive attack on either of them. This, however, did not affect his appreciation of Conrad's ability, patriotism and integrity. Writing to Conrad when he was convalescing after an illness in February 1908 he said

> Before anything else I want to tell you how glad I am that you have fully recovered . . .. To this I join the request that you will get yourself really fit . . .. Men like you, who are dedicated to the army heart and soul, and who hold high the *schwarz-gelb* banner of Austria are becoming rare . . .. For purely selfish reasons too I ask you to look after yourself, for you know my high regard for you, and that I see in you my most reliable and valuable support in the struggle against all the declared and hidden enemies of our Habsburg Empire and our glorious army. Rather than knocking yourself up again it is much better for you to return to Vienna a few weeks later. I too was once very ill, and I know how long convalescence takes.

From Conrad the Archduke received far more information than from his predecessor. But even Conrad did not keep him fully in the picture. He was often forbidden to do so by the Emperor and made no bones about it, saying on one occasion when Franz Ferdinand complained about being left in the dark, "I tell Your Imperial Highness everything I am permitted to". This, if reluctantly, His Imperial Highness accepted; it did not impair his belief that Conrad was the best man for the job of Chief of Staff.

With Aehrenthal Franz Ferdinand's relations were not cordial. The Foreign Minister welcomed unsolicited views from him no more than he did from anyone else, and the Archduke did not hesitate to voice them. It annoyed Aehrenthal to be told, for example, that to have the Italians as allies was deplorable, "I can have no love for the Italians and never will, for I cannot love people who behave badly and infamously towards everything which is right". At the beginning of April 1908 he said, tartly, that he had "again" urged His Imperial Highness to stop opposing and working against Government policy "for ultimately the will of the Emperor is decisive". He sent the heir to the throne only such copies of memoranda and despatches as he thought fit, and did not seek his views as to the desirability or otherwise of annexing Bosnia and Hercegovina, a subject about which he was determined the Archduke must not be allowed to interfere. When the Emperor in principle agreed to the annexation, he asked Franz Joseph to tell Franz Ferdinand only the bare minimum about this, and not until he was about to leave to attend the German army manoeuvres in Alsace, where for a time he would be out of the way.

The Archduke therefore first learnt that the annexation had definitely been decided at the beginning of August, when he called on the Emperor at Bad

Ischl on his way to Germany. In the train between Salzburg and Munich he scribbled a pencilled letter to Aehrenthal saying that he must without delay make his position clear, and stated that he was *not* (underlined) in favour of the annexation

> In general, in view of the deplorable internal situation, I am absolutely opposed to all such dissipations of strength. I consider that only a consolidated strong state can indulge in them; since we, thanks to the struggle between the two halves of the Monarchy, the attempts to disrupt its unity, the chaos, are neither consolidated nor strong, I would prefer that no action be taken. If, however, those who advise the Crown nevertheless consider that the annexation is absolutely necessary, then I am against any kind of mobilisation, for this could give grounds for quite unnecessary interpretations, and only in favour of calling up some reserves, which can be done without seeking the consent of Parliament.

He could, he stressed, only agree to the annexation if Bosnia and Hercegovina "are declared part of the territory of the Monarchy, that is to say as belonging to both halves of it". In any event the present "disastrous system" in the occupied provinces must be done away with, the Minister of Finance who was responsible for it sacked, and Feldzeugmeister Varešanin appointed Governor in Sarajevo with full powers. Apologising for his bad handwriting because the train was jolting, Franz Ferdinand ended with a plea to Aehrenthal

> This is my carefully considered belief about the affair, and I hope your Excellency will think it over and perhaps agree with me. I request your Excellency to keep me fully informed, for this is a matter of great importance which will be decisive both *now* and for the *future*.

It was a courteous letter and, all things being considered, restrained. He could have pointed out that few people would be more affected than him by the annexation of Bosnia and Hercegovina, for this would add over a million South Slavs, many of them doubtfully loyal to the House of Habsburg, to his future subjects.

Aehrenthal had no intention of keeping Franz Ferdinand fully in the picture. In addition to putting paid to Serbian claims for a Greater Serbia, he saw the annexation as an opportunity for giving a much needed lift to the prestige of the Monarchy which he was determined to exploit. He planned to ignore the stipulation in the Treaty of Berlin that no alteration to the status quo in the Balkans could be made without the agreement of the signatory Powers, and to present them with a *fait accompli*, thereby demonstrating that Austria-Hungary was capable of asserting itself and acting independently of any of them, including her ally Germany. It would be a coup which would establish him as a statesman in the Metternich tradition, which he was confident of pulling off provided he could square the only Power likely to be troublesome – Russia.

This too he was confident of achieving; by the time he received the Archduke's letter he was engaged in perfecting an exercise in diplomatic brinkmanship with the object of outsmarting the Czar's Foreign Minister, Izvolsky.

Izvolsky, also with visions of a coup, was seeking support for his own pet project, freedom of passage through the Dardanelles for Russian warships, and had hinted that it might be useful if he and Aehrenthal had a friendly discussion about this, and about Bosnia and Hercegovina. Towards the end of August Berchtold, on leave from St Petersburg at Karlsbad, on Aehrenthal's instructions told the Russian Foreign Minister who was also in Karlsbad, that Austria would in principle support the free passage of Russian warships through the Dardanelles, provided Russia placed no obstacles in the way of her annexing Bosnia and Hercegovina. He had a castle at Buchlau near Karlsbad, and suggested it might be useful if Izvolsky met Aehrenthal there for an informal review of these matters of mutual interest. Izvolsky agreed, and the meeting at Buchlau took place on September 16th 1908. The two Foreign Ministers were alone together for six hours; neither kept a record of what was said. After it Aehrenthal told Berchtold that Izvolsky had agreed to the annexation, and he had informed him that it would take place before long, assuring him that he would be notified of the date well in advance.

Izvolsky departed to continue a leisurely tour of Western Europe. Aehrenthal went straight back to Vienna. On October 6th 1908, when the Russian Foreign Minister was in Paris, Franz Joseph without prior notification to anyone, proclaimed that the Austro-Hungary Monarchy had annexed Bosnia and Hercegovina.

9
The Post-annexation Crisis

T HE proclamation of the annexation of Bosnia and Hercegovina caused an uproar in Serbia. There were demonstrations in the streets of Belgrade, the Habsburg flag was publicly burnt, the Austrian Legation had to be placed under military protection. Reservists were called up; Parliament was hurriedly convened and voted additional credits for the army. Newspapers demanded preparations for a life and death struggle. Ministers demanded that Bosnia and Hercegovina be made "autonomous" and "compensation" be paid to Serbia. The Foreign Minister set out on a tour of Western European capitals to drum up support. Pašić, the leader of the Radical party, went to St Petersburg to appeal for help.

In Russia the Pan Slav press was vituperative about the annexation, and public opinion demanded action in the Balkans. The Czar and his Ministers, anxious to preserve Russia's image as the protector of the Balkan Slavs, but aware that military action was out of the question, hedged. Nicholas and Izvolsky both told Pašić that Serbia was and would continue to be an important factor in Russian foreign policy, but at present no armed intervention on her behalf was possible.

Pašić returned to Belgrade, and said that as nothing more than moral support would be forthcoming from Russia, public opinion must be calmed down. This was easier said than done; judging from the newspapers the entire nation was prepared to die rather than accept the annexation, and yet another organisation directed against Austria had been formed.

Forty-eight hours after the annexation was proclaimed, a group of prominent Serbians met in Belgrade to consider how the wave of hostility to Austria which was sweeping the nation could best be exploited. It included politicians, amongst them the Minister of Education and several ex-Ministers, civil servants, professors, the Mayor, army officers. They agreed to set up the Narodna Odbrana. Its President was a serving general, and no secret was made of its objectives. These were further to inflame the national consciousness, to conduct a subversive propaganda war against the Monarchy, to organise acts of sabotage in its territory, and to enrol and train volunteer bands of *komitádjis* (guerillas). The slogan of the Narodna Odbrana was "whoever is a Serb must be a soldier, prepared to sacrifice everything for the Serbian cause and his country; whoever cannot fight must finance this cause". A central committee was established in Belgrade to supervise the work of a hierarchy of local committees and confidential agents and build up links with ostensibly cultural associations, such as the Sokols and shooting clubs, which the Narodna Odbrana subsidised. A school for training *komitádjis* was started under the supervision of Major Vojin Tankosić, an army officer and founder member of the organisation. Before long the Narodna Odbrana had over two hundred committees in Serbia, a network of informants, and had established an underground route into Bosnia.

In Bosnia and Hercegovina the proclamation of the annexation was outwardly received with calm. There were no street demonstrations in Sarajevo. A Bosnian national consciousness did not exist and there were deep and bitter divisions between the inhabitants of the city – Catholic Croats, Orthodox Serbs, Muslims – stemming from age-old hatreds. A young Bosnian contemporary of Princip later described them

> Anyone who spends one night in Sarajevo sleepless on his bed, can hear the strange voices of the Sarajevo night. Heavy but steady strikes the clock on the Catholic Cathedral: it is 2 a.m. More than one minute will pass (exactly seventy-five seconds, I counted) and only then will the Serbian Eastern Orthodox Church announce itself. It strikes its 2 a.m. A while after, with hoarse faraway voice the Sahat Tower near Beg's Mosque, declares itself. It strikes eleven times, the eleven ghostly Turkish hours, according to some strange alien part of the world . . . . And thus even during the night, when everybody is asleep, in this counting of the hours in the dead part of the night, the difference which divides these sleeping beings has been emphasised . . . . And this difference, sometimes openly and visibly, sometimes invisibly and basely, approaches hatred, often identifying with it.

The division between the Croats, Serbs and Muslims of Sarajevo was a reflection of the differences separating the three communities throughout Bosnia and Hercegovina, which a shared dislike of the annexation did not bridge. Thus no indigenous organisation comparable to the Narodna Odbrana in Serbia to resist it was formed. Moreover, in his proclamation the Emperor promised to grant the two provinces a constitution and a parliament. This would place them on an equal footing with provinces such as Bohemia in the Austrian half of the Monarchy, and opened up a prospect of political self-expression which to some extent reconciled the older generation to becoming subjects of the Habsburgs. One small but significant protest against this was, however, staged.

At the end of a special service in the Orthodox Cathedral in Sarajevo, when the Metropolitan asked the congregation to fall on their knees and pray for God's blessing on the Emperor and his dynasty, a group of boys from the secondary school remained standing bolt upright.

The schoolboys in the Orthodox Cathedral did not agree with their elders' passive acceptance of the annexation, and neither did many of their contemporaries. Many of them, like Princip, the son of a *kmet*, came from poor families to whom the Austrian occupation had brought little material benefit. They were anti-clerical, all searching after some form of social justice and convinced it would never come from Vienna, all with visions of the day when there would be an independent South Slav state, but with differing ideas of the form which this should take, their minds a ferment of undigested radical, "progressive", revolutionary, theories which they debated endlessly. But none of them had any idea of how to set about establishing a resistance network within Bosnia and Hercegovina. Some went to Serbia to volunteer for guerilla training. The rest continued to read Greater Serbia propaganda, revolutionary and anarchist literature, to meet, to talk. By the end of the year their hatred of the Austrians had evoked a great deal of rhetoric but no significant action.

A few days after the annexation was proclaimed the Austrian and Hungarian Delegations met. Baernreither, a member of the Austrian Delegation, had visited Sarajevo during the summer and returned convinced that "all the indications were that the methods of government so far pursued in Bosnia were out of date", and while the national and religious groups were at loggerheads with one another, all of them wanted the same thing – independence from Habsburg rule. Echoing Aehrenthal he said

> We lost Lombardy because the living centre of the Italian idea came to be outside Austria. We shall now lose Bosnia and Hercegovina and compromise the whole South Slav question unless we succeed in placing the centre of the South Slav world inside Austria.

The attention of the decision makers in Vienna was not, however, concentrated on this 64,000 dollar question, but on the immediate problem of resolving what was beginning to be termed "the annexation crisis".

The annexation of Bosnia and Hercegovina upset the status quo in the Balkans and contravened the Treaty of Berlin. Austria's announcement of it out of the blue was therefore received with angry consternation not only in St Petersburg, but also in London, Paris and the capital of Germany. Aehrenthal found there were more chestnuts to pull out of the fire than he had anticipated. Adopting an air of injured innocence, he pointed out that it had long been tacitly assumed (which was true) that Austria would remain in the two provinces, dug in his toes, and when agreeing to a proposal by Britain and France that a conference, the sovereign panacea for international crises, be convened, stipulated that at it the annexation must be confirmed without argument.

One chestnut which urgently needed salvaging was the Austro-German alliance. Austria's position in this was similar to that of a married woman who, after years of loyalty to her husband, during which she had refused to flirt with anyone else and broken off contact with her former friends if they were not friends of his, had without informing him indulged in an expensive caper and needed him to back the bill which she had incurred. The first impulse of Wilhelm II, enraged by the lack of notification by his ally of an action which could threaten peace, was to let Austria stew. Happily for Aehrenthal, his Chancellor von Bülow, already alarmed by the prospect of the encirclement of Germany by the Triple Entente – Russia, France, Britain – managed to persuade the Kaiser that the preservation of the Austrian alliance must take precedence over all other considerations. Therefore, much though Berlin disliked Vienna's "stupidities" in the Balkans, the Wilhelmstrasse told the Ballhausplatz that German "support (what precisely this meant was not defined) would be forthcoming.

From St Petersburg all the indications were that Russia had no intention of recognising Austria's *fait accompli*. Nicholas II wrote to Franz Joseph about the "painful impression which it had made"; Izvolsky accused Aehrenthal of having deliberately misled him at Buchlau. Berchtold in a private letter to the Foreign Minister said that the continuation of an active Balkan policy would certainly have an unfavourable effect on relations with Russia. A month after the annexation there was no doubt that St Petersburg's attitude was encouraging Belgrade's hostility to the Monarchy, and no end to the crisis seemed to be in sight.

In Vienna Conrad and Aehrenthal continued to disagree as to what should be done about Serbia. Their conflicting views resembled those of the participants in the battle of the Milvian bridge

Those behind cried "Forward"
And those before cried "Back".

Aehrenthal was adamant that no military preparations should be made which could be construed by Serbia as a provocation. Conrad declared that troop reinforcements must be sent to Bosnia, and work started on the implementation of "Plan S" (war with Serbia). In view of the hostile attitude of the Serbian government, the Emperor reluctantly authorised him to draw up plans for a partial mobilisation and to put fifteen battalions in a state of readiness. This was as far as Franz Joseph was prepared to go. The last thing he wanted was war. He liked Aehrenthal, who assured him it would be avoided, and found discussions with Conrad, who told him it was inevitable, a trial. Professional military opinion generally backed the Chief of Staff. Even General Bolfras, the head of the Emperor's Military Chancellery, had doubts about the soundness of the Foreign Minister's judgement

The diplomatic and military views of the situation are diametrically opposed; the former at present prevails, if it proves to be correct, very well – but who today is prepared to guarantee this? – and if it does not, we shall have a great deal of ground to make up.

Franz Ferdinand was at Konopischt when the annexation was proclaimed. On the following day Brosch telegraphed to say that Conrad wished to know whether he would consent to becoming Commander-in-Chief in the event of war. No mention of this had been made to the Archduke by the Emperor; it appeared that Conrad was acting on his own initiative. Franz Ferdinand replied that he did not wish to anticipate His Majesty's decision; if he did assume supreme command he must have unlimited powers, "in particular to protect military interests against other elements such as the Ministry of Foreign Affairs, the Ministry of Finance, both Minister Presidents etc". He also stressed that the Chief of Staff must "be restrained from too impetuous action, for it is vital to avoid incurring the accusation that we are the aggressor".

A tendency to shrink from taking a major decision in the hope that some miracle would occur to render it unnecessary was a Habsburg family trait. A few days' reflection strengthened the Archduke's conviction that the consequences of "too impetuous action" by Conrad could be disastrous, and on October 20th he wrote again to Brosch

> Please *restrain* Conrad; he must stop agitating for war. It would be splendid, and it is very tempting, to cut the Serbs and Montenegrins to bits, but to acquire these cheap laurels would be useless if the result of doing so was a European conflagration in which we might find ourselves fighting on two or more fronts, which we could not do with any hope of success. Therefore Conrad must . . . make his operational staff work day and night to perfect the preparations, but otherwise keep quiet and not agitate for war. If it breaks out Italy will attack us . . . and we could have to fight on two fronts. That would be the end of the story.

Franz Ferdinand also ordered Brosch to keep in touch with Mandić, the leader of the Bosnian Croats, who had made contact with the Belvedere, saying that he found Mandić's reports interesting and intended to visit Bosnia and Hercegovina. In early November, when receiving the Muslim Mayor of Sarajevo in audience, he told Essad Effendi that he would come there in the following year.

At the end of the month General Appel, one of the senior officers in Sarajevo, said in a letter to Brosch that the Mayor was full of praise for the Archduke. Appel, who had served in Bosnia for nine years, wrote after returning from a tour of inspection, during which he had ridden along the Drina on the frontier between Bosnia and Serbia. He pointed out that although the troops guarding the frontier had been reinforced, it was impossible to prevent illegal crossings under cover of darkness, when there was a mist, or when the river was low and easily forded. Moreover, although the frontier demarcation line was supposed to be in the middle of the main channel of the Drina, there were islands belonging to Serbia to the west of it near the Bosnian shore, an anomaly which must be rectified when the situation permitted. But, the General implied, there was no great urgency about this. During his tour he saw no Serbian patrols on the far side of the river, and while marauding bands could not be stopped from crossing into Bosnia, he thought they were unlikely to do much damage or find much support. The countryside was quiet; there were no signs that Christians and Muslims were drawing closer together in opposition to the Austrians; while the attitude of the Serbs was hard to determine, they were making no trouble. In his opinion the inhabitants of Bosnia were unlikely to become "difficult" on their own initiative.

By the end of the year the situation in Bosnia as described by Appel must have appeared halcyon to Franz Ferdinand compared to the state of affairs elsewhere in the Monarchy. In Prague the North Slav Czechs demonstrated in favour of Serbia: troops had to be called out and martial law imposed to restore order. The Hungarians renewed their pressure for military concessions and (this infuriated the Archduke), Aehrenthal argued that to obtain their co-operation some must be made to them. In Croatia, not only was the *Sabor* still suspended, but at the behest of the Hungarians, who never did things by halves, a number of leading members of the Serbo-Croat coalition were being tried in Agram on a charge of organising a treasonable separatist movement in collusion with Belgrade. During the year when further appeals for help from opponents of the Serbo-Croat coalition who still looked to Vienna for salvation, reached the Belvedere, all the Archduke could do was to tell Brosch, "I am greatly concerned that the well disposed *schwarz-gelb* Croats should be convinced of my regard for them, so that they do not go over to the other camp, but stand firm until better times come".

In the middle of January 1909 Franz Ferdinand took his family to St Moritz. His departure to Switzerland while the annexation crisis was unresolved was widely criticised, but he still did not know what his military role would be if war broke out, and generally to remain in Vienna until something was clarified would be to continue to bang his head up against a brick wall. In addition, in the autumn Sophie had given birth to a stillborn son which greatly distressed them both; he was unable to throw off a heavy cold; for personal reasons they needed a change. Before leaving, the Archduke ordered Brosch and Conrad to send him full reports of all developments, and told the latter that if need be he would return at once.

A family group photograph taken while they were in St Moritz shows Sophie in a large befeathered hat, a tweed jacket adorned with a fur tippet and an ankle-length skirt, Franz Ferdinand in a knickerbocker suit and a check cap – two proud parents apparently enjoying a holiday with their offspring. But the Archduke was far from carefree and bombarded Brosch with letters about a variety of worries. He *must* – but how? – retain the loyalty of the minority nationalities in Hungary. "Austria must rule in Bosnia, not Hungary", therefore any attempt by Budapest to gain economic or other influence there must be checked. Had the time not come to launch a press campaign against Aehrenthal with the object of impressing on him that, if he was going to come down on the side of the Hungarians, he would make life very much more difficult for himself? The Minister of War must be stopped from giving up barracks in the centre of Vienna; it was essential that an adequate number of troops should be stationed near the Hofburg. The Emperor had told someone that troops in an infantry regiment in Dalmatia had been suborned by Serbian agitators. Why had he heard nothing about this from the Ministry of War? It was of the *utmost* importance that such agitation should be stopped; a close watch must be kept on the reliability of all units in which Serbs were serving.

When worried Franz Ferdinand tended, as he himself confessed, to lie awake and brood. That while in St Moritz, in addition to the shortcomings of Ministers and the iniquities of the Hungarians, he brooded about the prospect of the North and South Slavs within the Monarchy combining against the dynasty, is suggested by a letter which Wilhelm II wrote to him on February 12th, evidently in reply to one which he had recently received from the Archduke. The Kaiser commented to "Dear Franzi"

> The Slav danger has revealed itself amazingly in its delusions and violence within the last months. According to your presentation Belgrade and Prague conspire on the basis of a fixed programme . . . .. Behind both of them stands Moscow; how far Cracow and Lemberg are in the game I cannot judge. But apparently the *Pan Slav* danger is the greater one for Austria, since it pulls the lever in your own country through the Czechs . . . . It endangers the preservation of the Monarchy *because she has recently incorporated Slavonic lands*, and thus is in the process of becoming a second Slavonic Great Power.

Never backward in offering unsolicited advice, he recommended that, to strengthen her position in the Balkans, Austria should add to the Roumanian alliance "a good solid relationship" with Bulgaria, and concluded

> In addition, the hatred of the Hungarians against everything Pan Slav would prove a good support against all Slav intrigues and particularly in the South. After all, the chauvinism of the Hungarians derives from a glowing patriotism even though it has a separatist slant. Guided in the right direction it might well be possible to use it for the common good of the fatherland.

Franz Ferdinand had been on friendly personal terms with the Kaiser since 1903 when, the first reigning sovereign to do so, the latter called on Sophie at the Belvedere, a gesture which warmed the Archduke to him. They shared the conviction that the aristocracy and the army were the mainstay of their respective dynasties, but he could not quite forget the past humiliations inflicted on the Monarchy by the Prussian Hohenzollerns, and resented Wilhelm's unconcealed liking for the Hungarians. His advice was unhelpful; Franz Ferdinand neither liked nor trusted King Ferdinand of Bulgaria, and "glowing patriotism" was the last epithet which he would have applied to the Hungarians.

Wilhelm's letter was not cheering. Neither was the news from Vienna. Conrad and Aehrenthal continued to pull in opposite directions. The Chief of Staff maintained that Serbia should be attacked in March and annexed. The Foreign Minister said that the Monarchy could never absorb Serbia, and action must be restricted to consolidating the position in Bosnia and Hercegovina. Serbia was becoming more belligerent, and some people thought that a showdown with her was unavoidable, which could lead to a general conflagration in view of the "sphinx like" attitude of Russia. As tension increased a leading politician noted in his diary that "all eyes were fixed on the heir to the throne in St Moritz, who was believed to be in favour of war and who, it was generally assumed, would press for it on his return". In fact, as Brosch knew, the Archduke's attitude remained unchanged, "I still do not believe there will be a war with Serbia, it would in my opinion be disastrous to the present situation". When on February 16th, Conrad telegraphed asking him to return, he deferred his departure from St Moritz for a week, and then broke his journey in Salzburg summoning Brosch to meet him there.

Brosch, certain that there must be "a small but victorious war" and the sooner the better, arrived in Salzburg determined to persuade His Imperial Highness to change his mind. They argued; Franz Ferdinand refused to listen to him, and then left the room saying "There are various ways of looking at this, I am going to send my wife to talk to you." Sophie appeared and, evidently briefed, warmly supported her husband. Brosch finally cut short the discussion by saying he thought ladies should have no part in military decisions, was ordered curtly by the Archduke to return at once to Vienna, and wrote from there pointing out that his advice was useless if he could not say what he thought, and asking to be relieved of his post. When Franz Ferdinand arrived in Vienna a few days later, he berated Brosch for half an hour, but refused to accept his resignation. The latter only succeeded in getting him to agree that he would not attempt to exert influence one way or the other over the decision as to whether there should or should not be war with Serbia.

According to Brosch, because Franz Ferdinand constantly suspected that he was being underrated, he was jealous of any General or Minister on whom public attention was focused. When he returned to Vienna Conrad and Aehrenhal occupied the centre of the stage and his own position was undefined. Conrad found His Imperial Highness in a bad temper. He first complained that Schönaich the Minister of War and the Foreign Minister were intriguing against him, and later accused the Chief of Staff of conspiring with Aerenthal, saying that everything was being done over his head. Conrad protested that before a memorandum could be put up the relevant officials had to be consulted. This provoked an explosion from Franz Ferdinand, "If I was Commander-in-Chief I would do what I wanted and woe betide everybody who did not obey me. I would shoot the lot of them".

The Chief of Staff had his own complaint against Aehrenthal, who was insisting that no reinforcements should be sent to Bosnia and Hercegovina before mid-March by which time, if Serbia had not become more conciliatory, he proposed to send a stiff Note to Belgrade. Conrad hoped for the Archduke's support, but failed to enlist it. On March 12th he told the Emperor that matters how now reached a stage where one must ask Aehrenthal's permission to send a gun from Vienna to Dalmatia, and that further delay in sending reinforcements was folly. His arguments prevailed to the degree that Franz Joseph's attitude, by contrast with that of Franz Ferdinand, became what some went so far as to describe as "warlike". He agreed the despatch of reinforcements and, on March 22nd, approved the placing of further troops on the alert so that a million men could be mobilised against Serbia and Montenegro, saying "It is better to be safe than sorry . . . this war will inevitably come sooner or later".

Twenty-four hours later this precaution proved to be unnecessary. Considerable diplomatic pressure had been brought to bear by Berlin on St Petersburg, and Izvolsky informed the German Ambassador that Russia recognised the annexation. Abandoned by Russia, Serbia had no alternative but to climb down. In a Note to Vienna on the 31st, the Serbian government announced its acceptance of the annexation, declaring that Serbia would desist from subversive activities and wished to live on good neighbourly terms with the Monarchy.

The end of the annexation crisis was acclaimed by many patriotic citizens as a triumph for the Foreign Minister, and the Emperor made him a Count. Unfortunately Aehrenthal had constructed another house of cards, the collapse of which some months later did not enhance the prestige of Vienna in the South Slav world, and severely handicapped its capability of assessing the threat which was building up there.

10
A Man called Stefanović

ON March 25th 1909, a few days before the end of the annexation crisis, the *Neue Freie Presse*, one of the leading newspapers in Vienna, published a signed article by Dr Heinrich Friedjung attacking Serbia and accusing leading members of the Serbo-Croat coalition in Agram of conspiring with Belgrade. Friedjung, a corresponding member of the Imperial Academy of Science, an honorary doctor of the University of Heidelberg and an eminent historian, wrote that this accusation was based on authentic material in his possession. Fifty-two members of the coalition, amongst them its leader Franjo Supilo, the President of the *Sabor*, a senior General and several deputies, promptly denied it and brought an action against him for libel.

The article was commissioned by Aehrenthal when it became apparent that the Agram trial of members of the coalition for treasonable contacts with Belgrade (which was still dragging on) was being mismanaged. Much of the case against the accused rested on the evidence of a notorious informant, and a number of the documents which he produced were being shown up as forgeries. The partisan conduct of the trial was attacked by the Czech nationalist leader Masaryk in the Austrian parliament, condemned by liberal opinion in western Europe, and criticised as a travesty of justice throughout the Slav world. Aehrenthal was determined to counter this by exposing the extent of Serbia's seditious activities in Croatia. The authentic material to which Friedjung referred had been made available to the historian on his orders, and consisted of a selection of a series of documents forwarded to the Ballhausplatz by Forgách, the Austrian Minister in Belgrade, under cover of his most secret despatches. They all emanated from one agent, a man known to the Legation as Milan Stefanović and, with a very few exceptions, such as a report from Spalajković, the Secretary General of the Serbian Ministry of Foreign Affairs, to Pašić, consisted of minutes of the meetings of the Serbian secret society Slovenski Jug at which its contacts with the Serbo-Croat coalition in Agram were discussed.

Forgách told the Ballhausplatz that these documents were copies of the originals, which Stefanović insisted must be returned to the Slovenski Jug archives from which he had extracted them. He assessed them as high grade intelligence, but when he learnt that Friedjung's defence in the impending libel action would depend on them, took fright. Information derived from an agent could not be produced as evidence in court; Masaryk had warned the Austrian Parliament that it would be shown up as a fabrication. He wrote to Aehrenthal saying that Friedjung's trial would be a "political monstrosity" and must not be allowed to take place. The Foreign Minister replied that attempts to settle the action out of court had been rejected by the plaintiffs, and that both the Austrian and Hungarian Minister Presidents were for going through with the trial; the latter was most anxious to discredit the Serbo-Croat coalition.

In July Forgách went on leave. While he was away Stefanović produced for Swietochowski, the dragoman and his contact at the Legation, the minutes of a Slovenski Jug meeting according to which it had been decided that a band of *komitádjis* should blow up the Governor's palace in Agram if the accused in the treason trial there were sentenced. Unlike the Minister, Franz the Chargé d'Affaires and Gellinek the Military Attaché had been doubtful for some time about the authenticity of these minutes. Franz said so when forwarding this latest instalment of them to Aehrenthal, suggesting that they could be a deception ploy by the Serbian Government, designed to induce the authorities in Croatia to institute draconian repressive measures against the Serbo-Croat coalition, and so stimulate further international condemnation of the Agram treason trial. Gellinek when reporting on it to Conrad agreed with Franz, and also pointed out that Stefanović was being paid for each document he produced; therefore it would be worth his while to fabricate at least some of them.

Aehrenthal took no notice of Franz, nor of a report that Masaryk had arrived in Belgrade to work up the case for the plaintiffs and was spending a good deal of time in the Russian Legation. Conrad, stressing that its authenticity was doubtful, sent a summary of the information provided by Gellinek to Brosch who showed this to Franz Ferdinand. Since a close contact of the Belvedere, Dr Funder the editor of the *Reichspost*, was also being sued for libel because his paper had named four members of the Serbo-Croat coalition as being bribed by Belgrade, the Chief of Staff's report must have been of interest to the Archduke, but he made no comment on it.

The hearing of the libel action against Friedjung was due to begin in Vienna on December 9th 1909. On the 5th the historian wrote in some alarm to the Ministry of Foreign Affairs

> There are now only four days before the trial starts . . . proof of the authenticity of the minutes will be incontrovertible if it can be established that they have been written by the secretary of the Slovenski Jug, Milan Stefanović.

There was evidently no reaction to this appeal, for Friedjung followed it up with a further S.O.S.

All would be well if I at least had a note signed by Stefanović . . . he has been given thousands, but curiously it seems to be impossible to obtain an authentic signature from him!! This omission must now be repaired . . . my opponents will be obtuse if they do not fasten on it.

Nothing was forthcoming from the Ballhausplatz, and Friedjung (who on the 8th, presumably as a last resort, had asked for an appointment to see Brosch) faced a packed courtroom without this proof in his hands. Nevertheless, after pleading not guilty, he did not withdraw a word of his article, and in the course of a four-hour speech asserted that he had written it to expose Serbian seditious methods, which started with bribery, continued with guerilla activity and bombs, and would culminate in a military attack. He declared that he would unmask the treasonable activities of the Serbo-Croat coalition, would indict named members of it during the trial, and describe and produce documentary evidence of their contacts with the Serbian Government. When it became apparent that the only documents which he could produce were not originals but copies, he laid his academic reputation on the line and, referring to a receipt for a bribe said

I have seen the original . . . it was brought from Belgrade to Vienna and then taken back to the place from which it originated, the secret archives of the Slovenski Jug in Belgrade. As a scholar, I am convinced that this document is authentic, and in addition I can confirm that it was made out by the secretary of the Slovenski Jug, Milan Stefanović.

Counsel for the plaintiffs then played a trump card and asked Friedjung if he was certain that Stefanović existed. He could only reply that he was convinced that he did, but would check on this, and asked urgently for a summary of the Belgrade Legation's knowledge of Stefanović, including his present address. After four days the Ballhausplatz replied that the Legation's agent was indeed called Milan Stefanović, but it was not known where he lived since, like all students, he frequently changed his lodgings. They added that since his name had appeared in press reports of the action against Friedjung, he had not been seen in the cafés which he habitually frequented.

On the eighth day of the trial Friedjung said that, amongst others, Franz Ferdinand was aware of the Stefanović documents. One newspaper commented that it could not be assumed that the heir to the throne had made any effort to check their authenticity, but he was known to be keenly interested in the whole affair, and the documents had been made available to Brosch, the head of his Military Chancellery, who had used them to inspire the article in the *Reichspost*. This implication that the Archduke was associated with Aehrenthal in the Friedjung case was unfortunate in view of the evidence which was then given by two of the Serbian witnesses called by counsel for the plaintiffs. Professor Božidar Marković, the last President of the Slovenski Jug (it was ostensibly dissolved shortly before the trial opened), and a member of the Narodna Odbrana, stated that the minutes of a Slovenski Jug meeting referred to by the historian in which he was cited as the principal speaker, were false, because on the day when the meeting was alleged to have taken place he was in Berlin, as a letter from the Prussian Chief of Police confirmed. Spalajković, giving evidence on the orders of the Serbian Foreign Minister, stated that the copy of the report which he was alleged to have sent to Pašić was, on grounds of form and content which he cited, a fabrication, and the signature on it was not his. In view of these statements Friedjung's defence collapsed. He was compelled publicly to acknowledge that the documents were false and the case was settled out of court. At the same time the sentences in the Agram treason trial, which had been referred to Vienna, were quashed on grounds of inconclusive evidence.

The Friedjung trial had disastrously misfired. That Serbians of the status of Marković and Spalajković were prepared to appear as witnesses in Vienna, and able to demonstrate that the documents on which the historian's article was based were forgeries, was a damaging loss of prestige and credibility for the Austrian Government for which Aehrenthal was blamed. The Foreign Minister, on the basis of never apologise never explain, had maintained that the libel action against Friedjung had nothing to do with him. But when it was over he decided that, in case there were further repercussions, it was desirable to establish whether the documents could at least be regarded as sufficiently founded on fact to be taken seriously. The Austrian Minister in Belgrade was therefore instructed by the Ballhausplatz to give the reasons which led him to vouch for their authenticity, to supply detailed information as to how the Legation had established contact with Stefanović, and to explain why the latter had disappeared and not taken up an offer of asylum in Austria, made to him when it became known that the information which he had provided would be quoted during the libel action, and therefore that he was blown.

Forgách when answering these questions with, no doubt, an eye on his career, did his best to pass the buck where possible. He replied that Major Wilhelm Cvitas, now dead, Swietochowski's predecessor as dragoman at the Legation, had recruited Stefanović in 1907, and after some initial doubts, rated him the best available agent. For two years the information provided by Stefanović had been considered useful and valuable by the Ministries to whom it was circulated. As an "outstanding and experienced historian", Friedjung should have realised that "agent material whether false or true, was unsuitable for production in court". The reason why the agent had not fled from Serbia was that he was "afraid of being caught in a trap". The Minister did not enlarge on what he meant by this, and ended his report by saying "Stefanović is at present living *undisturbed* in Belgrade . . . there has been no report that any of the many Milan Stefanovićs (86 are registered!!) have been subpoenaed (by the Serbian authorities)".

Had Stefanović been acting on his own initiative with the object of making as much money as he could out of the Austrian Legation, or had he passed information to the Austrians on the instructions of the Serbian authorities – was he in other words a double agent? The fact that he had elected to remain in Belgrade suggested the latter. But then why had the Serbians ordered him to pass information which, whether it was true or false, must be assumed would cause the authorities in the Hungarian half of the Monarchy to redouble their efforts to uncover and suppress contacts between the Serbo-Croat coalition and Belgrade? Forgách did not discuss these questions; Aehrenthal took the line that no further analysis of the unfortunate affair was necessary. Neither reconsidered the suggestion by the Chargé d'Affaires that Stefanović had been used for purposes of deception, in a ploy which would today be classified as a disinformation operation.

In 1909-1910 the term "disinformation" had not been introduced into the vocabulary of the European intelligence services. Derived from the Russian *"dezinformatsia"*, it denotes an area of intelligence activity which includes the dissemination of provocative information which may be partly or wholly false, by a variety of means such as forged documents or the propagation of misleading rumours, with the object of discrediting a foreign government, exacerbating opposition to it, fomenting discontent, riots, and disorder amongst the various groups and communities of the inhabitants of the target country. An essential feature of a disinformation operation is that it must be non-attributable – its true origins must be concealed. To achieve this, in addition to undercover agents, use is made of agents of influence (a term also not in the intelligence vocabulary in 1909), individuals who are inhabitants of the target country and not officially connected with the government originating the operation, but prepared to further it because it coincides with their own beliefs.

By these criteria the activities of Masaryk in support of the Serbo-Croat coalition in both the Agram and Friedjung trials were those of an agent of influence, and Stefanović, of whom no proof had emerged that he had been acting under official Serbian control, was a disseminator of disinformation. The result of the Friedjung affair was not only to increase the mistrust of the South Slavs of both Budapest and Vienna, but also to exacerbate the friction which already existed between Conrad and Aehrenthal on the subject of counter-espionage and intelligence operations, an additional dividend which was to be further exploited by Belgrade.

The Intelligence Bureau of the General Staff had the dual function of obtaining information about foreign armies and the intentions of their governments, and of conducting counter espionage operations within the Monarchy. When Conrad became Chief of Staff at the end of 1906, he found that the Bureau was short of personnel (it had a staff of 15 officers), short of agents in the field, and its budget was totally inadequate. Its work abroad was handicapped by the Emperor's aversion to the involvement of Military Attachés in any form of espionage, which he considered to be a breach of the hospitality of the country to which they were accredited. In addition, in two key capitals, St Petersburg and Belgrade, their movements were restricted and they were subjected to close surveillance. The information which they provided tended therefore to be confined to what they could glean from overt publications and gossip picked up from their social contacts.

To compensate for the restrictions on Military Attachés, officers were sent abroad on intelligence missions, particularly to Italy and the Balkans. Conrad considered this indispensable; these officers had the professional knowledge to evaluate on the spot an agent's report on, for example, a new fortification, and the training to observe technical details which an inexpert agent might miss. Inevitably from time to time one of them was blown, and the government of the country in which he had been operating lodged a formal protest about his activities. Such incidents were much disliked by the Ministry of Foreign Affairs. When one occurred in June 1908 shortly before the annexation, Aehrenthal complained bitterly to the Chief of Staff. Conrad replied that, while he would do everything in his power to avoid a repetition of it, he could not agree to a restriction of these intelligence missions

> Unfortunately intelligence work necessarily means contact with individuals who are frequently of a most dubious character, so leaks can occur. But under no circumstances will I abandon my officers who have to carry out these unpleasant tasks for, anything else apart, this would damage the operations of the service.

This reply annoyed the Minister, already intent on curtailing the activities of the Intelligence Bureau: some of the information which it produced was political, and he insisted that the procurement of this fell within his sphere. The Ballhausplatz had a large "Information Fund" at its disposal for the payment of agents producing political information such as Stefanović, money from which was in theory to be made available to the Bureau to finance operations abroad involving expenditure on a scale for which its own budget was inadequate. In practice this was rarely forthcoming; Aehrenthal saw to that. Finally, at the end of November 1909, Conrad went to the Emperor, stressed the importance of obtaining military intelligence, the imperative need of more funds for this, and the necessity of continuing to send officers abroad on intelligence missions. No more money was immediately forthcoming, and the aftermath of the audience was "a bitter blow"

> Count Aehrenthal succeeded in getting His Majesty to forbid such missions, particularly in the Balkans. From then onwards we were in many respects militarily blind and reduced to relying on what the Military Attachés could observe, and on agents' reports which could not be checked.

Soon after adminstering this "bitter blow" to Conrad Aehrenthal, his fingers badly burnt by the Stefanović affair, issued an order forbidding members of the

Belgrade Legation staff henceforward to have anything whatsoever to do with agents. This rendered the Ballhausplatz in many respects as politically blind in Serbia as the General Staff was militarily blind, and at a time when Nikolaj Hartwig, the newly arrived Russian Minister, an ardent Pan Slavist prepared, as one of his contacts said, to stand facts and truth on their heads to suit his ends, was settling down to make Belgrade the centre of Russian activities in the Balkans.

The Emperor's Foreign Minister by now had it seemed one overriding objective, which was to avoid any initiative which might be regarded as provocative by any foreign country – Russia, Italy, above all Serbia. He told Conrad that anything which might give the impression of "imperialist" action in the Balkans was to be avoided. The Balkan states should be left to sort themselves out; consolidation was the watchword; relations with Serbia would be improved by the commercial treaty which was being negotiated with Belgrade.

Urbanski, the head of the General Staff Intelligence Bureau, said that the Ballhausplatz's determination to avoid any kind of diplomatic incident "hampered every form of intelligence activity . . . every initiative evoked a vehement protest from the Foreign Minister". He was referring not only to operations abroad, but also to counter espionage within the Monarchy, into which during the year after the annexation of Bosnia and Hercegovina, what he described as "an army of spies" flooded from Italy, Russia and Serbia. A total of 60 cases of suspected espionage in 1908 rose by the autumn of 1909 to over 1,000. The limited resources of the counter-espionage section of the Bureau were stretched to the limit, and its work was not helped when the Ballhausplatz insisted on the release of Italian officers caught spying in frontier areas, and opposed surveillance of the Russian Military Attaché in Vienna who was known to be running agents, nor by the fact that within the Monarchy the maximum prison sentence for espionage was 5 years, as compared to 15-20 years in Russia and Serbia.

In addition, the number of Serbs supplying "information" to the Bureau's contacts, increased to a degree which led a senior General to comment that it almost seemed as though most members of the Serbian Intelligence Service were either double agents or traitors to their country. This included accounts of what purported to be the Serbian Government's plans for exploiting the post annexation situation in Bosnia and Hercegovina. A report in June 1909 quoted a Serbian Minister as saying that the "stupidity" of the Agram treason trial had caused many Serbs in the annexed provinces to turn to Serbia; the obedience of their leaders to instructions fully justified the confidence placed in them by Belgrade, and more material help would be given to them. In early 1910 an agent reported that, according to a senior Serbian official, Belgrade would only sign the commercial treaty with Austria if Vienna agreed to the opening of Serbian Consulates in Sarajevo and Mostar which, while ostensibly concerned with trade, would in fact have the task of stirring up unrest against the Austrians amongst both Serbs and Muslims. Another agent confirmed this, adding that

Belgrade also planned to establish a "financial institution" in each town, from which Serb and Muslim merchants and peasants could obtain interest-free loans. He quoted the Serbian Consul-General in Budapest as describing the relationship between Serbia and the Monarchy as no more than "an armistice", and saying that Serbia, already "much stronger" than before the annexation, would be in an even better position when a Parliament was set up in Sarajevo. It would provide a forum for national self expression, which Vienna would find "most disagreeable", and enable "our friends" in Prague, Agram, Slovenia and Dalmatia to criticise "every unlawful and unjust act" of the Austrian administration, thereby increasing the discontent of "our Serb and Muslim people".

The Intelligence Bureau when circulating these reports, did not attempt to assess whether their content was wholly or partly disinformation of the kind so successfully disseminated by the Stefanović forgeries. Aehrenthal after his unhappy experience of these, regarded all agents' reports as suspect, and asserted that if the Serbian Consulates were established in Sarajevo and Mostar they would not engage in political activity. Information reaching Franz Ferdinand's Military Chancellery from Brosch's contacts in Bosnia to some degree bore them out. Support there for a Greater Serbia was growing. Hopes that the Croats and Muslims could be relied on to provide a solid counter-balance to the Serbs were not being fulfilled. The former had split into two factions and were engaged in a series of internecine quarrels; the attitude of the latter was uncertain. But that was all. None of Brosch's correspondents said that Belgrade was sending "material assistance" – arms or money – to the Bosnian Serbs, nor that agitators were being infiltrated over the frontier. Nobody suggested that serious trouble was to be anticipated in the near future.

The Archduke ordered Brosch to support representations by Conrad and the Minister of War opposing the establishing of Serbian Consulates in Sarajevo and Mostar. Aehrenthal (whom he referred to as "an old woman"), who had pushed through the annexation with such a flourish, now seemed to think that all which was now necessary to consolidate this was to appease Belgrade, and with this he did not agree. But the unsatisfactory situation in Bosnia and Hercegovina seemed to him to be peripheral by comparison with the state of affairs in Croatia. A friend and shooting companion, Count Bombelles, had written to him in despair about this, saying that the Governor was a tool of Budapest and engaged in selling out Croatia to the Hungarians. Outwardly everything might appear to be quiet, but beneath the surface there was a seething mass of discontent, which was not voiced only because people feared to lose their jobs, their land, to be arrested and tried for treason. There was bitter criticism, both of the Emperor and himself as heir to the throne, for allowing this situation to continue.

Bombelles wrote this in the spring of 1909; by now, a year later, the situation in Croatia had further deteriorated. Franz Ferdinand, his attention still concentrated on what he believed to be the root cause of the trouble, those "Huns and Asiatics" the Hungarian politicians in Budapest, did not yet fully appreciate that the position there could not be considered in vacuo, and that the rot in Croatia could spread to Bosnia and Hercegovina. But neither did anyone else. In the Monarchy there was no coordinated consideration of the South Slav problem as a whole. Schooled by the Emperor's insistence that each should confine himself to his own sphere, the Minister of the Interior, who was responsible for Dalmatia and the Slovene areas of Austria, and the Joint Minister of Finance, responsible for Bosnia and Hercegovina, did not consult with one another, and there was no question of either having contact with Budapest on the subject of the Croats and Serbs in the Hungarian half of the Monarchy. Although the Stefanović case had demonstrated the need for an improved flow, circulation, and evaluation of intelligence about Serbian subversion and Greater Serbia propaganda, nothing had been done about this. The overall result was that there was no awareness in Vienna of the increasing grass roots resentment amongst the younger generation of both Serbs and Croats to Habsburg rule. It first became apparent in June 1910 when these young South Slav subjects of the Emperor acquired their first martyr.

11
"The Smell of Blood"

ON February 20th 1910, nearly eighteen months after the annexation, an Imperial decree was issued granting Bosnia and Hercegovina a parliamentary constitution. It laid down that Parliament would have no control over the administration, and of its 92 members, 20 would be appointed by the Emperor and the remainder elected on a very limited franchise. Officialdom described it as "an important step forward", a view with which those members of the younger generation of the inhabitants of the two provinces who resented Austrian rule did not agree. Impatient, inspired by the success of the demonstrations in Russia in 1905, they were convinced that nothing could be achieved by any form of legal action; the struggle against their oppressors must be carried on outside Parliament. There were also adverse reactions from some older Serb radicals, who said the constitution was a "caricature". The authorities in Sarajevo, however, informed Vienna that the decree had been generally well received; deputations of the senior members of all communities had asked Varešanin, the Governor, to convey their gratitude to the Emperor and assure him of their loyalty.

A visit by a member of the Imperial Family would, it was thought, strengthen these sentiments of loyalty to the Crown. Franz Joseph was eighty and in frail health, but he decided that it was his duty to undertake this arduous journey to a remote part of the Monarchy, thought of by most people as 'oriental', and appear in person before his new subjects. At the beginning of March it was announced that the Emperor would visit Bosnia and Hercegovina between May 30th and June 5th.

During the second half of May, two warnings of plots to assassinate Franz Joseph reached the Ballhausplatz. The first of these, from the Austrian Embassy in Paris, quoted an Austrian student as saying that the assassination was being planned by a South Slav "anarchist" organisation there, four members of which, whom he named and described, had already left for Bosnia. The second, from the Embassy in Sofia, said that the Ambassador had been told by a left-wing journalist with Serbian connections that an assassination was being planned in Belgrade by the Slovenski Jug, emissaries from whom had been sent to Bosnia. According to both reports the attempt to kill the Emperor would be made while he was in Mostar, the capital of Hercegovina, but both Embassies were doubtful about the reliability of their informants; each of them had asked for money.

The Sarajevo police could not trace the alleged assassins from Paris. Aehrenthal thought that the Sofia information resembled the Stefanović forgeries of the previous year, telling the Austrian Minister in Belgrade that it gave the impression "that they want to start their old tricks again in Serbia on the occasion of the Emperor's journey to Bosnia, and were beginning with attempts at intimidation". He instructed Forgách to call on the Serbian Foreign Minister, raise the question of this report of a conspiracy to kill the Emperor, and draw attention to the fact

> that we see through these tactics and will not be deflected by them. But we expect from the Serbian government a correct neighbourly attitude, and a watchful eye regarding the revolutionary activities which are apparently going on, and which seem to have their origin in Belgrade.

Forgách saw the Foreign Minister and reported the latter as having assured him that "the Serbian government will take all necessary measures and will either prevent every departure of elements suspected in any way or inform the Austrian government immediately".

By the time this assurance reached Aehrenthal, Franz Joseph was about to start on his long train journey to Bosnia. There was a tacit agreement that, in view of his age, the Emperor should not be told of anything upsetting. When therefore the reports of plots to assassinate him were passed to Count Paar, his General Adjutant, it is possible Paar did not show them to him. If he did, Franz Joseph, who accepted that assassination was an occupational risk of monarchs, took no notice. No last-minute alterations were made to his itinerary. It did not apparently occur to anyone that since details of it had been published in the press, a potential assassin would be well informed of his movements.

On arriving in Bosnia, Franz Joseph stopped for half an hour at Bosna Brod the frontier station to receive loyal addresses, and then continued his journey to Sarajevo. His special train halted at a number of stations en route in order that as many people as possible should have a chance of seeing him, if from afar, and reached the Bosnian capital, where he was to stay at the Governor's residence, the Konak, at 3 p.m. on the afternoon of the 31st. Stringent security precautions were in force during the three days he spent in Sarajevo. All known suspects were ordered out of the city for the duration of his visit. When he drove from the station to the Konak in a four-horse carriage, the route was lined on both sides by a double rank of soldiers, and over a thousand uniformed policemen and plain-clothes detectives mingled with the crowds. It was considered too dangerous for him to enter the narrow streets of the old town, and the programme included only one short excursion into the surrounding countryside, which was to Ilidže, a spa a few miles outside Sarajevo. Onlookers were kept at a distance at the parade staged in his honour. He watched a torchlight procession from the safety of the Konak, where he received leading members of all the communities.

Franz Joseph was reported to have told Varešanin before he left for Mostar that his visit had made him feel twenty years younger. He spent only a few hours in Mostar, and from there returned straight to Vienna. No doubt to the unbounded relief of all concerned, his tour of Bosnia and Hercegovina had passed off without incident.

In a confidential letter to Brosch, General Appel summed up the Emperor's visit to Sarajevo as "a triumphal progress". If in places the crowd which turned out to watch him drive from the station to the Konak had been somewhat thin, this was due to the fact that because of fear of disturbances and other "excesses", people from the surrounding countryside were not allowed into the city until the following day. The reason why at first there was comparatively little cheering was that this was not the way in which these 'oriental' people greeted their superiors, "many old Turks and Serbs did not trust themselves to call out his name and stood with folded arms and downcast eyes as though they were greeting a Turkish pasha". The General also said that the attempt by one of the Croat factions to make political capital out of the visit by hailing the Emperor as "King of Croatia", had angered both Serbs and Muslims. But this was the only discordant note in three unforgettable days. Most of the public had expected to see a bent old man who could barely sit on a horse, and when His Majesty galloped on to the parade ground they were speechless with admiration. After the parade, which all "the leaders of the former Serb and Turkish opposition" turned up to watch, Serbs said that "St George had come amongst them", and an old Turk maintained that there must be a mistake in the Emperor's date of birth, for if he rode like that he could not possibly be more than fifty.

Appel was certain that the graciousness and dignity of "our good All-Highest Ruler" had made a "deep and lasting impression" on the Bosnians and captured their hearts. He was personally delighted that his judgement of their mentality had been justified. In a postscript to his eight-page euphoric letter he urged Brosch to visit Bosnia to confirm this for himself and, having done so, to propose to the Archduke that he should come there. He suggested that Franz Ferdinand should bring Sophie and the children with him. They could stay at Ilidže while he inspected troop units, and this would "give the population great joy" and strengthen the bond between the heir to the throne and the new provinces. He concluded, "I will vouch for the security of such a visit with my head". That he could scarcely have made a more ill-judged statement became apparent a few days later when, on June 15th, Varešanin narrowly escaped assassination.

The Governor, accompanied only by his A.D.C. and without an escort, was driving back to Konak after opening Parliament. As his carriage was crossing the Kaiser bridge over the Miljačka which ran through the centre of Sarajevo, he heard a pistol shot which was rapidly followed by four more and then, after a pause, by another. On the far side of the river Varešanin ordered his coachman to pull up, and regardless of the possibility that a further attempt might be made to kill him, calmly walked back to the bridge, where he found a young man lying in the middle of the road, blood streaming from his mouth, having committed suicide by shooting himself in the head. His pockets were found to contain an identification card with a photograph which showed him to be Bogdan Žerajić, a law student at Agram University, 110 kronen in paper money, and a small circular cardboard badge on which was a portrait of a grimacing man carrying a scythe.

Having established the identity of his would-be assassin and ordered the police to start their investigations, the Governor proceeded on foot to the Konak. His report to Vienna three days later contained a series of neat diagrams showing the trajectory of the bullets, two of which he pointed out would have hit him in the head had he not leant forward after hearing the first shot with the intention of jumping out of the carriage and grappling with his assailant. He said that investigations to date pointed to the probability that the attempt to kill him was "a carefully planned anarchist plot", and that a nationalist political motive or a personal act of revenge seemed to be ruled out. Attempts were being made to discover whether Žerajić had any accomplices.

Within a few days the police reported that Bogdan Žerajić, a Serb, was born in 1887 at Nevisinje, a small town in Hercegovina. His father was a poor *kmet*. He was at Mostar secondary school from 1900 until 1907 before going to Agram University. His uncle, a doctor in the Serbian government medical service, had helped to pay for his studies, and he had made several visits to Belgrade. On May 28th he left Agram to return home to Hercegovina. Attempts to find out why Žerajić had attempted to kill Varešanin, and whether he had any accomplices, continued for a further six weeks, during which the police interviewed people in Bosnia and Hercegovina believed to be friendly with him, sent agents to Serbia and Croatia to investigate his past, and sought the help of their colleagues in Vienna, Budapest, and "known anarchist centres in Europe" in an endeavour to discover whether he had anarchist connections.

On August 5th after the police investigation was concluded, the Provincial Government of Bosnia summarised its findings in a report to Vienna. The cardboard badge found in Žerajić's pocket was identical with the cover of a book by Kropotkin, the well known Russian anarchist writer, and anarchist literature had been found in his lodgings in Agram, but no contact between him and known anarchists had been traced. Expert examination of his pistol showed that it was a Browning, hundreds of thousands of which were produced annually in Liège and exported all over Europe; it was impossible to discover how he had obtained it.

There were other questions which the police were unable to answer. Žerajić left Agram on May 28th because he was penniless. How had he since acquired the not inconsiderable sum of money which was found on him after he committed suicide? When he reached the Bosnian frontier on the 28th he left the train and stayed in Bosna Brod until June 1st, during which time the Emperor stopped there briefly on his way to Sarajevo. Why had he done this? Why had he then again broken his journey and remained in Sarajevo while the Emperor was there? In spite of these unanswered questions the report nevertheless stated unequivocally that all available evidence pointed to the conclusion that he had no accomplices, had confided in no one, and his attempt to kill Varešanin was unpremeditated. It could be regarded simply as the act of a man who, ground down by poverty, obsessed by political fantasies, had been seized by a momentary fit of paranoia.

The Provincial Government stressed that this conclusion was based largely on information about Žerajić provided by people who knew him. Statements published by some of them many years later suggest, however, either that they were not all contacted by the police, or when interrogated did not tell the truth.

One of these statements was made in 1927 by Vasily Grdjić, a leading Serb intellectual and member of Parliament, who as secretary of the cultural society Prosvjeta was in contact with a number of students, one of whom was Žerajić. He described the feeling of many Serbs during Franz Joseph's visit

> Everyone was obsequious. Even the opposition press – at the time *Srpska Riječ* – had, it was said to greet the new sovereign . . .. Our hearts were filled with bitterness against everything. We hated even our own lives.

On the evening of June 14th, in a mood of black depression, he went to dine at Katić's restaurant, and on entering one of its smaller rooms, saw Žerajić.

> Žerajić got up, approached me . . .. We were alone. He stopped beside me and whispered: "He was so near me – I could almost have touched him", and with his right hand he made a gesture as if he was aiming a pistol.

With a flash of insight Grdjić realised that "he" was the Emperor. He asked "Where?". Žerajić replied "At Mostar railway station". Grdjić wrote

> I cannot even today assess this event properly. We agreed completely. We are slaves . . .. We have no heroes who could start great fights. We have no man, who, all alone, asking no one, could perform a memorable deed. Žerajić . . . looked at me speechless, and we departed almost without saying goodbye.

Pero Slijepčević recalled in 1933 that when he saw Žerajić at some time during the same evening, the latter read out an extract from an article in the June 1st edition of the leading Serbian review in Sarajevo

> In our immediate past and in contemporary times we can boast no bright examples to prove we are a people fighting for our rights; there is not one single tragedy of the kind which are so often necessary to spur people on to action

and then said "But there will be tragedies". Another friend, Jovan Starović, asked about Žerajić in 1963, said that when he returned to Sarajevo from Mostar, he confessed that he had intended to assassinate the Emperor, and they then agreed that he should try to kill Varešanin.

The passage of time can blur memory and increase bias. The possibility cannot be discounted that these statements may not be wholly accurate. But their implication that Žerajić was not, as the Provincial Government believed, alone in his "fantasties" was correct. The "disgust" for his "base act" expressed by a leading Serb during the first session of the Sarajevo Parliament was not shared by a number of the younger generation.

The nationalist students of Bosnia and Hercegovina had read with admiration of the exploits of revolutionary terrorists in Russia, but none of them dreamt that it would be possible to attempt anything similar in Sarajevo, a city swarming with Austrian troops and, they believed, police informants. Žerajić's "act of courage" captured their imagination. Some of them took off their caps in homage to him when they passed the scene of his death. They discovered his unmarked grave in the remote part of the cemetery reserved for criminals and suicides where the Austrians had secretly buried him, and came by night to put flowers on it; within two years it became a place of pilgrimage for some young Bosnians.

Vladimir Gaćinović, Danilo Ilić's friend, was one of the pilgrims to Žerajić's grave. He was a contemporary of Žerajić at Mostar secondary school where they both belonged to the schoolboys' secret society. When the annexation was proclaimed he fled to Serbia to volunteer for the Serbian army, and after the crisis was over attended lectures on Serbo-Croat literature at Belgrade University. Financed by a Serbian Government stipend, he then went to the University of Vienna, from where he made secret visits to Bosnia. He kept in touch with Žerajić after they both left Mostar, and wrote three essays on the significance of his death, describing him as "a man of action, of strength, of life and virtue, a type such as opens an epoch, proclaims ideas and enlivens suffering and spellbound hearts, preaching the new ethic of dying for an ideal, for freedom".

Copies of Gaćinović's essays, the first of which was written in November 1910, were smuggled into Bosnia. They built up the legend of Žerajić's martyrdom in the minds of those students whose thinking, as a result of his death, was shifting to the conviction that, as one of them said, liberation could never, as they had hitherto believed, be achieved by a cultural revival; to arouse their countrymen against the Austrians there must be "the smell of blood" – another assassination must be attempted. By the end of 1911 unending discussions behind closed doors had not resulted in any plan for action. But, unknown to those who took part in them, one young Bosnian Serb, Gavrilo Princip, the *kmet*'s son who while lodging with Ilić had listened to Gaćinović expounding his political theories, had made up his mind to emulate Žerajić.

In June 1910 when Žerajić attempted to assassinate Varešanin, Princip was barely sixteen. He had an inferiority complex because he was small for his age, was not getting on well with his teachers and so in trouble with his brother who was paying for his education, restless and introverted. A photograph of him taken at that time shows a solemn youth, neatly dressed in a thick dark suit, sitting bolt upright holding a large book and staring into the middle distance. Possibly he asked to be photographed holding the book; he aspired to become a professor, and much to his brother's annoyance, immersed himself in reading. His choice of literature was indiscriminate, and still included such anarchist, socialist and nationalist pamphlets as came his way the contents of which, however, he discussed with nobody. He belonged to no student political groups. Absorbed with his personal problems, in August he transferred to the secondary school in Tuzla, a town in northern Bosnia. This was not a success, and by the end of the year he was back in Sarajevo.

Princip later said that 1911 was a critical time in his life. His outlook widened; he joined a secret student political group, brooded about what he referred to as the miseries of the Bosnian Serbs, his people, and the Žerajić legend acquired a personal significance for him. He began to visit Žerajić's grave, and after a long vigil there one night, swore that he would follow his example, avenge him, and kill one of the oppressors of their people. The degree of Princip's resolution when he took this oath was similar to Franz Ferdinand's when he swore to renounce the succession to the throne for his children – it was a sacred pledge which could never be broken. How he was going to implement it he then had no idea.

12
"History moves too slowly: it needs a push"

(i) Serbia

WHEN first reporting Žerajić's abortive attempt to assassinate Vare-šanin, most Belgrade newspapers accepted the official Austrian explanation, and described it as the act of a deranged youth. But two months later on August 18th *Politika*, which was generally assumed to reflect the views of the Serbian government, published a large photograph of him with a laudatory article, "Today we too light a candle at his grave and cry 'Honour to Žerajić'." To add insult to injury, August 18th was Franz Joseph's birthday, but the Ballhausplatz did not protest about the article. The Serbian Prime Minister had already told Forgách that he regretted his government had no control over the press; Aehrenthal was informed by the Foreign Minister that as a gesture of friendship, the King of Serbia wished to visit the Emperor.

The Count decided to take the Serbian government's apparently more conciliatory attitude at its face value, and hope for the best in an admittedly imperfect world. Forgách, after what he described as a "friendly confidential" talk with Spalajković at the Ministry of Foreign Affairs, was optimistic that there would be no official Serbian support for "revelations" by former agents. There had been a newspaper report that a brochure by someone called Vladimir Sergian Vasić, entitled "Behind the Scenes of Austrian Diplomacy" was about to be published, and that it would contain a sensational chapter on the "secret subversive activities" of the Austrian Legation in Belgrade. But by the time Forgách saw Spalajković it had not appeared, and the latter assured him that nothing which Stefanović could reveal would be damaging.

Then disaster struck. The manuscript of the brochure got into Masaryk's hands, and when the Delegations met in November 1910 he made a speech which within hours was reported in Belgrade in a special edition of *Politika*. Referring to the Friedjung trial he said that the contention that Forgách, Aehrenthal and the Ballhausplatz had been misled did not hold water, because the Stefanović forgeries "emanated from the Imperial and Royal Legation in

117

Belgrade" where, with the Minister's knowledge, Swietochowski the dragoman, and Vasić the author of the brochure, had fabricated them. A thorough
investigation in Belgrade left him in no doubt that this was correct. Twenty-
four hours later, on November 9th, another special edition of *Politika* announced in banner headlines that a young man had gone to the police and
revealed that he was the Vasić named by Masaryk. He was being held in police
custody. *Politika* demanded that he should be given the opportunity of describing to a court how the forgeries had been executed in the Legation, and that
Forgách, who had turned the Legation into "a forger's workshop", should leave
Belgrade immediately.

A Vienna newspaper, quoting as its source a "private telegram" from Belgrade, published what purported to be a summary of Vasić's statement to the
police. According to this, Vasić said that on Forgách's instructions, Swietochowski dictated to him the text of the forged documents, and he was paid a
monthly salary plus substantial bonuses. Eventually the Legation ordered him
to take a number of documents to Agram, where he came to the notice of the
police and fled back to Belgrade. After his return the Legation refused to pay
him; he became smitten with remorse for his "unpatriotic" action and, when
he learnt of Masaryk's disclosures, decided to reveal the operation.

The files of Franz Ferdinand's Military Chancellery contain a cutting of this
report, annotated by him "Is this true?!", together with the assessment which
the Intelligence Bureau then produced of it. In this the Bureau stated that
Vasić, a Serbian student, was identical with Stefanović, had approached the
Austrian Legation, said that he was a friend of the secretary of Slovenski Jug,
and offered to supply them with information. Forgách authorised his recruit-
ment, Swietochowski ran him, and he was paid a basic salary for delivering
minutes of Slovenski Jug meetings. After the Legation broke off contact with
him when the Friedjung libel case blew up, he went to Agram, represented
himself as a Ministry of Foreign Affairs agent, and offered to spy for Austrian
Military Intelligence. When inquiries by Corps H.Q. in Agram revealed that
the Ballhausplatz "disavowed" him, he was imprisoned and then expelled from
Croatia. The Legation was in no way involved with the production of the
forgeries, the Intelligence Bureau was emphatic that any question of this could
be ruled out

> for many reasons, and particularly in view of the latest reports from the
> Military Attaché in Belgrade. It is far more likely that when Vasić fabri-
> cated the Slovenski Jug minutes and sold them to the Legation, he was
> acting under instructions from the Serbian government, whose objective
> was either to alarm us into taking measures which would be construed as
> provocation, or to mislead us.

While the Intelligence Bureau was producing this assessment Forgách, also
convinced that Vasić was identical with Stefanović, sitting it out in Belgrade as

best he could, was taking a somewhat different line. He informed the Ballhausplatz that the "revelation" was a put up job, concocted by Masaryk and "certain people". The Serbian Prime Minister termed it "derisory", his colleagues were taking it calmly; no attention should therefore be paid to it.

Forgách's hope that the whole affair would go away was not realised. The Serbian government had no intention of letting the Austrians off the hook. The Ministry of Foreign Affairs published a ruling that it was against the interests of the State to pass information, whether true or false, to a foreign Legation, and it was announced that Vasić would be tried for this offence. To the Ballhausplatz, devoutly hoping that Vasić/Stefanović would sink without trace, this was unwelcome news; there was no knowing what further "revelations" he might produce in court, a forum where no intervention could be made to refute them. But nothing could be done to stop the trial; the only course was to ignore it.

The trial opened in Belgrade on December 22nd. Asked to describe how the forging had been carried out, Vasić enlarged on his statement to the police

> Swietochowski, the Legation dragoman, translated typed drafts in German into indifferent Serbian which was intermingled with Croatian expressions. I put the bad translations into good Serbian, and signed the forged Slovenski Jug minutes "Secretary Stefanović". The other signatures were copies from specimens of original signatures and added partly by Swietochowski and partly by me. Count Forgách often watched the work and checked it. The original German texts came from his secret archives.

Vasić was found guilty of "high treason of a special kind", and sentenced to a term of imprisonment which was not enforced. Having ruled that the members of the Austrian Legation whom he had named "could not be held responsible", the court made no attempt to determine whether his allegations about them were or were not true. The trial therefore left the question of whether Forgách and his staff were simply gullible and inept, or whether they had been engaged in what would today be termed "dirty tricks" wide open. While most people thought that Vasić was lying, there were others who maintained that he was not, amongst them Masaryk who, accompanied by members of the Serbo-Croat coalition who had been unsuccessfully prosecuted for treason in Agram, attended it. The Ballhausplatz remained silent. For the Serbian government Vasić's trial was, in a disinformation context, a most satisfactory epilogue to the Friedjung case.

"Our diplomatic service in the Balkans requires thorough reorganisation. Intelligent handling of national self-consciousness ought to play a part in our diplomacy there." Baernreither, still one of the few members of the Upper House of the Austrian Parliament who paid attention to the Balkans, noted this in his diary on June 5th 1911, six months after Vasić's trial, after talking to a senior Serbian diplomat in preparation for a fact-finding visit which he was about to make to Belgrade. He also noted the diplomat's criticism of "the line taken by Austrian diplomacy in Serbia, and its lack of interest in the country, the people and its intellectual life", ignorance of which had led Forgách to make "many mistakes".

Baernreither spent ten days in Belgrade. He thought the view over the Hungarian plain from the fortress set high on a cliff dominating the junction of the Save and the Danube superb, and was charmed by the old palace, a magnificent example of Turkish architecture surrounded by a park full of beautiful trees. The city he described as "unfinished"; the process of transforming Belgrade from a Balkan town into the Serbian idea of a "Europeanised" capital was still in midstream; electricity and water supplies functioned sporadically; although many of the streets were lined with newly planted trees, the road between them was still a mass of potholes. Most of the attractive old Turkish houses had been demolished, and the architecture of the rash of modern buildings was in indifferent taste.

On the morning after his arrival, Baernreither called at the Austrian Legation which was "neither roomy nor representative", particularly when compared with the "great new palace" which the Russians were constructing at vast expense. A Serb said to him

> The Russian Minister keeps open house for everyone in Belgrade. The French Minister is a learned historian who has travelled all over the country and knows it better than most. He is also in close touch with the intellectual life of Belgrade and much looked up to on that account. The English do less of this, the Germans still less, and the Austrians nothing at all.

Other Serbs to whom Baernreither talked during his stay all told him with varying degrees of vehemence that Serbia felt herself hemmed in, threatened by Austria of whom there was universal mistrust, deprived of the rights to which every nation was entitled. It was still hoped that, at some future date, "a great transforming war" might force the Monarchy to give up Bosnia and Hercegovina. Immediately, Austria must renounce any attack on Serbian independence, give Serbia guarantees for the future, and understand her aspirations. A professor engaged in the compilation of a Slav encyclopedia said that the purpose of this was to forge an intellectual bond between Serbia and Croatia, and so act as a counterblast to the Monarchy's "divide and rule" South Slav policy. The President of the Academy of Science was convinced that cultural unity between Serbs and Croats would be achieved, and that any attempt to prevent it would be a dangerous mistake. Politicians stressed that Serbia must have an outlet to the Adriatic, and declared the position of the Serbs still under Turkish rule in Macedonia to be intolerable. When, as was inevitable, Macedonia was partitioned, Austria must support Serbia's demand for a share of that province.

All of them maintained that small nations "must not be driven or sacrificed by the great" and that Serbia must have "life, light and air".

Was it still possible "to redeem the sins of omission and commission on both sides which had led to such bitterness and so many misunderstandings"? Pondering this question on his journey back to Vienna, Baernreither came to the conclusion that, provided Austria took the initiative, posted to Belgrade diplomats who knew the language and were prepared to learn about the country, and generally demonstrated good will, there was a slim chance that this might slowly be done. He did not know, because all his contacts in Belgrade were civilians, that there was an undercurrent of opinion amongst Serbian officers which made the odds against success very long indeed. Had he been aware of this, he might have wondered whether the comment about the Balkans made to him by the German Minister, "the best thing which could happen would be for the whole cauldron to be filled with petrol and then set on fire", might not be particularly applicable to Serbia.

Although the army had carried out the coup d'état in 1903 when King Alexander Obrenović was murdered and Petar Karadjordjević installed on the throne, it then left the politicians to run the country. By 1911, however, there was a growing divergence of views between Serbian political leaders and a number of army officers. It stemmed from the government's curtailment of the activities of the Narodna Odbrana in accordance with Austrian demands at the end of the annexation crisis. As a result of this, the Narodna Odbrana ceased to train *komitádjis* and saboteurs. While it maintained its underground routes, these were not used to smuggle arms into Bosnia. Sabre-rattling and violence as a means of realising the vision of a Greater Serbia and the unity of all South Slavs were abandoned; the emphasis shifted to cultural education and propaganda, from deeds to words. This was unacceptable to those officers who maintained (as did some civilians) that Serbian ambitions could only be achieved by revolutionary action. On May 9th 1911, ten of them signed the secret statutes of a new terrorist organisation, the Ujedinjenje ili Smrt, "Union or Death", which became generally known as the Crna Ruka, the Black Hand.

Article 1 of the Black Hand's statutes declared its aim to be "The realisation of the national idea, the union of all Serbs". Article 2 read "This organisation prefers terrorist action to intellectual propaganda". Several articles dealt with the nature and scope of its operations, and left no doubt that these would not be confined to "influencing politicians and the whole social life of the Kingdom of Serbia". They were listed as including the organisation of revolutionary activity "in all the lands inhabited by Serbs"; fighting "with all means" all those abroad who opposed the realisation of the Serbian national idea; supporting "in every way" all those who were "struggling for national liberty and unity". The organisation of the Black Hand was set out in detail. Supreme power was vested in the Central Committee in Belgrade which directed the work of district committees, both within Serbia and abroad, each of which controlled a number of cells of 3-5 members. One delegate from each of the "Serb lands abroad" – Bosnia and Hercegovina, Croatia, Dalmatia, the Voivodina in southern Hungary, Macedonia and Montenegro, was to be sent to the Central Committee.

The Black Hand demanded absolute loyalty and obedience. "Every member on entering the organisation must realise that by this act he forfeits his own personality, that he may expect within it neither glory nor personal profit, either moral or material" (Article 30). The initiation ritual for each new recruit which was laid down in a "Special Regulation" attached to the Statutes emphasised this. In a darkened room, lit only by a small candle, before a table on which was laid a cross, a dagger, and a revolver, in the presence of a masked member of the Central Committee, he swore an oath the text of which was given in Article 35

> I swear by the sun that warms me, by the earth that nourishes me, before God, by the blood of my ancestors, on my honour and on my life, that I will from this moment till my death be faithful to the laws of this organisation, that I will always be ready to make any sacrifice for it. I swear before God on my honour and my life that I will take all the secrets of the organisation with me into my grave. May God confound me and my comrades in this organisation judge me if I trespass against or either consciously or unconsciously fail to keep my oath.

Two other articles left no doubt of what this judgement would be. No excuse including "the most frightful torture" would be accepted for treason; the punishment for this was death and it would be executed without fail.

The statutes of the Black Hand have been described as "combining the self-effacing loyalty of the Jesuits, the ruthless spirit of Russian nihilists and the symbolism of the American Klu Klux Klan". Its seal, engraved with a skull and crossbones flag, a dagger, a bomb, and a bottle of poison, suggested that it would not be squeamish about the means which it employed to achieve its aims. Of its ten founders who signed the statutes, several were officers who had taken part in the murder of King Alexander in 1903.

One of these regicides, Dragutin Dimitrijević, a thirty-four-year-old major, dominated the Black Hand's Central Committee. Often referred to as Apis, a nickname given to him at school which stuck to him for the rest of his life, after the coup d'état, in which he was seriously wounded, he established a reputation as an outstanding officer. He was intelligent, personally courageous, an excellent organiser, and a fanatical Serb patriot. A contemporary described him as a man who, although he was professionally ambitious, worked to secure promotion for his subordinates, not for himself, a modest man who never boasted of his own achievements, "one of those leaders who accomplish more than they speak ... what one calls a good friend". But, this same contemporary added

As all fanatics, he valued the success of a cause more than the lives of men . . .. Friends were for Apis at the same time very dear and very cheap. His friendship had a dangerous quality; but this made his personality very attractive. When he wanted to draw his friends into a conspiracy, or into some other adventure, he behaved like a seducer.

Apis excelled at verbal seduction; he had a great deal of personal magnetism and was a persuasive talker. But he was also completely ruthless, certain that in the pursuit of patriotic aims there was no room for moral scruples, reckless and impatient. For the achievement of those aims as he conceived them the Black Hand was tailor-made.

The Central Committee was insistent that the Black Hand remained an élite organisation. Therefore many applications to join it were rejected and, while no reliable figures are available, it is unlikely that its total strength was ever much in excess of 2,500. Of the 300 people admitted to membership during the first few months of its existence the majority were army officers, but there were also some diplomats, journalists, lawyers, and university professors. Some of them were members of the Narodna Odbrana, which Apis and his colleagues penetrated in order to exploit its organisation for their own purposes. One of them was a Hercegovinian – Gaćinović the panegyrist of Žerajić. The establishment of contacts with student societies in the two provinces annexed by Austria was one of the first subjects discussed by leaders of the Black Hand. Gaćinović, still at the University of Vienna, was making secret visits to Sarajevo during which, one of his associates wrote, "he speaks, offers encouragement, and disappears again . . . as if the earth had swallowed him up, since he forever fears he is being followed by Austrian agents". He was appointed delegate for Bosnia and Hercegovina by the Central Committee.

On September 3rd 1911 a new newspaper appeared in Belgrade. It was financed by the Black Hand, and edited by a member of the Central Committee. Named *Pijemont* after the Italian province which was the cradle of the Risorgimento, its purpose was to publicise the overt political aims of the organisation. In its first issue it proclaimed its opposition to all political parties, because all of them "have shown in practice their immorality, their lack of patriotism and understanding of culture". War against Austria, the "aggressor" and "infamous opponent" was inevitable.

Reports about the Black Hand, most of them based on information derived from the Belgrade press, then began to appear in newspapers in various parts of the Monarchy, in Germany and France. They were unanimous that some of its members had taken part in the assassination of King Alexander, and that its aim was the fulfilment of the Serbian "national mission" to liberate and unite all Serbs. Some of them named Dimitriyević, alias Apis, as one of the "small group" who directed its operations, said that it was endeavouring to forge close links with the Narodna Odbrana, owned *Pijemont*, and had considerable financial backing. In November 1911 some quoted Belgrade sources as saying that its leaders were planning assassinations, which suggested that their political philosophy resembled that of Zhelyabov, the Russian revolutionary who played a leading role in the murder of Czar Alexander II – "History moves too slowly: it needs a push".

(ii) The Monarchy

THE Press Section of the Ballhausplatz maintained a file of newspaper reports of the Black Hand, but nobody in Aehrenthal's Ministry took much interest in it. Within the Monarchy during the greater part of 1911 history seemed barely to move at all. The Emperor spent most of his time in Schönbrunn, his palace on the outskirts of Vienna, and seldom came to the Hofburg. He was subject to attacks of bronchitis, and it was said that he occasionally nodded off during audiences. Those who had not seen him for some time found him much aged. Franz Joseph was very tired, but he still began work in the early hours of the morning, papering over the cracks in the machinery of government, making it function by sheer perseverance. His long reign was the thread of continuity in the lives of all his subjects, many of whom had not been born when he came to the throne. During it he had brought his multinational realm through manifold hazards into the second decade of the twentieth century, and he toiled on to hold it together for such years as remained to him.

By mid 1911 there was a great deal in the Monarchy which Franz Ferdinand was in no doubt urgently needed a push. Much of it concerned the armed forces. Although the building up of the navy, to which he had devoted over ten years of unremitting effort was progressing, and the first 20,000-ton battleship was about to be launched, there was still a long way to go before it could be any match for Italy's fleet in the Adriatic. Russia and Italy were each spending a quarter of their revenues on armaments, the Monarchy barely an eighth. The navy apart, large extra credits were urgently needed for every kind of military equipment, but the Council of Ministers refused to grant them. The man-power situation was even worse. The navy had to borrow 3,000 men from the army to man new ships. It had only been possible to form a few much needed extra batteries of artillery by cutting down the number of regimental bands and replacing soldiers wherever possible by civilians. All units were below strength. But when a new army law increasing the annual quota of conscripts was presented to the Parliaments in Vienna and Budapest it was rejected, as so often before, by the Hungarians.

The Archduke blamed the Minister of War for this state of affairs. He had long made no secret of his view, in which he was vehemently supported by Conrad, that Schönaich was useless, "weak" with the Hungarians, an "aprés moi le déluge" man, only concerned to hang on to his job. He must go, and be replaced by someone capable of standing up to Aehrenthal, who opposed any large expansion of the army or increase in its budget on the grounds that this

Left: Franz Ferdinand and Sophie shortly after their marriage.

Below: Franz Ferdinand with his wife and children in the music room of the Belvedere, 1910.

Emperor Franz Joseph in 1910.

Left: Janaczek in his House Steward's uniform.

Below: Konopischt.

Above: Franz Conrad von Hötzendorf.

Left: Alexander Brosch von Aarenau.

Above: Alois Aehrenthal.

Right: Oskar Potiorek.

Kaiser Wilhelm II with Franz Ferdinand in the garden at
Konopischt, June 1914.

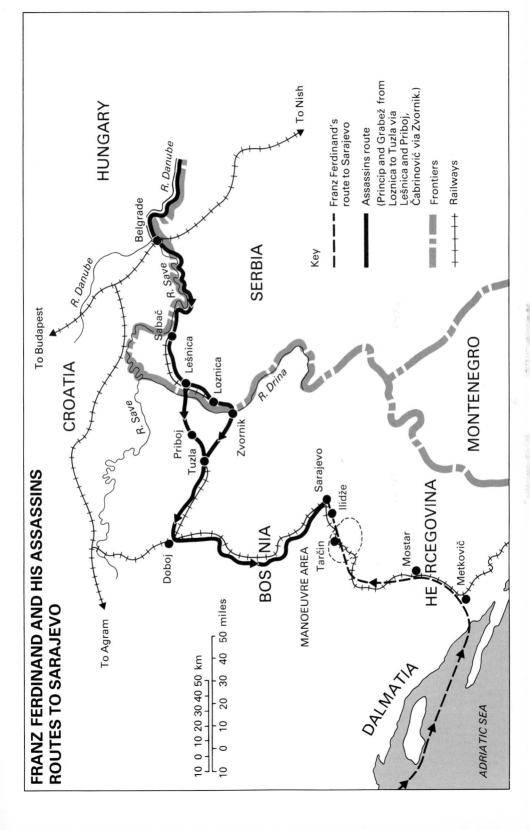

FRANZ FERDINAND AND HIS ASSASSINS
ROUTES TO SARAJEVO

HUNGARY

CROATIA

SERBIA

BOSNIA

HERCEGOVINA

DALMATIA

MONTENEGRO

ADRIATIC SEA

R. Danube

R. Danube

R. Save

R. Save

R. Save

R. Drina

Belgrade

Šabač

Lešnica

Loznica

Zvornik

Priboj

Tuzla

Doboj

Sarajevo

Ilidže

Tarčin

Mostar

Metković

MANOEUVRE AREA

To Budapest

To Agram

To Nish

Key

- - - Franz Ferdinand's route to Sarajevo

—— Assassins route
(Princip and Grabež from Loznica to Tuzla via Lešnica and Priboj, Čabrinović via Zvornik.)

Frontiers

+++ Railways

10 0 10 20 30 40 50 km

10 0 10 20 30 40 50 miles

Above: Sarajevo: the Appel Quay is on the right bank of the
river.

Right above: 28th June 1914: Franz Ferdinand and Sophie
leaving their train at Sarajevo.

Right Below: 28th June 1914: the departure of Franz
Ferdinand and his wife from Sarajevo Town Hall, with
Count Harrach standing on the running board of their car.

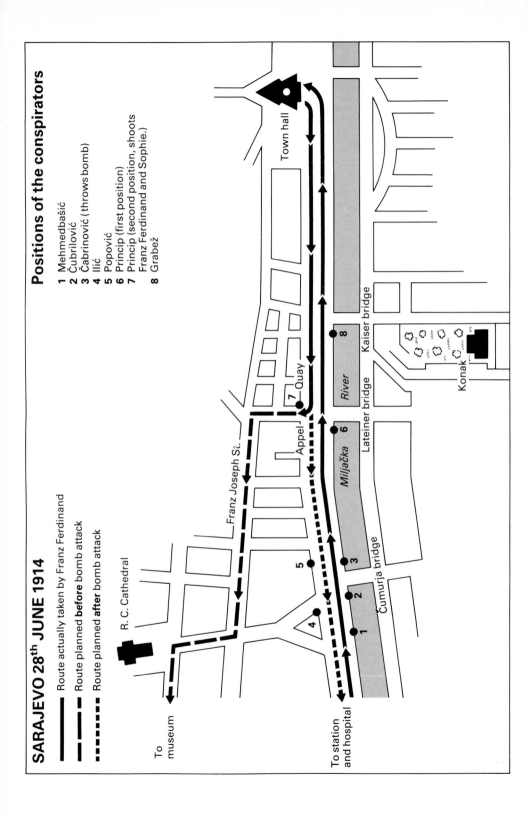

SARAJEVO 28th JUNE 1914

— Route actually taken by Franz Ferdinand

▬ ▬ ▬ Route planned **before** bomb attack

▪▪▪▪▪ Route planned **after** bomb attack

R. C. Cathedral

To museum

Franz Joseph St.

Appel Quay

To station and hospital

Miljačka

River

Čumurja bridge

Lateiner bridge

Kaiser bridge

Konak

Town hall

Positions of the conspirators

1 Mehmedbašić
2 Čubrilović
3 Čabrinović (throws bomb)
4 Ilić
5 Popović
6 Princip (first position)
7 Princip (second position, shoots Franz Ferdinand and Sophie.)
8 Grabež

28th June 1914: Franz Ferdinand's car on the Appel Quay a few seconds before the assassination.

Above: Gavrilo Princip after his arrest.

Left: (Left to right) Nedeljko Čabrinović, Milan Ciganović and Gavrilo Princip in a Belgrade park, spring 1914.

The trial in Sarajevo of those involved in Franz Ferdinand's assassination: *Front row, left to right*, Grabež, Čabrinović, Princip, Ilić, Veljko Čubrilović. *Second row*, Miško Jovanović, Jakov Milović.

would cause the Monarchy to be accused of aggressive aims and encourage neighbouring states to increase their arms build up.

After three months badgering by his heir, the Emperor in September reluctantly ordered Schönaich to resign, and appointed Auffenberg, the Archduke's nominee whom he personally disliked, Minister of War. A few days later Italy seized Tripolitania and Cyrenaica, the Sultan's North African provinces, and declared war on Turkey.

The outbreak of the Italo-Turkish war confronted the Monarchy with two unpleasant possibilities. The first of these was that Serbia and Montenegro might take advantage of it to 'liberate' their Slav kinsmen who were living under Turkish rule in Macedonia, thereby destabilising the fragile status quo in the Balkans; the second that Italy might grab another Turkish province, Albania, on the eastern shore of the Adriatic. Although Albania had been part of the Turkish Empire for hundreds of years, Constantinople had never fully succeeded in subjugating the tribes who inhabited its barren mountains. In the eighteenth century Gibbon described it as "a country within sight of Italy which is less known even than the interior of America", and in 1911 it was backward even by Balkan standards. But it was of vital interest to the Monarchy because its Adriatic coastline, on which there was a good harbour, extended from the frontier of Montenegro to the northern confines of Greece and was opposite the heel of Italy. If Italy gained a foothold in Albania she could close the Straits of Otranto, and the Adriatic could become an Italian lake.

Conrad at once wrote to Aehrenthal saying that a pre-emptive attack on Italy should be made while she was involved in war with Turkey. The Count promptly complained to the Emperor about the Chief of Staff's interference in foreign affairs. Franz Joseph instructed the head of his Military Chancellery to order Conrad on his behalf to stop sniping at Aehrenthal and, with reference to his continued complaints about the Foreign Minister's hindrance of military intelligence operations, to send him a written apology for some intemperate comments which he had made.

The Chief of Staff said he would sooner cut off his right hand than apologise to Aehrenthal, and took no notice of the Emperor's displeasure. His next move was to take up with the new Minister of War the subject of the subvention, which Franz Joseph had agreed when banning the despatch of officers on intelligence missions abroad, the Ministry of Foreign Affairs should pay so that more agents *sur place* could be recruited, and which in spite of repeated representations had not been forthcoming. He told Auffenberg that as a result of this, at a time of international tension when intelligence was urgently needed, funds were exhausted, and the utmost pressure to pay up must be brought to bear on the Ministry of Foreign Affairs. On October 11th the Minister sent a stiff note to Aehrenthal, with copies to the Emperor's and Archduke's Military Chancelleries, saying that in view of the current situation it was essential to increase the flow of information about both Italy and the Balkans, and for this purpose his

Ministry must immediately make 200,000 kronen available. If this was not done the consequence, for which the Ministry of War could not be held responsible, would be that no accurate appraisal could be made of military developments in states adjacent to the Monarchy.

A few days later the Italian Government lodged a protest with the Austrian Embassy in Rome alleging that the Military Attaché was engaged in espionage. The Ballhausplatz promptly agreed to recall him. Conrad wrote to the head of the Emperor's Military Chancellery

> It is no concern of mine that our Minister in Belgrade was away on his honeymoon when the 1909 crisis broke, nor that during the present crisis arising from the Italian annexation of Tripolitania, our Ambassadors in Rome and Constantinople are both on leave, but I must insist on being consulted about anything to do with Military Attachés for whom I am responsible, and the more so as in everything which affects intelligence work every conceivable obstacle is being put in my way.

He continued to reiterate that Italy should be attacked, and as soon as possible. On October 22nd Aehrenthal riposted with a letter to the Emperor saying that there was now a "War party" led by Conrad in the General Staff. The existence of this led to one inescapable conclusion

> It is high time that all concerned should be left in no doubt that the execution of foreign policy is the responsibility of the Minister to whom it has been entrusted by His Imperial Majesty. It is the duty of the Chief of Staff to make military preparations for any possible war, but this does not confer on him the right to influence the decision as to whether or not, or against whom, hostilities should be declared.

Conrad was summoned to the Emperor, who told him curtly that he and he alone decided foreign policy, that his policy was one of peace, and that it was being carried out to his full satisfaction by Count Aehrenthal. The Chief of Staff took no notice of this warning, and in November hammered the final nail into his coffin by urging in his annual report to the Emperor that pre-emptive attacks should be made on Serbia and Montenegro in addition to Italy. At the end of the month Franz Joseph sacked him.

The controversy between the Chief of Staff and the Foreign Minister had lasted for the better part of five years. During it, on the crucial issue which divided them – the desirability or otherwise of a preventative war – Franz Ferdinand's Habsburg caution led him consistently to agree with Aehrenthal. The purpose of building up the army was to enhance the Great Power status of the Monarchy, ensure its defence, and provide the Crown, should the need arise, with a means of enforcing internal order; it must not be hazarded in a foreign adventure. On their other major differences he sided with Conrad, and made a number of scathing comments about the Foreign Minister during 1911.

His policy of bending over backwards to avoid any semblance of provocation towards Italy was "incredible", "cowardly", "atrocious"; he was "weak" with the Hungarians at the expense of the army; he interfered in the military sphere "losing no opportunity of behaving as though he was Commander-in-Chief". As for the Balkan policy of "this Count and master of diplomacy" as Brosch derisively called him, it was "a series of failures".

Referring to Serbia, Aehrenthal said "My policy deals with the present, the future will take care of itself". This also summed up his general attitude to the Balkan situation which Franz Ferdinand criticised as being unjustifiably optimistic and, after the Italo-Turkish war broke out, dangerous. He agreed with Conrad that more information about Serbia and Albania in particular was urgently needed, and in a letter to the Emperor pulled no punches about the Foreign Minister's lack of co-operation over every aspect of military intelligence, as a result of which "it is not surprising that latterly our intelligence service has produced virtually nothing".

This was on October 30th. Nothing happened until December 14th, when the Ministry of War sent the Belvedere a copy of a Note which had at last been received from Aehrenthal. In this the Foreign Minister said he agreed on principle that Austrian diplomatic representatives abroad should do more to assist the Military Intelligence Service, but the risks of compromise and consequent damage to relations with the countries to which they were accredited were such that he must maintain his refusal to permit this. Should the situation change he would of course reconsider his decision. He made no mention of any financial subvention.

When submitting this document to the Archduke, the head of his Military Chancellery commented that it was "a typical Aehrenthal note" and totally unsatisfactory

> The fact that the Russian Consulates in Galicia are engaged in espionage does not seem to worry the Count. All he minds about is preserving his image and retaining the esteem of foreign governments. That he is thereby making us a laughing stock is not of the least concern to him.

Franz Ferdinand agreed, but all he could do was to record his views in a minute to the Ministry of War, which stated that His Imperial Highness considered that the Foreign Minister's agreement in principal that Austrian diplomats abroad should assist the Military Intelligence Service was, in view of the reservations with which he had hedged it, *absolutely worthless* (underlined).

This caustic minute was drafted by Bardolff, a General Staff Colonel who on December 1st succeeded Brosch as head of the Military Chancellery. Brosch left the Belvedere at his own request. When broaching this to the Archduke, he explained that he was anxious to return to regimental duties, and if he did not do so risked damaging his career. In addition, after six years of exacting office work, he was suffering from eye strain and nervous exhaustion. He assured His Imperial Highness that in Bardolff he had found the ideal man to take over from him.

Franz Ferdinand agreed to let Brosch go, but did so with great reluctance. He was his right hand both politically and militarily, totally loyal and trustworthy, and he had become a family friend. Sophie liked him and he got on well with the children; his daughter remembers that he was always a welcome visitor to Konopischt. After his departure the Archduke wrote to him

> I cannot tell you often enough how much I value the way in which you never spared yourself, working day and night with absolute devotion, sacrificing everything to your duty, and thereby rendering me and our beloved Austria inestimable service.

One of the subjects which constantly preoccupied Franz Ferdinand during the years Brosch was with him, was how to restructure the Monarchy – restructured it must be if it was to survive – when he came to the throne. One of the services which Brosch performed for him was to clarify his thinking on this, and find experts to advise him on subjects such as constitutional law. Both of them were in no doubt that Hungary must be cut down to size and forced to accept a new *Ausgleich*. The South Slav problem was a good deal more difficult. For a time the Archduke hoped that Trialism – the conversion of the Dual Monarchy into a Triple Monarchy by the creation within it of a South Slav kingdom consisting of Croatia, Bosnia and Hercegovina, Dalmatia, and Krain (the Austrian littoral on the northern Adriatic) – might provide a solution. But then evidence began to accumulate that anti-dynastic feeling was making headway amongst the Croats, and in June 1910 Brosch, engaged in drafting a blue print for action to be taken by the Archduke on his accession, pointed out to Franz Ferdinand

> Who can guarantee that a state composed of Croatia, Bosnia, Dalmatia and Krain, which would cut Austria off from the sea, will always be loyal and support Austria and the dynasty? The Croats are at present entirely in the hands of the Hungarian government – a new situation could develop overnight. And what would be the effect on Bohemia, which looks back to its historic past as an independent kingdom, if a new state is established in the south while it remains a province?
>
> In my opinion Trialism is extremely dangerous. It would also mean that taxes and conscript quotas would have to be agreed by three Parliaments, and it is already difficult enough to get them agreed by two.

Developments during 1911 provided further evidence of the intractability of the South Slav problem. In Croatia the *Sabor* refused to pass the budget and was, yet again, suspended. In Sarajevo Parliament barely functioned. The Serbs dominated it, and supported by a faction of the Croats, consistently obstructed its proceedings; the Croat-Muslim alliance opposing them was fragile. Croat, Serb and Muslim deputies from time to time ganged up to attack the Provincial Government, which was accused by radical politicians of administering Bosnia and Hercegovina on colonial lines, and whose employment of large numbers of "foreign" officials was widely resented. Outside Parliament there was friction between senior members of the civil administration (who also squabbled amongst themselves) and the army.

Brosch told Franz Ferdinand in February 1911 that the situation in Bosnia and Hercegovina was "extremely difficult". This was a masterpiece of understatement. Both provinces were, as a memorandum sent to the Belvedere said

> Politically unconsolidated, culturally and economically under developed, rent by political dissension, and wide open to foreign subversive influences.

The majority of their inhabitants had no sense of dynastic allegiance, and no progress was being made with the crucial problem of how to foster this. Vienna decided that Varešanin must be replaced by a "strong" Governor, and on May 10th it was announced that Feldzeugmeister Oskar Potiorek had been appointed to succeed him.

Potiorek was fifty-seven, and in the opinion of most of his army contemporaries likely eventually to crown a brilliant career by succeeding Conrad as Chief of Staff. But, while they acknowledged his professional ability, few of them liked him. He had no social graces, and Auffenberg voiced the opinion of many when he said that Potiorek was arrogant, over self-confident, and cut himself off from people and reality, implying that he might not be best man for the job.

Before long there were indications that Auffenberg might be right. Potiorek shut himself up in the Konak in Sarajevo, and seemed to be uninterested in building up contacts with leaders of the political parties and religious communities. That he was ignorant of feeling amongst them became apparent before the end of the year. When Franz Ferdinand suggested that it might be desirable for him to visit Bosnia, Potiorek pressed him to come, assuring him that his presence in their midst could not fail to encourage sentiments of loyalty to the Crown amongst all sections of the community. Sunarić, a leading Bosnian Croat, when consulted by an emissary of the Archduke's about the reception he was likely to receive, flatly contradicted the Governor, and was emphatic that Serb hostility to the dynasty was such that the safety of His Imperial Highness could not be guaranteed. Franz Ferdinand did not pursue the project; Potiorek by the end of the year had come up with no other proposal for improving feeling in Bosnia and Hercegovina.

For the Monarchy 1911 was a year virtually devoid of achievement. The conscript quota had still not been raised; the armed forces were still short of money; nothing had been done to improve the assessment and flow of intelligence about developments in Russia, the Balkans and Italy; Croatia, Bosnia and Hercegovina continued to fester. The decision-makers in Vienna seemed by the end of it to be capable of thinking only in terms of marking time and hoping every-one else would follow suit. Unfortunately, as they were to discover during 1912, marking time was something which Serbia and many South Slavs had no intention of doing.

13
South Slav imbroglio

O N January 29th 1912, Potiorek sent the Ministry of War a report about widespread rumours in Hercegovina of a Russian backed uprising in the Balkans which, it was said, would take place in the spring with the objective of carving up Turkey and detaching Bosnia and Hercegovina from the Monarchy. He commented that although these rumours were probably merely subversive propaganda, they demonstrated "the tense atmosphere in the Balkans, and the inescapable fact that there is unrest within the Monarchy".

Within 48 hours there were signs that Croatia was becoming the flash point of a new kind of unrest. After the victory of the Croat-Serb coalition in another election in December 1911 Baron Cuvaj, yet another new Governor nominated by the Hungarians, appointed by the Emperor with a mandate to restore order, had suspended the *Sabor* and banned all political gatherings. On January 31st the students of Agram University organised a meeting to protest against this, and when it was broken up by the police there was street fighting, during which policemen were stoned and some students injured; it took the authorities thirty-six hours to restore order. In mid-March trouble flared up again when several thousand secondary school pupils went on strike. The government closed all schools indefinitely, and banned youths under eighteen from appearing on the streets after 7 p.m. On April 4th the Croatian constitution was suspended, a State of Emergency proclaimed, and Cuvaj appointed Royal Commissioner with powers to rule by decree.

Meanwhile, the trouble in Agram had sparked off demonstrations against Cuvaj's "lawless system of terror" by South Slav students and schoolboys in other towns in Croatia, and in Dalmatia, Slovenia, Bosnia and Hercegovina. The most violent of these took place on February 18th-19th in Sarajevo where all the schoolboys – Croats, Serbs, Muslims – struck. The army and the police had to be called in and twenty boys were expelled, some of whom went to Croatia to continue their studies, others to Belgrade. One of the latter was Princip, who had not done well at school in Sarajevo since returning there from

Tuzla. He left without telling his brother and walked to Belgrade; according to one account, when he crossed the frontier he fell on his knees and kissed the soil of Serbia.

There were many young Bosnians in Belgrade. The majority of them were desperately poor – some slept rough in whatever street corner they could find because they were unable to afford the price of a bed – most of them, Princip included, were generally hungry. They foregathered in cheap cafés – the *Zlatna Moruna* (Golden Sturgeon), the *Žirovni Venac* (Acorn Garland), the *Zeleni Venac* (Green Garland) – where, for the price of a cup of coffee, they could sit for hours, talking about the iniquities of the Austrians, plotting, scheming, arguing as to how their vision of a future in which they would be free citizens of an independent South Slav state could be realised.

Princip frequented the *Zeleni Venac*. Shortly after his arrival a group of 150 Croatian students visited Belgrade and were given an enthusiastic welcome. Apis presided over a reception for them at the Officers Club; *Pijemont*, the Black Hand's newspaper, published an article by a Croat poet entitled "Croatia in the Struggle for Liberty" advocating violence, "in Croatia we must answer the system by force, rebellion and terror". In a preface to a pamphlet on the schoolboys' strike in Agram which was widely circulated in Belgrade, Luka Jukić, a 25-year-old Croat student from Bosnia, wrote

> We rose up against our oppressors in order to convince them that they have not succeeded nor will they succeed with their method of occupation. The struggle is in the hands of the youngest fighters for liberty.

The initiative of their contemporaries in Agram added a new dimension to the discussions of Princip and his compatriots in Belgrade, but discussions and no more they remained. Gaćinović's third eulogy of Žerajić, "Death of a Hero", made a profound impression on them when it was published in *Pijemont*, but how to emulate him was another matter. The next attempt to do so was made in Croatia, where on June 8th Jukić shot at Cuvaj from a distance of a few feet as the Governor was driving through the streets of Agram, missed him but seriously wounded an official who was sitting beside him, fled and was captured after a chase of twenty minutes, during which he killed one policeman and wounded another: eleven schoolboys, aged between fifteen and eighteen, were also arrested.

Jukić came up for trial at the beginning of August. He appeared in court wearing a black suit with a red rose in his buttonhole, and was defiant throughout the proceedings, saying when he was sentenced to death, "You cannot judge me, my judge is my country, Croatia". As he left the courtroom a girl threw him a fresh rose and he turned back shouting "Down with tyranny!". One of his associates wrote that he "completed Žerajić's deed. The Serb bullet was echoed by a Croat one – the goal is the same".

Princip had recently failed his end of term examinations, but did not return home and hung about in Belgrade. Serbia had reached an understanding with Bulgaria; there were rumours that the day of liberation for Serbs under Turkish rule in Macedonia might be at hand; excitement mounted in the Serbian capital. When the army began to mobilise he decided to volunteer for the *komitádjis*. There seemed to be no foreseeable opportunity of following Žerajić's and Jukić's example and, as he had sworn on the former's grave, assassinating a tyrant, but at least he could give his life on the battlefield for his beliefs.

The *komitádjis*, amongst whom were a number of Bosnians, were concentrated in southern Serbia, poised to advance into Macedonia under the command of Major Vojin Tankosić. Described as being kindly and gentle in private life, Tankosić could give the impression of being a retiring, almost timid, man. This was deceptive; he was a harsh commander, prepared to commit murder. or any form of atrocity in the pursuit of what he conceived to be his patriotic duty. A close associate of Apis, he had played a prominent part in the murder of the King in 1903, was a member of the Black Hand Central Committee, and the leading expert on *komitádji* operations in the Serbian army. When Princip appeared before him, he took one look at this pale weedy boy, told him he was unfit for any kind of military service and sent him packing. Princip returned to Bosnia in a state of black misery.

In Vienna during the early months of 1912 not much notice was taken of the demonstrations and strikes by South Slav students and schoolboys; it was assumed that the local authorities were competent to deal with them. Two events made the headlines. Aehrenthal, fatally ill with leukaemia, resigned and the Emperor appointed Count Berchtold, who until 1911 had been Ambassador in St Petersburg, to succeed him as Foreign Minister. The army law raising the annual conscript quota was at last pushed through the Austrian and Hungarian Parliaments.

Both these developments were highly satisfactory to Franz Ferdinand. Berchtold, tactful and a good listener, from the outset made a practice of keeping him informed and giving him that insight into foreign affairs which, the Archduke told him, "I only too often lacked when your predecessors were in office". Progress could now be made with bringing the army up to strength. Shortly after the law was passed he left on a private visit to England. In early June, when Princip and his friends were mulling over their hatred of the Austrians in a sleazy café in Belgrade Franz Ferdinand, accompanied by Sophie, was much enjoying himself at the Chelsea Flower Show.

The Archduke and his wife stayed in England for a fortnight, returning to Konopischt a few days after the attempt to assassinate Cuvaj. Nobody as yet realised the implications of this; Franz Ferdinand carried on with his annual shooting programme. If necessary Bardolff could be summoned to wherever he might be, and as a matter of routine daily reports, together with files from Ministries requiring his attention, were sent to him by his Military Chancellery. He complained to Brosch, with whom he kept in touch, that the amount of work these entailed was increasing, "My spare time gets less and the reports get thicker". Bardolff complained of the difficulty of getting His Imperial Highness to deal promptly with files and memoranda, and suspected that if the subject did not interest him, he sometimes initialled them without having studied them.

In August Bardolff submitted a memorandum to which Franz Ferdinand did, however, pay attention. Its subject was a development in the South Slav provinces of the Monarchy which had not hitherto come to notice

> The investigation of Jukić's assassination attempt in Agram has led to the discovery of a secret South Slav youth organisation extending throughout Croatia and Dalmatia and possibly into Bosnia. The statutes of this organisation, which were drawn up in 1909, are not subversive, but during the past year schoolboys in Dalmatia have formed a new secret revolutionary offshoot of it – "Jugoslavia" – whose declared objective is the establishment of a republican state consisting of Croatia, Dalmatia, Bosnia, Hercegovina and Macedonia, in conjunction with Serbia and Montenegro.

Bardolff went on to say that "Jugoslavia" was in contact with Belgrade and irredentist circles in Italy. A number of its members had been arrested. He pointed out that, while it would no doubt be argued that a "Schoolboys' Revolution" presented no threat to the State, it must be borne in mind that these youths would soon be occupying posts in public life in which they would be in a position to influence the situation in Dalmatia. The root of the trouble lay in the schools; it must be assumed that the teachers knew what was going on, and possibly in some instances were encouraging it. Therefore, he submitted, it was urgently necessary to ensure, both in Croatia and Dalmatia, that teachers who were in any way politically active were removed, and that henceforward emphasis was laid on "healthy non-political subjects" – religion, literature, natural history, sport.

Franz Ferdinand agreed, and authorised Bardolff to put up his proposals for reforming the educational system in Croatia and Dalmatia to the Minister of the Interior. No similar action seemed to be needed in Bosnia where, according to Potiorek, the situation gave no cause for alarm and he had it fully under control. He informed the Minister of War – on what grounds it is difficult to surmise – that the Croats and Serbs generally remained aloof from political activity, and that the majority of the radical students, of whom there were only a few, were Muslims. In his opinion the source of the student trouble was undoubtedly in Dalmatia, not Croatia.

Reform of the educational system was a long-term measure; in Dalmatia Count Attems the Governor was beset by more immediate problems. All the schoolboys who had been arrested were connected with some influential member of the community, and every politically active Croat and Serb in the province supported them. Therefore if they were tried they were certain to be acquitted, and the administration would suffer a devastating loss of prestige. The only means of getting off this hook seemed to be to have them tried outside Dalmatia, but before a decision had been reached about this, violent demonstrations broke out in Ragusa. The police failed to control them and the Emperor asked for a report. Attems wrote to the Minister of the Interior and said that the demonstrations had got out of hand because the police were incompetent and unreliable. He stressed that the unrest, which was prevalent not only in Ragusa but throughout Dalmatia, was a direct result of the State of Emergency in Croatia, and that the situation would only improve when this was lifted. Franz Joseph's attention was drawn to this, but without effect; he received Cuvaj and assured the Governor that he had the utmost faith in him. Tension increased in Dalmatia where the saying now was "The Emperor hates the Croats".

How could the Emperor be made to understand that Cuvaj must go? Franz Ferdinand considered a direct approach to his uncle, and found a letter which Bardolff drafted for him excellent

> I believe I can best make Your Majesty aware of the situation in Croatia by humbly reporting that the Royal Commissioner, Herr von Cuvaj, is universally hated there . . .. The reason for this is . . . his attempt to exert his power by ruthlessly hounding down his political opponents, muzzling the press, and totally suppressing all forms of political freedom . . .. The Hungarian Government may assert that Croatia is quiet, but it is only being kept so by force.

If the Archduke finally sent this letter to Franz Joseph it also had no effect. When in early October, Montenegro, Serbia, Bulgaria and Greece attacked Turkey, setting alight a conflagration of unpredictable dimensions in the Balkans, Cuvaj was still in office, the State of Emergency was still in force in Croatia, the situation in Dalmatia was unchanged, and an increasing number of the inhabitants of these South Slav provinces were becoming His Imperial Majesty's most disloyal subjects.

In Vienna, information to enable an assessment to be made of how the war was likely to develop was not available. Military intelligence could produce practically none about what was occurring on the far side of the 260-mile long frontier with Serbia. Nothing was being provided by the Legation in Belgrade; the Military Attaché was away attending manoeuvres in Roumania, and Aehrenthal's ruling that diplomats should have nothing to do with intelligence activities was still in force. Potiorek telegraphed to the Minister of War saying that he was completely in the dark, and a surprise move by Serbia against Bosnia could not be ruled out. Neither could the even more serious possibility of some hostile move by Russia in Galicia. There were indications of some increased Russian military activity along the frontier, but these were derived from visual observations by low level agents and it was impossible to estimate their significance. The Intelligence Bureau had no agents in key positions and with access to documents in Russia, and during the first half of October the Military Attaché in St Petersburg was away shooting in the Caucasus.

Bardolff submitted a memorandum on this unsatisfactory state of affairs to the Archduke. He stressed that the Intelligence Bureau was not to blame; it was the result of the "separation of the diplomatic from the military information services and the attempts of the former to suppress the latter, both of which were the work of Count Aehrenthal". It must be made clear to Berchtold that this must cease, that as much money as possible must be made available for foreign intelligence, all consular officials must cooperate with the Bureau, and there must be no restrictions on sending officers on intelligence missions abroad.

Franz Ferdinand annotated this reiteration of the arguments which Conrad had put up, unavailingly, for years, "Absolutely right. I completely agree". At this stage, in spite of the absence of information about Russian intentions, he still hoped, as he had earlier told Berchtold, that the Monarchy could stay clear of Balkan entanglements, "Let these ruffians bash in one another's skulls; we will watch from the stage box".

During the next few weeks this hope evaporated. The Serbs and their allies occupied a large area of Macedonia, and the Serbian army, together with the Montenegrins, advanced through Albania towards the Adriatic. The Russians reinforced their troops in Galicia, and the Emperor was compelled to order the reinforcement of the Austrian army corps both there and in the South Slav provinces of the Monarchy. It seemed that Pašić, the Serbian Prime Minister and his government either would not or could not control the army, whose officers were punch drunk with victory. The Austrian Military Attaché in Belgrade took a gloomy view of the situation

> The prestige of the Monarchy in Serbia has never been lower. Nobody takes us seriously; it is believed that we are only bluffing, and because of Russia's attitude will not dare to back up our threats by force of arms . . .. Victorious nations tend to expand rapidly and I have a feeling that the Serbs will be no exception to this rule . . .. After a few years we must reckon that Serbia will present us with a grave threat.

The Serbian army had acquitted itself well, captured a great deal of arms and equipment from the Turks, and its morale was high. The only way to restore the prestige of the Monarchy was to send an ultimatum to Belgrade demanding Serbia's immediate withdrawal from Albania.

This was at the end of November. Hard intelligence about Serbian troop movements was still lacking. The Military Attaché was under surveillance and his movements outside Belgrade were restricted. Information produced by such low grade agents as the Intelligence Bureau still possessed in Serbia could not be checked and took days to reach Vienna – the Minister of War complained that by the time he received it, he had often already read it in the newspapers. But there was no doubt of the reaction of the Emperor's South Slav subjects to Serbia's victorious progress. Reports reaching the Archduke's Military Chancellery described "fanatical enthusiasm" for a Greater Serbia in southern Hungary and Croatia amongst Serbs of all classes from the intelligentsia to peasants. The entire younger generation in Croatia were said to be dedicated to the realisation of a united South Slav state. There were instances of disaffection amongst South Slav troops. From Bosnia young men flocked to join the Serbian army. The frontier could not be closed because the Monarchy and Serbia were not at war; the Ministry of Foreign Affairs dithered about introducing passport controls on the grounds that this might be regarded by Belgrade as a provocation, and in any case, given the difficulty of the terrain, illegal crossings were impossible to prevent. Reports of subversive contacts between Belgrade and dissidents in the South Slav provinces, of plots to stir up unrest, of preparations for uprisings when – it was "when" not "if" – Serbian troops arrived to liberate their oppressed kinsmen, multiplied.

Contrary to what Franz Ferdinand had hoped Serbia, far from being weakened by the campaign in Macedonia and Albania, had gained a great deal, was hell bent on gaining more, and was stepping up what amounted to a Cold War with the Monarchy. The Archduke decided that in view of this menacing situation, Conrad, the ablest General in the army, must be reinstated as Chief of Staff. He argued Franz Joseph into agreeing to this, summoned Conrad to the Belvedere, told him of their joint decision and left him with no alternative but to accept it.

Conrad's appointment was gazetted on December 12th. He at once reiterated to the Emperor that Serbia must be smashed, and the sooner the better. Three days later he dined with a friend who noted in his diary

> The atmosphere was like a funeral. Conrad was in despair at having once again to take on the job of Chief of Staff. Everyone expects action from him and his hands are tied. The Emperor wants peace at any price and will not listen to his proposals. He maintains, in a state of black pessimism, that he has no hope of getting them accepted. The rot is worse than ever.

At the end of January 1913 the British Ambassador, writing to the Foreign Office about the fear in Vienna that Serbia would be the cause of a European war, said

> I cannot describe how exasperated people here are by the unending trouble which that small country, incited by Russia, is fomenting for Austria.

He thought it would be a near miracle if war between the Monarchy and Serbia was averted.

Conrad by then had already pressed three times for an immediate attack on Serbia. He continued to do so; Franz Joseph continued to refuse to contemplate it. Franz Ferdinand, who in view of the tense situation had not taken his family abroad for their annual winter holiday, agreed with the Emperor

> Even assuming that nobody hinders us from settling accounts with Serbia, what shall we have gained at the end of it? A collection of robbers and murderers and a few plum trees, and that at great cost in lives and money.

The Monarchy already had a next to impossible situation on its hands in Bosnia; it would be idiocy to acquire another hostage to fortune in the Balkans. There could be no question of annexing even a square metre of Serbia. Moreover

> If we move against Serbia we shall have war with Russia. Are the Emperor of Austria and the Czar to topple one another from their thrones and leave the way wide open for revolution?

The Archduke told the Chief of Staff outright that what he called his "Hurrah" policy was crazy, and consistently turned down his proposals for aggressive military action. This, however, was not widely known. It was generally assumed that because Franz Ferdinand had been responsible for Conrad's reinstatement as Chief of Staff, therefore he agreed with him.

During this winter of 1912-1913 Princip lodged with his brother at Hadžići outside Sarajevo. In the Bosnian capital people queued outside tobacconists to read reports of the advance of the Serbian army which were displayed in their windows; each victory was greeted with an outburst of rejoicing; in the streets children sang the old songs about Kosovo; every day more volunteers left for Serbia. Princip sought refuge in reading and made no further attempt to take part in the war, neither was he involved in any conspirational activity against the Austrians. Many of his friends were away at the battlefront. But throughout the winter he brooded over the bitter humiliation of Tankosić's rejection of him and, as the months went by, his determination increased that one day, by some means, he would accomplish a great deed and prove himself a hero.

In the summer of 1913 Princip was back in Belgrade. The war ended on May 30th. Turkey was forced to cede to her opponents most of her possessions in Europe, but Serbia and Greece were dissatisfied because Bulgaria got the lion's share of Macedonia. At the end of June they attacked her, Roumania and Turkey joined in, and the Second Balkan War began. Franz Joseph was not alone in finding the situation "very confusing". After a month Bulgaria was forced to capitulate, and at the Peace of Bucharest Serbia gained a very much larger area of Macedonia.

According to a military intelligence report, the Serbs had suffered heavy casualties and were short of equipment. The Deputy Director General of the Ministry of Foreign Affairs, however, told the Austrian Minister that Serbia was "well used to war and well able to embark on another one". The Military Attaché reported that the attitude of army officers was summed up by an article in *Pijemont*, which declared that any reconciliation with Austria was out of the question. Articles in other Belgrade papers referred to the Austrians as "The Imperial and Royal Turks", and to the Emperor as "The Padishah in Schönbrunn". One of them came out with a swingeing attack on Franz Ferdinand, saying that he was

> so arrogant and haughty that nobody can stand him . . .. Rulers shun him. The Czar has twice refused to receive him. During the last six months he has lost his only friend, Kaiser Wilhelm . . .. Nobody trusts him. A man whose speciality is forging documents is to be avoided. No decent person can have anything to do with a man who interferes in Chancelleries solely in order to slander entire nations.

"After Turkey it will be the turn of the Monarchy; Serbia will take Bosnia and Hercegovina"; this was the thesis which Hartwig the Russian Minister was reported to be plugging. Little else was talked of in the cafés of Belgrade. The Serbs, intoxicated by victory, were filled with what someone described as "joyous hope" for the future.

From this heady atmosphere Princip returned at the end of the summer to a Bosnia in which there seemed to be less hope than ever. At the beginning of May Potiorek had declared a State of Emergency. It was repealed after a fortnight, but the measures enacted while it was in force were not. All Serb associations of any kind, even those concerned with welfare, were dissolved; strict government control was imposed on the administration of all schools, and the secondary school in Mostar was closed for a year. Although the Joint Minister of Finance remained nominally responsible for the administration of Bosnia and Hercegovina, both provinces were now run by what Baernreither described after another visit to Sarajevo as a "militarist-police regime" headed by Potiorek.

After returning to Sarajevo Princip spent much of his time with Ilić, whom he spoke of as "his best friend". During the summer Ilić, travelling on a false passport, had visited Switzerland, where according to some accounts he saw Gaćinović and met a group of Russian Social Revolutionaries, after which he served briefly as a stretcher bearer with the Serbian army. They discussed the intolerable situation, and decided that one or other of them must attempt to assassinate Potiorek. Then both had second thoughts. Ilić backed down, arguing that it was useless to attempt this before a political organisation to exploit the deed had been created. Princip decided that he was incapable of carrying out the assassination by himself, and made up his mind to return to Belgrade in the new year to study and attempt to pass another exam.

Potiorek, Baernreither noted, "likes to hear himself speak and lives in a very restricted circle". That old Bosnian hand, General Appel, enlarged on this in a letter to his friend Brosch, saying that the Governor rarely appeared in public, did not receive people, shut himself up in his office, and formed his judgement of what was going on from reports in the files in which he immersed himself, and what his senior officials, many of whom were new and understood what the mass of the population were thinking as little as he did, told him. The tenor of the information which reached Potiorek was that the situation, while leaving much to be desired, could be worse. There were reports of trouble in the schools sometimes fostered by nationalist teachers, "treasonable" expressions of disloyalty to the Monarchy, subversive literature from Belgrade circulating amongst students. But they referred to isolated instances and the Governor, unaware that they were symptomatic of a deep-seated disaffection, agreed with his officials that no great importance was to be attached to them.

By mid-September, when Potiorek left for a visit to Vienna, there was no doubt that under the "hypnosis" of Serbia's military successes, Serbs and Croats throughout Bosnia and Hercegovina were becoming more restive. But there had been no attempt to assassinate him or any of his officials – by contrast with Croatia where a second attempt to kill Cuvaj had been made followed by another to murder his successor – no large scale demonstrations, and no evidence to suggest any form of organised revolutionary activity. Therefore, when the General was told in Vienna that Franz Ferdinand proposed to attend the manoeuvres in 1914 of the Army Corps under his command, it did not occur to him to suggest that, while in Bosnia, His Imperial Highness's life might be at risk.

Part Three
Encounter at Sarajevo

14
Decision making

(i) Vienna and Sarajevo

A FEW weeks before Potiorek arrived in Vienna, the Emperor appointed Franz Ferdinand Inspector General of the army, a post which had been vacant since the death in 1895 of its only previous incumbent, Archduke Albrecht. This meant that Franz Joseph vested in his heir responsibility for its administration, training, equipment and morale, a recognition of the Archduke's dedication to its interests which the latter greatly valued.

One of the first decisions which Franz Ferdinand then took was that he must visit what amounted to the forgotten corps in Bosnia. The troops there were serving in conditions not dissimilar to those of the British army in India, stationed in a remote part of the Monarchy the language of whose inhabitants many of them could not speak, and kept constantly on the alert. The morale of some units was said to be low. When the Archduke told Conrad in mid-September 1913 that in the following year he proposed to attend routine training manoeuvres of the corps under Potiorek's command and would take Sophie with him, the Chief of Staff's reaction was "that an imperial prince should at least visit Bosnia again . . . seemed only natural in the interests of the dynasty".

After his return to Sarajevo Potiorek began to plan the manoeuvres. They must demonstrate "the power of the dynasty and the Monarchy". Therefore they must be on the largest possible scale, and he applied to Conrad for a grant of one million kronen to finance them. The Chief of Staff slashed this by over half, saying that to transport brigades from outlying stations by rail to the area west of Sarajevo where they were to be held was far too expensive, and ruled that they should last for two days only instead of the four envisaged by Potiorek. For similar reasons of economy, Franz Ferdinand later ordered that the troops engaged in them should not wear their best uniforms.

Having not done as well as he hoped over the public relations aspect of the manoeuvres, Potiorek then turned his attention to the programme for the Archduke's visit. He belonged to the school of thought, to which a number of his senior officers also adhered, which held that the light of a Habsburg countenance could work wonders in a difficult situation. If, in addition to attending the manoeuvres, His Imperial Highness appeared in Sarajevo and made some expeditions into the surrounding countryside, thereby giving the civilian population a chance to set eyes on him, this would encourage the Muslims to support the dynasty and, hopefully, strengthen the wavering loyalty of some of the Croats. The draft programme which he sent to the Belvedere for approval accordingly included a visit to Sarajevo, and several excursions and shooting expeditions to different parts of Bosnia.

On February 17th 1914, Bardolff wrote to tell Potiorek that the Archduke had read the programme with interest, but decided that he could not arrive in Bosnia as early as His Excellency suggested, must curtail the length of his stay, and so would have time only to attend the manoeuvres and after them to make a brief visit to Sarajevo. He would probably be in Bosnia from June 23rd-29th, but the exact dates had still to be fixed. At some future date, perhaps later in the year, he would hope, together with the Duchess, to make an unofficial tour of other parts of the province.

This uncertainty over dates caused Potiorek some alarm. The Archduke and the Duchess were to stay at Ilidže, the spa a few miles outside Sarajevo, where the principal hotel was being commandeered for them. The spa season, he explained, must open on July 1st at the latest, and there would be "much unpleasantness" if they had not left by June 29th. With reference to the question of a later unofficial tour, he asked Bardolff to inform His Imperial Highness that, while he confidently undertook *full responsibility* (underlined) for his forthcoming visit, because he had been informed of it well in advance and so had time to plan the necessary security measures, he could not assume similar responsibility for a further unofficial visit made at short notice.

On March 12th Bardolff wrote that Franz Ferdinand had finally decided to come to Bosnia on June 25th. He would go straight to Ilidže, attend the manoeuvres on the 26th and 27th, give a large dinner party for senior officials and local dignitaries, and visit Sarajevo on Sunday the 28th. This meant that he would be in the Bosnian capital on Vivodan, the anniversary of the annihilation of the Serbian army by the Turks at Kosovo in 1389 and the most emotive day in the Serb calendar, but Potiorek did not draw attention to this. If he recollected a report from the Ministry of War on the Black Hand, warning that this Serbian secret society might attempt to assassinate prominent personalities in the Monarchy, he disregarded it. It was dated February 1912, and since then no activity attributable to the Black Hand had come to notice in Bosnia or Hercegovina. The possibility that the Serbs might try to make some sort of trouble could not be entirely discounted, but security measures were only one item in the long list of preparations which must be made for the Archducal visit, to the detailed planning of which he now devoted the greater part of his time and attention.

(ii) Belgrade

IN October 1913 Gellinek, the Military Attaché in Belgrade, informed Vienna that the Serbian government was under increasing pressure from the army, and that this was spearheaded by what he described as an "undercurrent" of the Officers' Corps, the Black Hand. For over a year despatches from the Belgrade Legation had made no mention of that organisation; presumably the appointment in the previous June of Colonel Dragutin Dimitriyević, alias Apis, who had been mentioned in the press as one of its founder members, to the key post of Director of the Military Intelligence Department of the Serbian General Staff, had passed unnoticed. Confirmation of the Military Attaché's report was, however, provided by an agent at the end of January 1914, who stated that the membership of the Black Hand was increasing and it had a growing number of adherents in political circles. By then Gellinek was in no doubt that all political parties and the entire press were rabidly anti-Austrian. The British envoy summed up the mood of the general public, "The Serbs already see themselves at the gates of Vienna".

Princip returned to Belgrade in February 1914. He lodged in a house occupied by several other young Bosnians, sharing a room with Trifko Grabež, the son of a Serb Orthodox priest. Grabež, a few months younger than Princip, was continuing his studies in Belgrade after having been expelled from school in Bosnia and held under arrest for 14 days for hitting a professor. He was a defiant, somewhat surly youth, of medium height with a shock of black hair and a small moustache – someone said he looked like a gipsy. He had been in Belgrade for about a year, and told Princip that the sense of freedom and hope in Serbia made him realise the intolerable oppression of their compatriots in Bosnia. They had long discussions about the liberation and political union of all South Slavs.

Princip's friends in Belgrade at this time included Nedeljko Čabrinović, whom he had known since 1912. Čabrinović's father owned a fourth rate café in Sarajevo, which he had obtained a permit to open from the Austrian police on condition that he acted as one of their informants. His home life was unhappy. He was on bad terms with his father, who when he was a boy often beat him, and took him away from school at the age of fourteen when he failed to pass his exams.

Čabrinović was then apprenticed as a typesetter in the Serbian printing press in Sarajevo, but left after two months when a foreman boxed his ears. Thereafter he had a chequered career. He was taken on by another printing firm, but denounced to the police as a trouble maker when he became leader of the students' branch of the printers union. Leaving Bosnia, he went illegally to Belgrade and found work with a firm specialising in anarchist literature, much of which he read far into the night, but fell ill and was forced to return home. When he recovered he got a job with yet another printer in Sarajevo, but this came to an abrupt end when, having been involved in a strike, he was banished from the Bosnian capital for five years and, handcuffed, sent under police escort to Trebinje in Hercegovina. Bitterly resentful of the injustice to which he felt he had been subjected, he again made his way illegally to Belgrade, but failed to find work, and hearing that the banishment order against him had been rescinded, decided to go home. He walked to Sarajevo having spent such money as he could scrape together on buying books by Kropotkin and other socialist and revolutionary authors; when his mother discovered them she burnt the lot, and there were more quarrels with his father. In the autumn of 1913 he returned illegally to Belgrade for the third time, and managed to get a job with the Serbian Government printing press; the hours were long and the pay barely enough to live on but he stuck to it – anything was better than returning home.

Now aged nineteen, Čabrinović was a handsome dark young man, less farouche in appearance than Grabež. He had added to his hotchpotch of socialist and anarchist ideas a passionate hatred of the Austrians, was an ardent convert to Serb nationalism, and thought of Princip as his best friend. In the cafés – the *Zlatna Moruna*, the *Živorni Venac*, the *Zeleni Venac* – where in early 1914 they and other Bosnians continued to gather, *komitádjis* back from the war boasted of their exploits against the Turks and Bulgarians, and talked ceaselessly of the time when they would repeat these against the Austrians. But when that would be nobody knew, and meanwhile life was harder than ever in Belgrade; prices had risen and there was little work for Bosnians who, having served with the *komitádjis*, were afraid to return home. Other younger Bosnians like Princip, Čabrinović and Grabež, had in addition to endure the galling experience of being mocked by their Serbian contemporaries for their failure to make any contribution to the liberation of their kinsmen. This stimulated them to think in terms of violence, but how to translate thought into action they had still no idea; all they could do was to wait and hope that something would happen which would give them a chance to prove themselves.

In the spring of 1914 the chance appeared. On about March 22nd Princip read in a German newspaper that Archduke Franz Ferdinand, accompanied by his wife, would come to Bosnia for several days in the middle of June, and while there would attend the summer manoeuvres of the 15th and 16th Corps. No precise dates were given for the visit; official confirmation of these was still awaited. Similar reports appeared in newspapers in the Monarchy, and some ten days later Čabrinović received a cutting of one of them, which was posted to him anonymously from Bosnia. He later said that when he saw Princip at midday in the *Živorni Venac* and mentioned it to him, the latter seemed to take no interest in it, but when they met at another café in the evening, said there was something he wanted to discuss. They went out and sat on a bench in the square, and Princip asked Čabrinović to join him in a plot to assassinate the Archduke. Čabrinović's initial reaction was that more might be achieved by killing Potiorek, but after a few minutes argument agreed Princip's proposal.

They swore to one another that they would abide by their decision, shook hands and parted. Grabež was not in Belgrade, having gone home for the Easter holiday. When he returned Princip asked him if he would join the plot, and he agreed to do so without hesitation.

Princip had already written to Ilić telling him that the assassination would take place, that when before long he came to Sarajevo he would bring the weapons for it, and asking him to find some more conspirators. But by the time he recruited Grabež at the beginning of May, little progress in obtaining the weapons was being made. They must be pistols or bombs; the Archduke would be surrounded by guards and it would be impossible to get near enough to kill him with a dagger. Pistols, and bomb casings which could be filled with explosives, were obtainable at arms shops in Serbia, but Princip and his fellow conspirators had no money to buy them. A suggestion that it might be possible on some pretext to get cash from the Narodna Odbrana, which from time to time produced grants for students, had come to nothing. The only hope seemed to be to get hold of some of the bombs which *komitádjis*, who had been equipped with them for guerilla operations in Macedonia, had failed to hand in at the end of the war, and an approach to one of them, Milan Ciganović, had been made, but whether it would produce anything remained to be seen.

Ciganović, referred to by his associates as "the handsome Cigo", was a 26 year old Bosnian Serb who had a minor post in the Serbian State railway. He had emigrated to Serbia in 1908, volunteered for the *komitádjis*, served with them during the Balkan wars, and was well known to their leader, Major Tankosić. When Princip revealed to him that he, Čabrinović and Grabež had resolved to kill Franz Ferdinand, and asked for his help in obtaining weapons, "Cigo" was evasive and said he must consult someone (whom he did not name) about this.

For about three weeks nothing happened. Then, on May 24th, Ciganović came to Princip and told him that Tankosić wished to see one of the conspirators. Princip contacted Grabež, and no doubt with memories of the time when Tankosić had turned him down for the *komitádjis*, declared that he would not go. They agreed that Čabrinović, who was liable to get over excited and talk too much, would make a poor impression; Grabež therefore must represent them. In the evening Ciganović took Grabež to Tankosić's house. The Major kept them waiting for half an hour, greeted Grabež curtly, and in the course of a brief interview, asked whether he and his fellow conspirators could shoot. Grabež had to admit that none of them had ever handled a pistol. Tankosić gave one to Ciganović, ordered him to see that all three were taught how to use it, and concluded the interview by saying that Grabež need not come to his house again. The latter returned to Princip and Čabrinović and told them that Tankosić made an "evil impression" on him.

On the following day the three youths had a short lesson in shooting, organised by Ciganović, in a wood on the outskirts of Belgrade, where they practised firing at a tree. Forty-eight hours later, in a café garden, "Cigo" produced the assassination weapons. These consisted of four Browning pistols each loaded with seven bullets, four loaded reserve magazines, and six bombs filled with nails and pieces of lead, each of which weighed about two pounds, was the size of a large cake of soap and fitted with a safety cap. Ciganović said that Tankosić had cashed a cheque to buy the pistols. His instructions on handling the bombs were brief – unscrew the safety cap, knock the bomb against something hard, and it would then explode in 10-13 seconds. He told Princip and his friends that they must take this armoury with them; there was not, as they had hoped, any possibility of forwarding it separately to Sarajevo.

Briefing them on their journey, Ciganović stressed that they must on no account be caught by the civilian authorities in Serbia with the assassination weapons on them. On the following day they were to board the Save river steamer and travel to Šabac, a small town about 45 miles upstream from Belgrade. He gave them a card with his initials on it – M.C. – and said they should show this to Captain Rade Popović, the frontier gendarmerie commandant in Šabac, who would arrange to smuggle them safely over the border into Bosnia. Once in Bosnia they should make for Tuzla where, if they could not transport the weapons from Tuzla to Sarajevo, Miško Jovanović, a local merchant, would help them.

Ciganović also gave them a small sum of money saying, when Princip complained that it was totally inadequate, that it was all he had. With regard to carrying out the assassination he had only one chilling comment to make. In order to ensure that none of them under interrogation gave away the others, after the attempt had been made they must all commit suicide, for which purpose he handed them a phial of cyanide, saying that it contained enough poison to kill many people. He then departed. The conspirators took the pistols and bombs to Princip's room, where he hid them under his bolster, and solemnly vowed that they would never betray one another, and would tell nobody of their journey and its purpose.

The foregoing description of the inception of the plot to assassinate Franz Ferdinand, and the means by which the weapons for this were obtained, is based on reports of what Princip, Čabrinović and Grabež later said when they were interrogated at length by Austrian police and officials, and at their trial. From time to time their statements differed over points of detail, but they were unanimous that they, and they alone, had conceived the idea of the assassination

> If it is asserted that somebody talked us into committing the assassination I can only say that this is not true. The idea of it was born in our hearts, and we realised it.

According to one account, these were Princip's last words to the court before he was sentenced. Many historians and writers who have contributed to the vast literature on the plot maintain, however, that he and his fellow assassins concealed the truth, and that the decision to kill the Archduke was made by Apis. A confession by Apis himself provides some support for this contention, but it is not conclusive. It occurs in a four-page document which he wrote during the war in 1917, when he was being tried by a Serbian Military Tribunal in Salonica for conspiring to murder the Crown Prince. The text of this was not released by the Yugoslav Government until 1953 and, to quote one expert, "must be treated with reserve until more is known about the circumstances of its composition . . . .. More light is certainly needed before this version is acceptable".

Two years earlier, according to Cedomir Popović, also a member of the Black Hand Central Committee, Apis had related another version of his role in the inception of the assassination. He told Popović that one day Tankosić (whom he did not mention in his 1917 "confession"), came to his office, said that he was being pestered by some young Bosnians who wanted to return home, and asked whether they should be allowed to go. Apis said he authorised this without stopping to think. When Tankosić added that these youths, together with their associates in Bosnia, intended to attempt "something" against Franz Ferdinand, his reaction was that the Archduke would be so closely guarded that they would have no chance of trying to assassinate him, let alone succeeding in doing so. They might just conceivably stage some sort of incident. If they did, so much the better, it would serve as a warning to His Imperial Highness and his entourage that the Serbs were not to be trifled with.

It has been suggested that his 1917 "confession" may have been extorted from Apis, or that he was induced to make it by an appeal to his patriotism. At that time there was a slight hope of concluding peace with Austria, the terms for which might be improved if he admitted responsibility for the assassination of Franz Ferdinand. Both these theories, however, remain unproven. There is also no collateral for Popović's account of what he alleged Apis told him, and the possibility cannot be ignored that he may have invented or distorted it. But of the two versions it is the more plausible, for it does suggest an explanation of why the three Bosnians who set out from Belgrade to eliminate Franz Ferdinand were not battle-hardened *komitádjis*, but three youths not yet out of their teens, untrained in the use of the pistols and bombs which they were carrying, very short of money, and quite unbriefed as to how to plan the assassination.

149

15

The Assassins and their Target

(i)

ON the morning of Ascension Day, May 28th, Princip, Čabrinović and Grabež, the pistols and bombs concealed about their persons, embarked on the steamer for the first stage of their journey to Sarajevo. In the evening when they arrived at Sabač, they contacted Captain Popović, showed him Ciganović's card, and told him that they wanted to cross the Drina secretly into Bosnia. Popović advised them to go by train to Loznica, about 40 miles south of Sabač, and gave them a note to Prvanović, the frontier gendarmerie captain there: "Look after these men and take them across where you think best". When Princip said they were short of money, he made out a warrant stating that they were three customs officials, and so entitled to a reduction in the price of their tickets.

At Loznica next morning Prvanović, presented with Popović's note, was equally obliging, said he would consult his sergeants in charge of frontier posts as to where the three of them could best cross the Drina unobserved, and told them to return to his office at noon on the following day.

By the following day Princip and Grabež were, however, barely on speaking terms with Čabrinović. He was a loquacious youth, and on the journey they had already rebuked him for striking up conversations with strangers. While they were filling in time at Loznica, in what seemed to be holiday mood, he wrote half a dozen postcards to friends in Sarajevo and elsewhere, on two of which he quoted lines from Serbian nationalist poems. This was the last straw. They told him that his indiscretion could wreck the whole venture; he must give them the bombs which he was carrying, cross the frontier on his own and meet them in Tuzla. Provanović, when told by the young Bosnians of their decision to split up, gave a sulky Čabrinović a letter of introduction to the customs officials at Zvornik, a few miles down the river, and handed Princip and Grabež over to Sergeant Grbić, who took them to his post on the bank of the Drina where they spent the night.

Čabrinović had a trouble-free journey to Tuzla. A convention had been concluded between Vienna and Belgrade whereby a passport was not necessary for crossing the frontier; almost any kind of identification document would do. Since Čabrinović possessed none having entered Serbia illegally, Grabež had given him his school registration card – they were almost the same age and looked much alike. The Serbian customs officials were helpful and on good terms with their Austrian opposite numbers. One of them saw him through the Austrian check point at Zvornik (where Grabež's registration card was accepted without question) and introduced him to the mayor's secretary there who put him up for the night. Next morning he caught the mail wagon, and by the evening, thirty-six hours after having parted from Princip and Grabež, was comfortably lodged with a friend of the latter's in Tuzla.

Princip and Grabež spent May 31st, the day on which Čabrinović was making his way to Tuzla, on an island in the middle of the Drina belonging to Serbia, to which they had been ferried by Sergeant Grbić. It could be reached from the Bosnian shore by wading across the river, and was therefore a convenient staging post for smugglers, Narodna Odbrana couriers, Serbian agents, and anybody else who wished to cross the frontier illegally. There was a small tavern on it which was frequented by Bosnian peasants because it sold cheap plum brandy. When one of them, a young baker, appeared, the sergeant told him that there were two students on the island who must cross into Bosnia and travel secretly because they had no identification papers, and sent him off to fetch another peasant, Jakov Milović, an experienced smuggler.

Some hours later the baker returned with Milović. They both realised that there was something unusual about the students; one of them was practising shooting with a pistol and there were some bombs lying around. Grbić impressed on them that they must say nothing about this to anyone. In fact they had no intention of doing so – they had the instinctive conviction of illiterate peasants that the way to survive was to keep one's head down and ask no questions. When the students said that they wanted to go to Tuzla, Milović undertook to guide them as far as Priboj, a small town not far from there, and put them in touch with Veljko Čubrilović, a Serb teacher and the local representative of the Narodna Odbrana, who occasionally employed him as a courier.

In Serbia, where they had been handed on from official to official, the first stage of Princip and Grabež's journey had gone smoothly. The next stage in Bosnia was, they soon discovered, considerably rougher. It began after nightfall when, festooned with pistols, bombs, and ammunition, led by Milović they waded across the Drina, struggled through a swamp on the far side of the river, and then followed their guide through a seemingly endless forest. The path was rough and barely visible in the darkness; they tore their trousers on bushes, and to add to their misery, after a while it began to rain. Eventually further progress became impossible; soaked to the skin they spent what remained of the night in a ruined hut. The going was no easier next day, and by the time they reached the house of a peasant known to Milović, they were too tired to care about security, no longer able to endure the weight of their weapons, and thankfully put them into two bags provided by the peasant. After some hours rest they set out once more, Milović and his friend carrying the bags, Princip and Grabež plodding behind them up a steep slippery track. It rained again, and footprints in the mud suggested the nearby presence of a patrol of Austrian gendarmes. Fear was now added to exhaustion; when at last they reached the outskirts of Priboj, Princip and Grabež refused to go into the town and hid themselves in a thicket.

The peasants went into Priboj and found Čubrilović who rode out with them to the students' hiding place, where he was confronted by two bedraggled youths who told him they must get to Miško Jovanović in Tuzla without attracting the attention of the gendarmes. This presented a problem. It would be apparent to anyone from their town clothes that they were strangers to the district; therefore they must be smuggled into Tuzla, and for this help was needed. The teacher paid off Milović and his friend, attached the bags which they had been carrying to his saddle, told Princip and Grabež to follow him, and set off for the house of a peasant well known to him, Mitar Kerović. The bags were suspiciously heavy. After persistent questioning Princip admitted that they contained pistols and bombs, telling the teacher to keep his mouth shut, and threatening that if he failed to do so he and his entire family would be killed.

Čubrilović had the impression that there must be some organisation behind these youths; one did not, he reflected pick up so many bombs in the street, but on arrival at Mitar Kerović's house merely said that he had with him two students from Tuzla who wanted to return there after midnight, and meanwhile needed to rest. Age old tradition decreed that shelter must be given to any traveller in need of it; Mitar told him to bring them in. Princip and Grabež, by then at the end of their tether, collapsed on to a bed and fell asleep. Their host produced some plum brandy and settled down with Čubrilović to gossip about local affairs.

The plum brandy session was prolonged – Mitar's philosophy was that once one began to drink one should drink as much as possible. After they were joined by three of his sons and a neighbour, the teacher opened the bags, showed the assembled company the pistols and bombs, and said that the students to whom they belonged had no permit for them, therefore they must be smuggled into Tuzla. After some discussion, during which money changed hands, two of the younger peasants agreed to drive them there in a farm cart. Čubrilović gave them a letter to Jovanović and went home.

Old Mitar Kerović had passed out. Grabež was still exhausted and incapable of thought; Princip, physically frailer but with more nervous stamina, took control of the situation. On his insistence, when they set out for Tuzla in the early hours of the morning, the peasants strapped the bombs and pistols round their waists, and he and Grabež concealed themselves under hay in the back of the cart. A detour had to be made to avoid a gendarmerie post, progress was slow and by the time they neared Tuzla it was beginning to get light. The youths got out of the cart telling the peasants to drive into the town and leave the weapons at Jovanović's house.

Miško Jovanović, a prosperous merchant regarded as a most respectable member of the community by his fellow citizens, was the Tuzla representative of the Narodna Odbrana. Shortly before 7 a.m. he heard knocking on his front door, went down to see who was there, and was confronted by two peasants who marched in, dumped an assortment of bombs, pistols, and ammunition on his kitchen table, gave him a letter and departed. Jovanović looked at the array on the table in horror. Disseminating propaganda for a Greater Serbia was one thing, involvement in anything to do with arms another – which he did not at all fancy. He opened the letter and found a note from Čubrilović saying that two students would come to see him about them in the Serb reading room at nine o'clock, stuffed the arms and ammunition into a box which he hid under the desk in his study, breakfasted, and feeling extremely unwell went to the Serb reading room.

Princip and Grabež meanwhile did what they could to make themselves look more presentable by washing in a stream, after which they walked into Tuzla, each bought a much needed new pair of trousers, had breakfast in a café and arrived punctually for their assignation with Jovanović. When he asked them what they wanted, they said that because they were travelling without identification papers, they would be in trouble if during their onward journey they were stopped at a police check point – would he therefore take the arms for them to Sarajevo? Jovanović, according to Princip "extremely agitated", flatly refused to do this, but reluctantly agreed to house them for a few days until someone, who would identify himself by producing a box of Stefanija cigarettes, collected them. He returned home, and after much pondering as to how best to conceal these incriminating objects, hid them in his attic.

Having deposited the pistols and bombs with Jovanović, Princip and Grabež were anxious to get out of Tuzla as soon as possible. It was not a large town, and having both for a time been at school there they were afraid of running into someone who knew them. To make matters worse, when they found Čabrinović they discovered that he had again been indiscreet. While waiting for them to arrive he had encountered a detective who knew his father and, without thinking, told him that he was on his way home from Belgrade. When they all caught the next train for Sarajevo Čabrinović, travelling separately from the other two on their insistence, found himself in the same carriage as the detective. The latter, however, displayed no more than a friendly interest in him, asked a number of questions about living conditions in Serbia, and was expansive about the arrangements which were being made for Franz Ferdinand's forthcoming visit to Bosnia.

There was no police check on the train, and the last lap of the three conspirators' week-long journey from Belgrade went without a hitch. When they arrived in Sarajevo they separated. Čabrinović went to his father's house, and Grabež to his parents at Pale a few miles outside the city. Princip made his way to his brother at Hadžići. By now because they had made no attempt to conceal this; at least ten people in Bosnia had seen that he and Grabež were carrying a suspicious number of pistols and bombs. But the possibility that one of them might report this to the police, and that it might accordingly be desirable to remain out of the Bosnian capital for the time being, did not apparently occur to him, neither it seems did he envisage that overt contact with Ilić, also actively involved in the plot to kill the Archduke, might endanger them both. After spending two days with his brother he moved into Sarajevo, rented the spare bed in Ilić's room from the latter's mother, and a few days later registered with the police as her lodger.

Ilić by then had recruited three more assassins. One of them, Muhamed Mehmetbašić, a Hercegovinian carpenter in his late twenties, was that rare phenomenon, a Muslim who was a fanatical Serb nationalist. According to his own account, in January 1914 he attended a meeting of several Bosnian revolutionaries in Toulouse at which it was decided to kill Potiorek, and was chosen to carry out the assassination. He left for Bosnia equipped with a dagger and a bottle of poison, but became alarmed when police boarded his train after it crossed the Austrian frontier, threw the dagger out of the window and flushed the poison down the lavatory. There is virtually no information to support Mehmetbašić's story of this fiasco, but he evidently impressed Ilić, who met him in Sarajevo after his return from France, as being someone who was prepared to commit an act of terrorism. After receiving Princip's letter he went to Mostar, and asked him whether he would take part in an attempt to kill Franz Ferdinand during the latter's visit to Bosnia in June. Mehmetbašić said that Ilić could rely on him; when summoned he would come immediately to Sarajevo.

The only other likely potential assassin personally known to Ilić was a student at the Teachers' Training College, who had declared in his presence that, if weapons could be found, Franz Ferdinand ought to be killed when he came to Sarajevo. But when told they would be available and that an assassination was being planned, he lost his nerve and refused to participate in it. On his suggestion Ilić then approached Vaso Čubrilović, aged seventeen, who at once agreed to take part in the attempt, and produced another willing collaborator, his eighteen-year-old friend Cvetko Popović. Ilić told them only that they would be supplied with weapons and would receive further instructions. He informed Princip that he had found three additional murderers, but did not give him their names, neither did he say that the trio consisted of a Muslim assassin *manqué* and two Serb schoolboys.

On June 6th, when Princip moved into Ilić's mother's house, the position therefore was that six assassins, if of somewhat varying calibre, had been lined up. The next problem was to transport the pistols and bombs from Tuzla to Sarajevo. After a week's havering Ilić set off to collect them. He arrived in Tuzla on Sunday, June 14th, identified himself to Jovanović by producing a box of Stefanija cigarettes, and said, to the latter's dismay, that because he was a stranger in the town the police might stop and search him: Jovanović therefore must pack the weapons in a harmless looking box and bring it to a station down the line where they could meet and safely effect the handover. Jovanović did not at all care for this proposal, but agreed because it seemed to be the only way of getting rid of the pistols and bombs. They arranged to travel separately on the early train next morning to Doboj, about thirty-five miles from Tuzla, and to meet there in the station waiting room.

This arrangement did not go according to plan; when Jovanović arrived at Doboj next morning there was no sign of Ilić. Very alarmed indeed, his sole thought was now to keep as far away from the weapons as possible. He left the sugar carton in which they were packed in the waiting room with his coat over it, searched the station and, having failed to find Ilić, humped it into the town and left it in the shop of a tailor whom he knew, saying that it would be collected before long. After calling on a business associate he returned to the station and met the next train from Tuzla, to find to his relief that Ilić was on it, having failed to arrive earlier because he had overslept. They retrieved the carton from the unsuspecting tailor and Ilić went off with it. Afraid that the express might be searched by the police, he changed to a local train, left this at a stop on the outskirts of Sarajevo and took a tram into the city. On arriving home he solved the problem of concealing the pistols and bombs from his mother by putting them under Princip's divan – when cleaning the house she was not in the habit of sweeping under the beds.

It was by then generally known that Franz Ferdinand would stay at Ilidže, attend the manoeuvres and probably visit Sarajevo on Sunday June 28th. Ilić and Princip assumed, as no doubt did Grabež, the only one of the other conspirators whom they in any way took into their confidence, that his hotel at Ilidže would be heavily guarded, during the manoeuvres he would be surrounded by troops, and therefore the attempt to kill him must be made when he came to Sarajevo. But to plan this in detail they needed to know the programme for His Imperial Highness's visit to the city, and this had not yet been announced. Until it was, there was nothing to be done but wait. Princip, convinced that Čabrinović was hopelessly indiscreet, did not tell him that the pistols and bombs had been brought to Sarajevo. On the principle that the less they knew the better, Ilić said nothing about this to his three recruits fortunately, for Čubrilović and Popović too were indiscreet and consequently at least five of their classmates (one of whom, a Croat, volunteered to hide Čubrilović's weapons for him), knew that they were involved in a plot to kill the Archduke.

Young Popović found that after he agreed to take part in the attempt to assassinate Franz Ferdinand his whole view of life changed

> Convinced that I had only until June 28th to live, Vivodan – St Vitus Day – I looked at everything from a different angle. I left my school books. I hardly glanced at the newspapers . . .. I failed to react to the jokes of my friends.

Princip, Čabrinović and Grabež, having all resolved to commit suicide after the attempt, also thought of June 28th as their last day on earth. While waiting for it to dawn, Čabrinović worked with a printer, and Grabež remained with his parents at Pale where he saw a good deal of a local girl. Princip, in order to avoid drawing attention to himself, latched on to a coterie of his school contemporaries who were more interested in wine than politics, and although a teetotaller, spent much of his time in the tavern which they frequented. Such money as he had was barely enough to cover his meagre living expenses; when, about a week before the Archduke was due to arrive, it ran out, he managed to get a job as a clerk.

During this last phase of waiting Princip had several long arguments with Ilić. The latter had begun to have doubts about the desirability of killing Franz Ferdinand, maintaining that it would achieve nothing, evoke a reaction from the Austrians which would certainly increase the sufferings of the Bosnian Serbs, and tried to persuade Princip not to go through with the assassination. Princip refused to listen, "I was not in agreement with the postponement of the assassination because a certain morbid yearning for it had been awakened in me". Ilić's doubts were not dispelled, but he continued to collaborate in the plot; of the two of them Princip was the stronger personality.

All Princip's thinking was now concentrated on June 28th when Franz Ferdinand's life and his would, for a few minutes, converge. The only facts which he (or his fellow conspirators) knew about the Archduke were that he was heir to the throne and Inspector General of the army. This he assumed meant that without his approval no important political or military decision could be taken. Therefore he was responsible for the annexation, Vienna's hostility to Serbia, the Agram treason trial and the Forgách "forgeries", for Hungarian oppression in Croatia, and for all the misdeeds of the Monarchy in Bosnia and Herce-govina. He did not know that the decision to annex these provinces had been taken over Franz Ferdinand's head, of his consistent opposition to war, his condemnation of Budapest treatment of the Croats and his conviction that the South Slavs of the Monarchy must be given more political and cultural autonomy, nor that the amount of influence which he could exert was limited and that ultimate power of decision rested not with him but with the Emperor. Princip was convinced that the Archduke was the principal enemy of the South Slavs, implacably opposed to their unification. Therefore he must be killed, and his assassination would be a great and noble deed, a "sweet and bloody revenge" for the sufferings inflicted by the Austrians on his countrymen in Bosnia and Hercegovina. He thought of Franz Ferdinand as a quarry to be brought down and destroyed, not as a human being.

(ii)

AT the beginning of April, when in Belgrade Princip and Čabrinović decided to assassinate the Archduke, Franz Ferdinand and his family were at Miramar, a Habsburg castle on the shores of the Adriatic near Trieste. To him the visit to Bosnia was simply an item in his summer programme, which towards the end of the month after he left Miramar it seemed possible might not take place. Franz Joseph was seriously ill and the doctors feared he might not recover.

The Emperor's illness lasted for over four weeks, during which Franz Ferdinand spent most of his time at Konopischt. No provision had been made for him to act as regent while his uncle was incapacitated, he was in daily touch with his Military Chancellery, if the need arose he could be in Vienna in a matter of hours. But his absence from the capital at this time was seized on by the many people who disliked him as added proof that, as a senior politician was reputed to have said, he had no serious understanding of his position, no desire to learn, no vision, and would allow nothing to interrupt his shooting. This was only one of the derogatory comments made about him. Others were that his judgement was superficial, that he was vain and unstable, that he wanted to control everything and admitted no contradiction.

Berchtold thought that by the spring of 1914, Franz Ferdinand "in spite of his complex personality had come to terms with himself". In many ways this was true, but the Archduke's temper remained unpredictable. He was still liable to lash out and, occasionally, to fly into what seemed to be an ungovernable rage: within the past year there had been three instances of this, all involving his protégé Conrad, which were much talked of by those who had no use for him.

The first of these was evoked by the Chief of Staff's handling of the Redl affair. In the early summer of 1913 it was discovered that Colonel Redl, the senior staff officer at Eighth Corps headquarters in Prague, formerly head of the Counter Espionage Section of the General Staff Intelligence Bureau, and generally held to be one of the most brilliant officers in the army, was clandestinely receiving large sums of money from abroad for selling military secrets to a foreign power. Informed while at a dinner party of the incontrovertible evidence of this, Conrad ordered that Redl should immediately be interrogated, forced to admit his guilt, and then "given the opportunity to judge himself". During the interrogation, which lasted for barely an hour, Redl said that he had been working for the Russians for about a year because he needed money to pay his debts, and named a few classified military documents which he had copied for them. He was not pressed for further details, but handed a revolver and left alone: forty minutes later he shot himself. Next day a search of his flat in Prague revealed that he was a homosexual, and produced evidence that his espionage activities were far more extensive than he had admitted.

Franz Ferdinand, informed by Bardolff of the Redl case, summoned Conrad to the Belvedere, and kept the Chief of Staff standing rigidly to attention for three-quarters of an hour while (with some justification) he castigated him about every aspect of it. Why had Redl's treason not been discovered sooner? Why had he not been subjected to an in-depth interrogation? Why had he not been tried by a properly convened military court? It was barbarous and a contravention of the laws of the Church to hand him a revolver and virtually compel him to commit the mortal sin of taking his own life. The whole affair demonstrated that, as he had long suspected, the General Staff was sloppy and incompetent. Conrad, who later wrote that this audience was the worst experience of his career, thought at one point that the Archduke was going to choke with rage. At a lunch party given by Berchtold on the following day, he was not reticent about it, with the result that before long yet another story of His Imperial Highness's inability to control his temper was circulating in Vienna.

The second and third instances of this occurred in public and in rapid succession at the end of the summer. At the September manoeuvres in Bohemia, Franz Ferdinand was extremely irritable, and lost no opportunity for finding fault with Conrad, reproaching him for failing to attend Mass "with unparalleled anger, even brutality". A month later, at a banquet given by Wilhelm II after the celebration in Leipzig to mark the centenary of the defeat of Napoleon, the Archduke was unwarrantably rude to the Chief of Staff in the presence of the Kaiser and a large number of senior German and Austrian officers.

Outbursts such as these fuelled rumours, which had been circulating for some time, that Franz Ferdinand was going mad. Conrad, who saw more of him than his detractors, did not subscribe to them, but thought that during the summer of 1913 he must be feeling ill. Eisenmenger, who having been his personal physician for nearly twenty years had few illusions about him, wrote that anyone who called "such fits of passion raving madness" and concluded from them that His Imperial Highness was going off his head, needed to have their own head examined – a refutation of the malicious rumours about him which is the more convincing in that it appeared in the doctor's by no means wholly eulogistic reminiscences of Franz Ferdinand which were published in 1930, when Eisenmenger had nothing to gain by it because the Monarchy had ceased to exist.

Members of the Archduke's staff who witnessed such explosions of temper did not doubt his sanity, neither certainly did anyone who met him in England, when, accompanied by Sophie, he went there on a private visit shortly after the incident in Leipzig. They stayed first at Windsor for a week's shooting, and then went on to Welbeck for a shoot with the Portlands. Count Mensdorff, the

Austrian Ambassador in London, was in no doubt that the visit was a great success. Franz Ferdinand got on well with King George V, who invited Asquith the Prime Minister, Grey the Foreign Secretary and other leading politicians to meet him. The Portlands introduced him to Lord Roberts and Lord Curzon, and took him to lunch at Chatsworth where he was entranced by the garden. The Duke thought him a first-class shot, and he and the Duchess agreed that Franz Ferdinand and Sophie – "a most charming woman always called Sopherl" – were delightful guests.

The impression made by Franz Ferdinand on a member of the house-party at Welbeck was that his "one aim in life was *peace*, his policy eminently constructive, and his greatest joy embellishing everything with which he came in contact". He made a similar impression on Baron von Morsey, a young civil servant whom he appointed to his staff early in 1914. When first approached by the Archduke, Morsey was doubtful about accepting the appointment, for everything he heard suggested that His Imperial Highness would be an exacting taskmaster. When told that he would be at his personal disposal when not acting as mentor to the children in their spare time, he protested he was too inexperienced and had never been a tutor. Franz Ferdinand persisted, emphasising that nothing would be better for the children than the company of somebody young, and he would learn the rest of his duties as he went along. He then said something which Morsey never forgot

> I am *schwarz-gelb* and a Catholic Austrian. This Monarchy can only be saved if all its nationalities are treated equally and granted the autonomy to which they are entitled. You are young and the future awaits you. Gather round you people who will work to bring this about.

Morsey accepted the post. At Konopischt, while it was uncertain whether the Emperor would recover, Franz Ferdinand talked to him about some of his hopes and fears for the future. The armaments race between the Powers would ruin them all and must cease. An Austro-Russian alliance would solve the South Slav problem and make it possible to build up a new relationship with the Balkan states. War with Russia was unthinkable

> even if we won it, and I am certain there is no chance of this – even the wildest optimist could not hope for it – it would be the ultimate disaster for the Monarchy.

As Prince Clary, a nephew of Sophie's recalled, the Archduke allowed young men who were invited to Konopischt to shoot, to stay and listen when, in the evening after the ladies had gone to bed, he had "serious conversations with his close friends and advisers". Franz Ferdinand repeatedly told Morsey to remember what he said and pass it on to his contemporaries with whom the future lay. To his accession to the throne, however, he rarely and very reluctantly referred, neither did he talk in detail about the plans which he was struggling to evolve for the enormous task of restructuring the Monarchy. At Konopischt in the spring of 1914 he seemed to both Clary and Morsey to be in excellent spirits, the kindliest of hosts, a happy family man who played and laughed with his children.

Towards the end of May the Emperor's doctors issued a bulletin stating that he had fully recovered from his illness, and on June 4th, the day on which Princip, Čabrinović and Grabež arrived in Sarajevo from Belgrade, an official statement announcing that the Archduke would attend the manoeuvres in Bosnia was published in Vienna. The interchange of correspondence between Potiorek in Sarajevo and the Military Chancellery in the Belvedere about the arrangements for the Bosnian visit, which had been in progress since March, continued. Although the programme for the Archduke's day in Sarajevo involved civilian officials and the city police, who came under the jurisdiction of the joint Minister of Finance who was responsible for the administration of the annexed provinces, Bilinski, the current occupant of that office, was not consulted. Franz Ferdinand disliked him and laid down that Bardolff should deal with Potiorek. This suited Potiorek who did not get on with the Minister, and sitting in his office in the Konak, like a snail in its shell, he supervised every detail of the arrangements for the visit. The stream of letters and telegrams sent on his instructions to the Belvedere contained suggestions for Franz Ferdinand's approval ranging from alternative routes for his journey to Bosnia to the siting of the military band which would play while he lunched at the Konak; requests for assistance, which included the despatch of an official from the Emperor's Lord Chamberlain's office to supervise the catering in the hotel at Ilidže, and the provision of two standards to be flown on the Archduke's car; queries, such as what was to be done about photographers?, was a saddle being sent from Vienna? if not, what was the length of His Imperial Highness's stirrup leathers?; personality notes on officials and local dignitaries.

Security measures were still by no means the only subject engaging Potiorek's attention. Planning them was simplified by the fact that throughout his visit the Archduke would be staying at Ilidže, would arrive there by train by-passing Sarajevo, and proceed from there direct to the manoeuvres, which were to be held on a bleak stretch of upland 14 miles further west of the Bosnian capital. At them he would be surrounded by officers, but as an additional precaution orders were given that all strangers were to be kept out of the area. A detachment of troops was detailed to mount a twenty-four hour "guard of honour and security guard" on the hotel at Ilidže, with orders to check on all visitors and report to Bardolff who would be accompanying Franz Ferdinand.

These arrangements seemed adequate to ensure the Archduke's safety from June 25th–27th, the greater part of his stay in Bosnia. How this was to be done when he visited Sarajevo on Sunday 28th was another question. As a preliminary precaution orders were given before the end of May that frontier crossings from Serbia were to be strictly controlled (which did not prevent Princip,

Čabrinović and Grabež from entering Bosnia), and that anyone arriving in Sarajevo from Serbia was to be closely watched (but Čabrinović, although he had told a detective in the train en route to Sarajevo that he was returning from Belgrade, was not kept under surveillance). The plan for the day itself was that all troops would remain in barracks, and the protection of the Archduke while he was in Sarajevo left to the police, whose total strength in a city of over 50,000 inhabitants was 120 men. The possibility of applying to Budapest for additional detectives was considered, but rejected when it was discovered that this would cost 7,000 kronen (about £700 at the 1914 exchange rate). The provincial government of Bosnia was short of cash: Potiorek, who had no intention of going hat in hand to Bilinski for a subvention, decided that the situation would be adequately covered by drafting gendarmes from the surrounding countryside into Sarajevo to reinforce the police.

Dr Gerde, the senior civilian official responsible for the police, believed there was a serious danger that an attempt might be made on Franz Ferdinand's life while he was in Sarajevo, did not consider the proposed measures to protect him were anything approaching adequate, and said so. He was told by army officers that he was "obsessed by phantoms". When Count Collas, the head of the political section of the provincial government, attempted to warn Potiorek of the strength of Serbian nationalist feeling amongst the younger generation of Bosnians, the Governor retorted that Collas was afraid of children. He took no notice of repeated warnings from Sunarić, the Croat Vice-President of parliament, who was well informed about local Serb irredentism, nor of reports from other sources of threats to kill the Archduke. One of these, from military intelligence, stressed that every precaution must be taken while he was in Sarajevo; Potiorek said the author of it was a pessimist and tore it up. He seemed to have an *idée fixe* that, regardless of any additional security risks, the more the heir to the throne saw of – and was seen in – Sarajevo the better, and on June 9th proposed that his programme there should be extended to include a morning and afternoon tour of anything of any conceivable interest in the city – barracks, old fortifications, the principal mosque, the carpet factory. When this was turned down he devoted himself to the final perfecting of the minor details of the visit. On June 19th, by which time the four pistols and six bombs designated for the assassination of Franz Ferdinand were reposing under Princip's bed barely a mile from his office, he instructed a member of his staff to telegraph the Belvedere asking whether the programme of music to be played during lunch on the 28th met with His Imperial Highness's approval.

Potiorek's line that the danger to which the Archduke would be exposed was minimal was not borne out by information which reached Vienna from a variety of other sources.

If the heir to the throne goes to Bosnia we will see that he pays for it . . ..
Serbs, make use of every available weapon, daggers, guns, bombs and

dynamite. Revenge is sacred. Death to the Habsburg dynasty. The memory of those heroes who rise up against it will live for ever.

This exhortation appeared in *Srboban*, the Serb emigré newspaper in Chicago, in December 1913 when it was first rumoured that Franz Ferdinand might before long go to Bosnia. During the next six months more threatening Serb reactions to the visit were reported by the police to the Ministry of the Interior, by consular officials in Serbia (who unlike the Belgrade Legation were permitted to be in touch with informants) to the Ballhausplatz, by various sources to the Ministry of Finance, by Military Intelligence to the Ministry of War. A number of people in Vienna – Ministers, the Chief of Staff, senior officials – were therefore aware that the Archduke's life must be considered to be at risk while he was in Bosnia, and so by implication that Potiorek's optimism was unfounded. Of these, Conrad ordered that the Belvedere should be kept fully informed of the content of reports which were flooding into the Intelligence Bureau, and thought that the visit should be cancelled. Berchtold was less apprehensive. The Ballhausplatz did not pay much attention to consular reports – the sole comment on one recently received from Belgrade was that the colour of the tape with which it was fastened should have been *schwarz-gelb*, not red. Since information from the Austrian Minister there was that the army was engaged in a power struggle with the government, apart from anti-Austrian polemics in the press, no provocative action was, he assumed, to be anticipated from Serbia while His Imperial Highness was in Bosnia. Bilinski took the line that, since he had not been consulted about it, he had no responsibility for the visit. The attitude of the Minister of the Interior was somewhat similar; Bosnia and Hercegovina did not come within his sphere. At departmental level interchange of information between Ministries was slow and often incomplete. The bureaucracy of the Monarchy, the largest in Europe after Russia, generated a vast amount of paper, but contained no adequate provision for co-ordinating and evaluating all information from all sources on any one subject.

There was thus no means of producing a comprehensive assessment of the danger to which the heir to the throne would be exposed while in Bosnia. Nor, if one had been submitted to him, is it likely that Franz Ferdinand would have paid attention to it. His reaction at Miramar in the spring, when his attention was drawn to the dangers of driving through an Italian irredentist area without at least informing the police was

> But of course we are going to Cividale! Precautions? Alerting the police director in Trieste? I have no use for any of that. One is always in God's hands . . .. Worries and precautions cripple life. Fear is always one of the most damaging things,

and on another similar occasion

> We are all constantly in danger of death. One must simply trust in God.

The Archduke was under no illusions about the possibility that he might be assassinated – there had been a number of threats to his life over the past few years – but, a man of unquestionable personal courage and sustained by his religious beliefs, like the Emperor he calmly accepted this as an occupational risk of his position. Countess Nostitz recalls having been told that before leaving for Bosnia, her father entrusted Janaczek with the key to his desk, saying that if anything happened to him, he was to give the papers in it to Karl his nephew who would then be heir to the throne, but he may have done this as a precaution rather than as the result of any definite premonition. His reaction to attempts by some of his friends to dissuade him from going on the grounds that it would be "frightfully dangerous" was that, as Inspector General of the army it was his duty to go, and go he would.

If Franz Ferdinand had any apprehensions about the visit, he was determined to conceal them from Sophie. She was worried about the effect of the heat in Bosnia in June on her husband's health, and desperately anxious about his safety. He intended that she should accompany him and she was determined to do so, believing that if she, a woman, was at his side, it was unlikely that anyone would attempt to shoot him because they would be afraid of killing her. But whether she could go was dependent on the Emperor's permission, which at the end of May had still not been obtained. Her fears may have been part of the reason why Franz Ferdinand then asked his uncle for an audience, and when the Emperor received him early on June 4th, the day the official announcement was due to be made, said that he was uncertain about attending the Bosnian manoeuvres because he was doubtful whether his health would stand up to the heat, and asked for permission if he went to take Sophie with him. Franz Joseph told him to do as he liked, and raised no objection to her accompanying him.

The Archduke decided to go through with the visit and, somewhat belatedly, to travel to Bosnia by a roundabout route – train to Trieste, sea on board the battleship *Viribus Unitis* to the mouth of the Narenta in southern Dalmatia, up the Narenta by shallow draught naval vessel to Metković in Hercegovina, from there by rail to Ilidže stopping en route for an hour in Mostar, the Hercegovinan capital. Sophie would come by train from Vienna direct to Ilidže. According to the official programme, she would be present at the dinner given by the Archduke for senior army officers, civilian officials and local dignitaries at Ilidže on the evening of Saturday June 27th, and accompany him on his visit to Sarajevo on the following day, but no other engagements were listed for her, and the guard at Ilidže was ordered not to present arms to her. Bardolff telegraphed Potiorek, who had submitted a draft of Franz Ferdinand's reply to the Mayor of Sarajevo's address to him for approval, to say that the latter part of the sentence "the loyal sentiments which you have expressed on behalf of the provincial government have given my wife and myself much pleasure", must be altered to read "have given me much pleasure". Sophie's part in the visit was to be kept in low profile.

After his audience with the Emperor the Archduke returned to Konopischt and turned his attention to a different subject – gardening. Wilhelm II had accepted an invitation to come there when, he hoped, all the roses were out, and was arriving on the 12th. Franz Ferdinand took great pride in his rose garden which now contained an infinity of different varieties, and was set in a five hundred acre park, also his personal creation, into which he had landscaped the surrounding fields by planting the hedgerows between them with roses and other flowers. Determined that the Kaiser should see all this at its best, he ordered the gardeners to use all conceivable devices to ensure that everything possible was in full bloom and, driving himself round in a trap, spent the next few days supervising their work.

Wilhelm arrived, and was at his most genial. Attired in the "hunting uniform" which he had designed for himself for country house visits, a green broad-brimmed homburg hat adorned with feathers, a green high-collared jacket from the belt of which were suspended a sword and a dagger, breeches and riding boots, he was escorted round the garden and park by Franz Ferdinand (who wore a lounge suit and a straw boater), and was unstinting in his praise of every feature of them. The Archduke and Sophie invited a number of Bohemian aristocrats and their wives to entertain him, their children were much in evidence, and their daughter was allowed to stay up for dinner. During this informal country house party, with one exception of barely an hour, Franz Ferdinand and Wilhelm had no tête-à-tête discussion.

The weather was fine, the garden had never looked more beautiful, the visit was a success. On his return to Berlin the Kaiser sent a fulsome telegram, "I want to thank you and your wife once again with all my heart for the exquisite hours which I was able to spend with you both in 'Klingsor's Magic Garden'". For the next three days Franz Ferdinand for the first time opened the park at Konopischt to the public. Crowds of people came to see it, special trains were run from Prague, he drove round talking to them and was astonished and delighted by their appreciative comments.

Altogether it had been a good week. Berchtold, who saw the Archduke at Konopischt towards the end of it, noted that he made no special reference about his forthcoming journey to Bosnia. Writing to an elderly cousin from Chlu-metz, where the children were to stay while their parents were away, two days before the start of it, Franz Ferdinand merely said, "I am about to go with Sophie for a short while to Bosnia", and went on to tell him about the family plans for the rest of the summer.

16
On Stage in Sarajevo

(i)

WHEN Franz Ferdinand's visit to Bosnia was announced in Vienna Baernreither wrote in his diary

> If things go on as they are with us the ground will slip from under the feet of Imperial authority. All this is being done in the name of the sick old Emperor.

When the Archduke succeeded to the throne, he must within the first few weeks show that "he intends to rule with the people". If he proved to be a reformer "there would certainly be an immediate swing in public opinion . . .. For him, and for us, it is a life and death question". On June 23rd this man on whom Baernreither and many others thought so much depended, set out on the first stage of his journey to Sarajevo.

Before leaving Chlumetz on the afternoon of the 23rd Franz Ferdinand gave Janaczek, his house steward and most stalwart friend, a gold watch – possibly in commemoration of 25 years of devoted service – and asked him never to leave the children. Then, accompanied by Sophie, he drove to the station, to be informed that his special coach was out of action; its bearings were overheating and it was emitting clouds of steam. The Archduke sometimes teased his wife by making up exaggerated stories of imaginary disasters. As their luggage was being transferred to a first class carriage on the train to Vienna, Morsey heard him say to her, "You see what we are in for. First an overheated coach, then an assassination attempt in Sarajevo and, to round it off, an explosion on the *Viribus Unitis*". The Duchess, visibly alarmed, did not find this amusing.

When they reached Vienna Franz Ferdinand left Sophie in the Belvedere, and with Baron Rumerskirch his Chamberlain, Bardolff and two other officers from the Military Chancellery, went on to the Südbahnhof to catch the night express for Trieste. On arriving at the station he was told there had been another mishap – the electricity on his coach had failed. His private secretary came to see whether His Imperial Highness had any final instructions, and found him surrounded by flickering candles complaining that their dim light made him feel as though he was in a vault.

The beginning of the journey was not propitious, but thereafter it went well. During his voyage down the Adriatic Franz Ferdinand received a telegram informing him that the King of Serbia had abdicated in favour of his second son and the Belgrade parliament had been dissolved. The Serbs, absorbed by this internal crisis, were unlikely to make trouble in the immediate future. It was a good omen for his stay in Bosnia, so was the loyal reception which he received during the hour he spent in Mostar. The scenery during the five-hour railway journey onward from there through the mountains was spectacular, and when his train pulled into the station at Ilidže at 3 p.m. on Thursday June 25th Sophie, who attended by Morsey and Countess Lanjus her lady-in-waiting, had arrived in the morning, was waiting to welcome him. The band struck up the Imperial anthem, he inspected a guard of honour, acknowledged the cheers of the crowd which had gathered outside the station, and drove to the hotel to greet his wife.

The Hotel Bosna, like its counterparts in other spas in the Monarchy, was a substantial edifice, to the façade of which were attached balconies surrounded by carved woodwork, of no architectural merit. At Potiorek's behest much effort and money had been devoted to preparing it for the Archduke's stay. One room had been converted into a chapel at, according to a local newspaper, a cost of 40,000 kronen, a report which if true might explain why the Bosnian government was unable to produce 7,000 kronen to pay for extra detectives. Franz Ferdinand and Sophie's suite was furnished "in the Turkish style" with carved tables inlaid with mother of pearl, Oriental carpets and *objets d'art* loaned by dealers in the Sarajevo bazaar. The sight of the assortment of copper ware, filagree boxes and other bric-a-brac with which it was crammed suggested to the Archduke, a keen if undiscriminating collector of orientalia, that the bazaar would be worth visiting. After the oppressive heat of the Dalmatian coast, Ilidže at an altitude of over 1,600 feet was cool and bracing. He was feeling well and delighted to be reunited with Sophie "my very best physician". At his suggestion they decided to fill in the time before dinner with a shopping expedition, and at 5 p.m. drove into Sarajevo.

News of the Archduke's unscheduled visit to the city spread rapidly, and when he and Sophie emerged from a leading antique dealer's shop the street was blocked by a large crowd. Franz Ferdinand, an indefatigable bargain hunter, nevertheless insisted on plunging on into the bazaar, a labyrinth of narrow lanes. Morsey and other members of their entourage "sweating with fear", had to push and shove to clear a path through the people who pressed in on them; but the crowd was friendly, there were welcoming shouts of "Zivio!", and the party returned safely to Ilidže.

When later in the evening the Archduke and his wife dined with their suite, both were in excellent spirits, and the atmosphere was that of a cheerful, relaxed family dinner party. Franz Ferdinand described their visit to Sarajevo and was evidently delighted by the friendly reception they had received. Although his day had started at five in the morning he did not seem to be in the least tired, and after dinner stayed up talking about his journey and the manoeuvres during the next two days, to which he looked forward with interest. Everything so far as he was concerned was going extremely well.

The manoeuvres, planned and directed by Potiorek, were held at Tarčin about 14 miles west of Ilidže, in difficult mountainous country interspersed with patches of woodland. About 20,000 men from the 15th Corps in Bosnia and the 16th Corps in Dalmatia, both of which were under Potiorek's command, were assigned to take part in them; they were an exercise in repelling an attack on Sarajevo by an enemy advancing from the Adriatic.

On the first day of the manoeuvres, Friday June 26th, Franz Ferdinand, accompanied by Conrad who had arrived to attend them, left Ilidže shortly before 6 a.m., and went by special train to the nearest point down the line to Tarčin, from where he rode to Potiorek's command post. During the night the weather had broken; instead of being hot as he had feared, it poured with rain for most of the day and there were occasional flurries of snow. The Archduke, undeterred by this, stayed with the troops until the late afternoon: the 20 gendarmes designated to guard him had, as he intended, for he detested any form of protective bodyguard, considerable difficulty in keeping up with him.

While Franz Ferdinand was out at Tarčin Sophie spent some time in Sarajevo. Morsey went with her, "I was ordered to accompany the Duchess into the city, and in particular to make sure that no official, no nationality and no religious denomination was overlooked". She visited the Catholic children's home of which she had been patron since 1912, schools – where she gave the older children photographs of the Archducal family and the younger ones sweets – the carpet factory, the Roman Catholic and Serb Orthodox cathedrals, and several mosques. Morsey said all these visits were "official, the Archduke represented the Emperor and allocated to the Duchess some of the duties which this entailed". They must therefore have been made with Franz Ferdinand's agreement which, in view of his devotion to Sophie, it is difficult to believe he would have given if he thought that during them she would be exposed to danger. Although nothing untoward occurred, the "extreme incompetence" of the Sarajevo police gave Morsey some anxious moments. When as the Duchess emerged from a building, the crowd of onlookers pushed forward to within feet of her car and the civilian detectives escorting her struggled to clear a space around it, they looked on and did nothing. Sophie remained unperturbed and "took the keenest interest in everything she saw", a comment by Morsey which suggests that she may have begun to share her husband's conviction that she had nothing to fear in Sarajevo.

Although on the second day of the manoeuvres, June 27th, the weather was fine, the Archduke ended them before noon. He never believed in driving the troops to the point of exhaustion, and they had been on the march since 4.30 a.m. Commanding that it should be translated into the various mother tongues of the soldiers who had taken part in them, he issued an Order of the Day saying that his high expectations of all units had been fully justified, praised Potiorek and, by contrast with the previous summer, was at his most charming to Conrad.

After returning to Ilidže, where Sophie was waiting for him after a further visit to the Bosnian capital, Franz Ferdinand telegraphed to the Emperor reporting that the performance of the troops had been "outstanding beyond all praise". They were highly trained, very fit and their morale was first class. He added, "I am visiting Sarajevo tomorrow and departing in the evening". This telegram was sent at 4 p.m. The Archduke was now on the last lap of his Bosnian visit, according to the plan for which within thirty hours he and Sophie would be starting their journey home to their children. Seven miles away in Sarajevo, at that time, on Princip's insistence the final steps were being taken to implement another plan, the intention of which was to ensure that within 30 hours Franz Ferdinand would be dead.

(ii)

THE official programme for the Archduke's visit to Sarajevo was announced there on June 24th, the day before he arrived in Bosnia. Dr Gerde had urged for security reasons that the announcement should be delayed until at least the 25th, but Potiorek, intent on orchestrating an enthusiastic reception for the heir to the throne, took no notice. In response to a broad hint from him, the city council on the 23rd renamed the principal thoroughfare "Franz Ferdinand Strasse", and the Mayor called on the inhabitants of Sarajevo to demonstrate their "gratitude, devotion and loyalty" to the Emperor and the Imperial Family by decorating their houses. On the following morning the official programme for the 28th giving full details of Franz Ferdinand's route, timed to the minute, was published in all the newspapers. The citizens prepared to hang out flags, people from outlying districts made plans to come in for the day (unlike the Emperor's visit in 1910 there was no ban on this), Gerde reflected that the security arrangements for the 28th really were in the hands of fate.

Princip and Ilić got down to planning the assassination. They now knew that the Archduke would arrive by train from Ilidže at 9.50 a.m. (whether Sophie would be with him was not stated), would proceed from the station by car, and would only be in Sarajevo for fractionally over four hours, during which he was scheduled to visit the Town Hall (10.10-10.30); open and tour the new museum (10.40-11.40); lunch with Potiorek at the Konak (12-2 p.m.), and directly after this return to Ilidže. There was no chance of getting near Franz Ferdinand at the Konak, the gates to which were guarded, but the attempt to assassinate him could be made at the station or when he was arriving at or leaving the Town Hall or the museum, on which occasions he would present an easier target than when seated in a car moving at an unpredictable speed. But, if Princip and Ilić considered the former possibility (there is no information to show that they did), they rejected it and made up their minds that he must be killed while he was driving through the streets of the city. The six potential assassins – Princip, Čabrinović, Grabež, and the Sarajevo trio Mehmetbašić, Čubrilović and Popović – could have been spread out along his route. They decided, however, that all six should be stationed within a space of 350 yards along the Appel Quay bordering the Miljačka, and successively fire their pistols and throw their bombs at the Archduke on his way from the station to the Town Hall.

It was an astonishing plan, and without precedent in the long list of assassination attempts in various countries since the turn of the century (the victims of which included 4 Kings, 1 Queen, a Crown Prince, a Russian Grand Duke, 3 Presidents and half a dozen Prime Ministers). Whether it was initially thought up by Princip or by Ilić, and what Grabež, who saw them when he came in from Pale on the 25th, contributed to it, is impossible to determine. The reasoning behind it can only be conjectured. Possibly they assumed that the Archduke would be guarded as closely as the Emperor in 1910, and therefore the best chance of killing him lay in making one concentrated effort. They may also have reckoned that the Sarajevo trio were incapable of achieving anything if they were stationed far away from the others, and the most which could be hoped of them was that their shots and bombs, however wide of the mark, would create confusion and open up a chance for one of their more efficient associates to kill Franz Ferdinand. Why they elected to stage this saturation assassination on the Appel Quay, rather than in the narrower streets between the Town Hall and the Museum through which the Archduke's car would be moving more slowly, remains a mystery.

By the time Franz Ferdinand arrived at Ilidže on the afternoon of June 25th, the position was that the inner circle of conspirators – Ilić, Princip, and Grabež – had agreed and worked out when, where and how he was to be killed. All that remained for them to do was to distribute the pistols, bombs and cyanide, and to brief those of the assassins – Čabrinović and the Sarajevo trio – who had been excluded from the initial planning, on their role. Ilić, who must deal with his Sarajevo recruits because none of the others knew them, was still being difficult, arguing vehemently that the Archduke's murder would only lead to terrible reprisals and the attempt should be abandoned. Princip continued to refuse to listen to him, and he made no appreciable headway with Grabež. Nevertheless their future – and Franz Ferdinand's – lay in Ilić's hands: to prevent the assassination he had only to remove the weapons from his house and hide them elsewhere. For some reason he did not do so; fate seemed to be on Princip's side.

Next day Princip met Čabrinović and told him that the assassination would take place; Ilić sent a telegram to Mehmetbašić summoning him to Sarajevo. Then, or on the following morning, they worked out a scheme for distributing the weapons and divided the cyanide into six portions, empackaging each in a slip of paper.

On the afternoon of Saturday, June 27th, when Franz Ferdinand was drafting his telegram to the Emperor saying that he would leave for home on the following evening, the distribution of the pistols, bombs and cyanide began. Ilić met his two youngest recruits, Čubrilović and Popović, in a café and doled out to each a packet of cyanide (with instructions to swallow the poison immediately after the assassination), a loaded pistol and a bomb. In an adjacent park he explained briefly how the bombs worked and how to release the safety catch on the pistols, from one of which he fired a shot in a tunnel saying "No medicine will help anyone who is hit by that". By this time Mehmetbašić had arrived in Sarajevo. Later in the evening, as they walked to his hotel, Ilić told him where he was to station himself on the Appel Quay and handed him his ration of cyanide together with a bomb; there were no pistols to spare since the remaining two were reserved for Princip and Grabež.

Princip meanwhile saw Čabrinović, told him to go to Vlajnić's patisserie on the following morning where he would be given a bomb, and handed him a packet of cyanide. When instructing him where he was to stand on the Appel Quay, he said, without going into details or making any mention of Ilić, that "all the others" had already been assigned to their posts.

After dealing with Čabrinović, Princip joined the drinking coterie in Semiz's tavern, which was within sight of where he would be stationed next day. One of them thought that at first he was withdrawn and silent, and noticed that he suddenly drained a glass of wine at a gulp. Then he gradually cheered up, at the end of the evening seemed reluctant to go home, and walked with two of his companions to their lodgings, where he embraced them telling them to go in at once, for they must not be seen with him.

While the drinking party was going on in Semiz's tavern, Franz Ferdinand was giving a large dinner at Ilidže for the leading dignitaries of Sarajevo. The Archduke, sitting between Potiorek and the President of Parliament, reiterated to the former his satisfaction with the manoeuvres, and said to the latter that Bosnia and its inhabitants had made an excellent impression on him. Sophie, the only woman present, had the harder task of making conversation to the Serb Orthodox and Roman Catholic bishops, and probably stuck to the safe topic of her children. After dinner was over, when Sunarić, the leading Bosnian Croat who had consistently warned about the dangers of the visit, came to pay his respects to her, she said to him with a radiant smile, "Dear Dr Sunarić you have been quite wrong, things have not turned out as you said they would. Wherever we have gone we have, to our delight, been spontaneously greeted by everyone, including the Serbs, with the utmost warmth and friendliness". Sunarić replied

"Your Highness, I pray God that if I have the honour of seeing you tomorrow evening, you will be able to say this again to me, for then a weight will fall from my heart".

The evening went well. After most of the guests had left, the Archduke told Bardolff how pleased he was with his expedition to Bosnia. Two members of his suite pointed out, however, that the risks inherent in his visit to Sarajevo next day could not be ignored, and suggested he should cancel it and leave in the morning. Franz Ferdinand was within an ace of agreeing; the weather had changed and it was likely to be hot; the prospect of sweating round the city in a thick full dress uniform making the sort of public appearance which he much disliked, was not attractive. Then fate, this time in the person of Potiorek's adjutant Colonel Merizzi, again intervened on Princip's side. Merizzi pointed out that the Croats, whose dynastic loyalty it was imperative to foster, would be affronted if His Imperial Highness cut short his programme. Franz Ferdinand decided to go through with it, and in excellent spirits stayed up talking until after midnight. A few hours after he went to bed dawn began to break over Sarajevo.

17
Sunday June 28th 1914

O N the morning of Sunday June 28th the sun shone in a cloudless sky;
it was a perfect summer day. At 8 a.m. Ilić met Grabež in the patisserie
and gave him a bomb and a pistol but not, as had been arranged, a packet
of cyanide. Saying that before leaving home he had again unsuccessfully attempted to argue Princip into abandoning the assassination, he urged Grabež
to take the weapons away and not to use them. To Čabrinović when the latter
arrived to receive his bomb and cyanide, he said nothing. His behaviour at this
eleventh hour was still, to put it mildly, equivocal.

Grabež was tense and feeling queasy. Ilić's arguments were undermining:
he went into a park and sat on a bench wondering what to do. Čabrinović, whom
Princip, Ilić and Grabež considered to be naive, boastful, unreliable and likely
to lose his nerve at the last minute, was untroubled by doubts. He had minded
parting from his grandmother and sister whom he was certain he would never
see again and of whom he was very fond, and after giving them most of what
little money he had, shut himself up alone and wept bitterly. But that moment
of sorrow was behind him. Buoyed up by the conviction that his part in the
assassination would ensure that his name was inscribed on the roll of Serb
heroes and martyrs, he had put on his best clothes for this crowning day of his
life, a black jacket, dark grey trousers, a white shirt with a stiff collar, and after
receiving his bomb decided to be photographed "so that a memory would
remain behind me". When he left the patisserie he ran into a friend whom he
persuaded to accompany him to a photographer where, having given a false
name, he posed sitting nonchalantly on the arm of a chair holding a rolled up
copy of a Serb newspaper, the bomb in the inside pocket of his jacket. Told that
the prints would be ready in about an hour, he asked his friend to collect them
and send copies to his grandmother, sister, and several other addressees.

While Čabrinović was having this record of himself made for posterity,
Princip, equipped with his bomb, pistol and packet of cyanide, was calmly
strolling round a park with two of his former schoolfellows talking about noth-

ing in particular. After a time he parted from them and made his way to the Appel Quay. There was not a soldier in sight, and not many uniformed policemen. Since it was already hot, the river side of the quay was practically deserted; most people waiting to see the Archduke were standing in the shade of the trees on the opposite pavement, but even there the crowd was not dense.

It was about 9.15. At the station, seven cars belonging to members of the Imperial and Royal Voluntary Automobile Corps, all reserve officers, who made their vehicles available to the Court and senior generals on manoeuvres and official occasions, were lined up in readiness for the Archduke's arrival. At Ilidže Franz Ferdinand had attended Mass with Sophie and dictated two telegrams to Morsey, one to a member of his staff at Konopischt, the other to his beloved thirteen-year-old daughter

> Mama and I are very well. Weather warm and fine. We gave a large dinner party yesterday and this morning there is the big reception in Sarajevo. Another large dinner party after that and then we are leaving on the *Viribus Unitis*. Dearest love to you all. Tuesday. Papa.

He was now preparing to start with his wife for Sarajevo.

They left Ilidže some minutes behind schedule. Franz Ferinand was in the full dress uniform of a cavalry general – a pale blue tunic with a high gold braided collar and gold braided cuffs, a sash with a large gilt tassel, black trousers with a double red stripe, a hat adorned with green plumes. Sophie wore a picture hat ornamented with feathers, a long white silk dress with a red sash and carried a parasol. When their special train arrived in Sarajevo they were formally greeted by Potiorek and the Archduke reviewed a guard of honour, the only troops he would see on that day. The procession of cars then set off for the Town Hall. Franz Ferdinand was seated in a black right-hand drive Graf und Stift belonging to Count Harrach, with Sophie on his right; Potiorek and Harrach were opposite them on tip up seats. Its hood was folded back, and two cars preceded it, in the first of which were police officers, in the second Gerde and the Mayor of Sarajevo. Behind it came four more cars, the occupants of which included Bardolff, Rumerskirch, Morsey and other members of the Archduke's suite, Countess Lanjus, Sophie's lady-in-waiting, and Potiorek's adjutant Merizzi.

By the time this procession left the station, all the youths who, with varying degrees of bravado and resolution, had declared they would kill Franz Ferdinand, were at their posts on the Appel Quay. On the right of the Archduke's route along it to the Town Hall the Miljačka was here successively spanned by the Čumurja, Lateiner, and Kaiser bridges. The first three assassins whom he would pass were all standing on the river side of the Quay near the Čumurja bridge, Mehmetbašić about 20 yards on the station side of it, Čubrilović on the corner of its junction with the quay, Čabrinović about a yard beyond this junction. Princip was a hundred yards further on at the corner of the Lateiner bridge. Grabež, who after all had more or less decided to take part in the assassination, the last of the line on the river side, was a hundred yards or so beyond Princip near the Kaiser bridge. The only armed member of the assassination conspiracy amongst the trees across the road was Popović, who was diagonally opposite Čabrinović. Ilić hovering near him, Grabež's packet of cyanide in his pocket, carried no weapons, seemingly one of those protagonists of political assassination such as Kropotkin who, while advocating it in theory, left it to others to wield the dagger, fire the pistol or throw the bomb.

One of the spectators waiting in the shade to see the Archduke looked across the quay, and noticed a youth on the far pavement "half a pace away from the Čumurja bridge" standing in the blazing sun, which seemed curious because he was

> rather strangely dressed. He wore a black jacket which resembled a dinner jacket and dove grey trousers . . .. The jacket was buttoned up, and as the youth looked in my direction I saw that he had thrust his right hand inside it, as though he wanted to hold on to something in his left inner breast pocket.

The youth was Čabrinović, who was clutching his bomb and had stationed himself on the edge of the pavement near a tramway mast.

A few minutes later the procession of cars came in sight. They were being driven slowly, probably at about 10-12 m.p.h., and spaced out at intervals of 30 yards. The third car in the procession was flying the black and yellow Imperial standard, passed Mehmetbašić who lost his nerve and did nothing, and Čubrilović who also did nothing, "When I saw the Archduke I could not bring myself to kill him". Then it began to draw level with Čabrinović who acted, took the bomb out of his pocket, banged it against the tramway mast, threw it straight at Franz Ferdinand and missed him by inches. The safety cap came off with a crack which sounded like a pistol shot, Harrach's chauffeur hearing this instinctively accelerated, and the bomb landed on the folded back hood of the car from where (pushed some eye-witnesses said by the Archduke) it fell on to the left-hand side of the road. A few seconds later it exploded. Čabrinović tried to swallow his cyanide but in his agitation spilt most of it, and without waiting to see what damage had been done, jumped over the parapet of the quay into the Miljačka. On the nearby pavement terrified spectators, a dozen of whom had been injured by flying splinters, jostled one another as they attempted to reach the safety of the side streets. Mehmetbašić, Čubrilović, and Popović panicked and fled; Ilić disappeared.

When the bomb went off the two cars at the head of the procession were some way up the quay. Their occupants – the policemen, Gerde, the Mayor – heard the explosion but it was not loud and they paid no attention to it (one of them thought it was part of an artillery salvo fired in the Archduke's honour) and drove on to the Town Hall. Franz Ferdinand, behind them, turned round, saw that the following car had halted, the air about it filled with smoke, and realised that an attempt had been made to assassinate him. Eight years earlier, in Madrid, he had witnessed a similar attempt when a bomb was thrown at the King of Spain, and described the scene to Brosch as "ghastly". The possibility could not be discounted that another assassin was nearby, and Sophie at his side was also in danger. Altogether it would have been understandable if the Archduke had driven on without stopping. But his immediate reaction was that of an officer responsible for his men: members of his suite might have been injured; if so he must ensure that everything possible was being done for them. Regardless of his own safety, he ordered Harrach's chauffeur to pull up, and told the Count to go back and find out what had happened.

Harrach found that the car behind his, which belonged to Count Boos-Waldeck, had taken the brunt of the explosion. Its oil sump was holed and it was out of action. Of its occupants, Boos-Waldeck was grazed by a number of splinters; Merizzi, Potiorek's adjutant, was streaming blood from a wound in the head which Countess Lanjus was stalwartly mopping as best she could with her pocket handkerchief; Bardolff and Rumerskirch, both unhurt, were hurrying forward to see whether Franz Ferdinand and Sophie had been injured, so were members of the suite from the other cars one of whom, Morsey, looked over the parapet of the quay and saw that Čabrinović, whose cyanide had failed to work, had been caught and was being manhandled by the police across the river, the water in which was low.

While this was going on Princip was in a state of some confusion. When he heard the bomb explode he was on the corner of the Lateiner bridge and the Appel Quay, his view of the road blocked because he was not tall enough to see over the heads of the people in front of him. Peering between them, he saw a car stop very nearly opposite him which, since he was unable to see who was in it, led him to conclude that the assassination attempt had succeeded. Unaware that Franz Ferdinand and Sophie, unhurt except for a slight scratch on her neck, were sitting within a few yards of him waiting for Harrach to return, he next looked over the parapet and saw that Čabrinović had been caught by the police. His immediate reaction was that he must kill him before he could talk, and after that commit suicide. Then the car started to move; Harrach having returned and reported that nobody had been killed and doctors were attending to the wounded, Franz Ferdinand had given the order to drive on. Princip could not see the Archduke, but he caught a glimpse of Sophie, and realised that the attempt had failed. Their car was accelerating and his field of fire was blocked; there was nothing he could do except stand and watch the remainder of the procession which followed it. Grabež, beyond him by the Kaiser bridge, also heard the explosion, and thought because a few minutes elapsed before any more cars arrived, that the attempt had succeeded. But then the Archduke passed him: less resolute than Princip and also in the middle of a crowd, he too took no action.

175

The question for both of them, each of whom was on his own and unaware of the other's whereabouts, was what to do next. Both decided to make another attempt to kill the Archduke. Grabež remained at the junction of the Kaiser bridge and the quay, which Franz Ferdinand must pass whether he carried on as planned and went to the museum, or to the Konak or straight back to the station. Princip, after some hesitation, crossed the quay and walked a few steps along the Franz Joseph Strasse leading off it opposite the Lateiner bridge. According to the published programme, the Archduke would turn right off the quay up this street on his way from the Town Hall to the museum. Banking on this occurring, he hung about outside Moritz Schiller's delicatessen shop endeavouring to make himself as inconspicuous as possible.

Sarajevo Town Hall was built by the Austrians at the turn of the century; its architecture was imitation Turkish and the result was unfortunate. Baedeker's Guide to Austria Hungary, noting that "it had a glass roofed arcade and fine council rooms" refrained from mentioning its façade, of which a later visitor wrote, "It is horribly particoloured and has a lumpish two-storeyed loggia with crudely fretted arches, and it has little round windows all over it which suggest that it is rich beond the dreams of avarice in lavatories". When the Archduke and Sophie arrived, a few minutes late, the Mayor and all the city dignitaries, the Muslims wearing their fezzes and attired in loose jackets, coloured sashes and baggy plush trousers, the remainder in frock coats carrying their top hats, were assembled in front of this edifice to greet them.

According to the programme the Mayor, a Muslim, was to read his loyal address on the steps of the Town Hall. It did not occur to Potiorek nor anyone else to suggest that for security reasons, this ceremony should take place inside the building. Fehim Čurčić Effendi, unaware of what had happened, prepared to launch into it, the Archduke and Sophie standing in front of him, a sitting target for any assassin who might be lurking amongst the spectators. Then the shock of realising that both he and his wife had narrowly escaped being blown to bits suddenly hit Franz Ferdinand who blasted off at him, "To hell with your speech! I have come to visit Sarajevo and am greeted by bombs, it is outrageous". Bardolff must have feared that this was the beginning of one of His Imperial Highness's outbursts of temper, which given the circumstances would have been neither surprising nor unjustified. But the Archduke paused, with a great effort regained control of himself, and said to the Mayor, "Very well, now go on with your speech". The latter, incapable of extemporising, ploughed through his prepared text

> Your Imperial and Royal Highness! Your Highness! Our hearts are filled with joy over your most gracious visit . . . .. Your Highnesses can read in our countenances our feelings of love and devotion, unshakeable loyalty and obedience to His Majesty our Emperor and King . . . . All the citizens of Sarajevo, overwhelmed with happiness, greet your Highnesses' most

illustrious visit with the utmost enthusiasm, convinced that Your High-nesses' stay in our beloved city of Sarajevo will still further increase Your Highnesses' most gracious interest in our progress and well being, and deepen that gratitude and loyalty which is for ever rooted in our hearts . . ..

When the Mayor finished this inappropriate peroration, Franz Ferdinand re-plied briefly in German, saying that it gave him great pleasure to accept these assurances of "unshakeable loyalty" to the Emperor, and that "this brief stay in your midst" had convinced him of "the satisfactory development of this magnificent region, in the prosperity of which I have always taken the keenest interest". Thanking the Mayor for the reception he had received he departed from his prepared text, adding that he did so all the more cordially because he saw in it "an expression of pleasure over the failure of the assassination attempt". He ended with a painfully learnt sentence in Serbo Croat asking the Mayor to give his warmest greetings to the inhabitants of "this beautiful city", and with Sophie entered the Town Hall. Harrach, to whom the Archduke had said after the bomb attack, "We are going to have some more of this today", thought they were both behaving with the utmost composure.

Inside the Town Hall, Sophie as already planned, went to the first floor to receive the wives of Muslim dignitaries. In order to forestall alarmist news-paper reports, Franz Ferdinand drafted a telegram to the Emperor giving a reassuring account of what had happened. His suite, handicapped by their lack of knowledge of the geography of the city, discussed how to get His Imperial Highness out of Sarajevo alive, and one of them suggested that he should re-main in the Town Hall until troops (who would have to be brought back from the manoeuvre area) had cleared the streets. The Archduke turned this down flat. In addition to courage he had a great deal of Habsburg pride, and nothing was going to induce him to skulk in the Town Hall. He asked Potiorek whether he considered another assassination attempt likely. Potiorek was by now unable to manage much in the way of coherent thought: it was well known that it did not do to make a hash of arrangements for members of the Imperial Family (a German diplomat once commented that if a fly settled on an Archduke's head when he was standing on a railway platform the station master got the sack), and he saw his career in ruins. Morsey had the impression that he was incapable of making a quick or firm decision. Certainly he lacked the moral courage to admit that his assertion that Franz Ferdinand would be in no danger in Sara-jevo had been wrong, and to tell him that the rest of his programme must be abandoned because his safety could not be guaranteed. According to Bardolff he replied that he was convinced that nothing more would happen, and then hedged, suggesting that His Imperial Highness should either go direct to the Konak, or to the museum "avoiding the town to punish it". Gerde, in spite of the failure of the police, backed him up.

Franz Ferdinand decided to carry on as planned, with one alteration; before going to the museum he would visit Merizzi in the military hospital. But he was determined to go there alone: Sophie must not be exposed to further danger, and drawing Morsey aside, he ordered him to take her to Ilidže or the Konak. Morsey took her coat and went upstairs, "I asked her to come with me, it was the Archduke's wish. She replied, quietly, but in a manner which brooked no argument, 'As long as the Archduke appears in public today I am not leaving him'"

Morsey bowed, went downstairs and told Franz Ferdinand of his wife's decision. Bardolff was summing up to Gerde a change of route which had been agreed by His Imperial Highness when Potiorek said, in reply to a sensible question from a member of the suite, that the hospital could be reached without going through the narrow streets in the older part of Sarajevo bypassing the Franz Joseph Strasse, along which the Archduke was to have driven to the museum, and continuing straight back along the Appel Quay. Morsey heard Bardolff ask Gerde, who would again be in the car immediately in front of Franz Ferdinand (no change in the order of the procession was planned) "to repeat his exact words". But the latter "without looking round or listening, only said 'Yes, yes, of course', and rushed out of the door".

A few minutes later Franz Ferdinand and Sophie, whose courage matched his beside him, walked down the steps of the Town Hall followed by the rest of the party. It was assumed that since Gerde knew of the change of route, it was unnecessary to brief the chauffeurs of this; all they had to do was, as before, to follow him. With one exception, nobody seems to have thought of taking additional precautions to safeguard the Archduke, such as arranging for an armed detective to sit beside Gerde's driver; closing up the distance between Franz Ferdinand's car and those behind it; arming his suite – all Morsey, for example, had on him in the way of weapons was an unsharpened ceremonial sword. The exception was Count Harrach. After Franz Ferdinand had been installed in his car, Sophie as before on his right, Potiorek on the tip up seat facing him, "because I was convinced that another assassination attempt would be made, I did not seat myself beside the chauffeur, but stood on the running board beside His Imperial Highness, so that on the left-hand side his body was completely shielded by my body". The Harrachs were one of the great aristocratic families grouped around the throne, utterly loyal to the House of Habsburg; in the family tradition the Count was prepared to sacrifice his life to save his future Emperor. When Franz Ferdinand smiled at him and said he should take his place beside the chauffeur, he refused to budge.

The column of cars started to drive back along the Appel Quay. Grabež by the Kaiser bridge saw it coming but did nothing. For the seventh time within an hour the Archduke drove safely past a would-be assassin, and there were none left on the Quay ahead. But fate then again took a hand and dealt Princip the ace of trumps. A hundred yards beyond the Kaiser bridge, for some reason which has never been explained, Gerde's car, instead of proceeding straight on, turned right into the Franz Joseph Strasse, and Loyka, Harrach's chauffeur, having been given no instructions to the contrary, followed it.

Potiorek realised what had happened, turned round and told the chauffeur to get back on to the Appel Quay. To do this Loyka had to pull up and change gear into reverse. He braked, and for a few seconds the car came to a halt by the curb of the right-hand pavement in front of Schiller's delicatessen shop outside which Princip, unable to think of anything else to do, was still waiting in the hope of getting another chance of assassinating the Archduke. The car stopped within five feet of him. He raised his revolver, saw that Sophie was seated on the near side of it, and for a split second hesitated. But "a strange feeling" came over him and "greatly agitated", he fired two shots in quick succession. Since he fired without taking aim, "I had turned my head away", the odds against either of them doing any serious damage were long, but the first went through the right-hand door of the car and hit Sophie, and the second hit Franz Ferdinand in the neck.

Potiorek ordered Loyka to drive straight over the Lateiner bridge opposite the Franz Joseph Strasse to the Konak. Neither he nor the officers of the Archduke's suite, who leapt out of their cars and rushed forward when they heard the shots, thought at first that either His Imperial Highness or his wife were injured. He continued to sit upright; when she collapsed across his knees everyone assumed, since she had no visible wound, that she had fainted from fright. Two of the younger officers, now more concerned that the assassin should not escape, flung themselves into the mêlée round Princip who, his revolver clenched between his knees, was struggling to resist arrest. Potiorek was occupied in directing the chauffeur as he reversed.

Harrach, who remained steadfastly on the running board after his gallant attempt to protect Franz Ferdinand had failed because he was on the far side of the car from Princip, was the first to realise what had happened

> As the car quickly reversed a thin stream of blood spurted out of His Imperial Highness's mouth on to my right cheek. With one hand I got out my handkerchief to wipe the blood from the Archduke's face, and as I did so Her Highness called out "In God's name what has happened to you?". Then she collapsed, her face between the Archduke's knees. I had no idea that she was hit and thought she had fainted from fear. His Imperial Highness then said "Sopherl! Sopherl! Don't die! Live for my children". I took hold of the collar of his tunic in order to prevent his head sinking forward and asked him "Is Your Imperial Highness in great pain?". He answered distinctly "It is nothing". Then he turned his face a little to one side and said six or seven times, more faintly as he began to lose consciousness, "It is nothing". There was a very brief pause, then the bleeding made him choke violently, but this stopped when we reached the Konak.

This account appears in a deposition by Harrach describing what he had witnessed during the day, which he made to a magistrate and was subsequently read out in court. A recent biographer of Franz Ferdinand's citing medical evidence, asserts that Harrach cannot have heard the Archduke say anything after he was hit, because the damage caused by Princip's bullet was such that, while he might have been able to move his lips, he could not have uttered a word. But there are instances when, briefly, things happen which according to medical text books are impossible; this could have been one of them. Harrach was an honourable man and, judging from his deposition, not given to dramatisation. It is dated June 28th, so it would seem reasonable to assume that he drafted it before the end of that momentous day, while its events were still vividly in his mind. If he did, for some incomprehensible reason, make up "Sopherl! Sopherl! Don't die! Live for my children", it was a brilliant fabrication, for it has the ring of total veracity. When strength ebbs people tend to turn to the mainspring of their lives. At the end of the day Franz Ferdinand's was his family. Janaczek, who knew him so well, later told Morsey that if, during that moment of decision in the Town Hall, he had reminded the Archduke of his children, and so by implication that for their sake he must not expose himself to further danger, the last fatal drive would not have taken place.

But it had taken place, and it was the end of the day. On arrival at the Konak Sophie was found to be dead; Franz Ferdinand died a few minutes later. At about 11.15, as the interrogation of Princip, battered, sick from the cyanide he had swallowed which had failed to kill him, but without a trace of remorse, began, the death knell of his victim, the heir to the Habsburg throne, tolled out over Sarajevo.

Epilogue
"The End of the Story"

(i)

WHEN the news of the assassination was broken to Franz Joseph in Bad Ischl early on the afternoon of Sunday June 28th, he closed his eyes and sat for a few moments in stunned silence, but showed no outward sign of sorrow for Franz Ferdinand. Neither did the majority of his subjects, shocked though they were by the news from Sarajevo, grieve for the heir to the throne. There were a number of people, particularly in Court and official circles, who disliked the Archduke, and he was not well known to the general public. In Vienna when the Emperor returned there on the following day, although black flags hung on all public buildings and the opera and theatres were closed, there was no atmosphere of mourning, nor any feeling of crisis. The inhabitants of the capital went about their business as usual, frequented their habitual cafés, planned their summer holidays. It did not occur to the average man in the street that the tragedy would in any way affect him personally.

It was decided that the bodies of Franz Ferdinand and Sophie should be brought back from Sarajevo by rail to the coast, then by sea to Trieste on board the battleship *Viribus Unitis*, from there by train to Vienna, the route taken by the Archduke on his way to Bosnia. When the cortège, headed by several battalions of infantry, set out from the Konak for the station, the streets were lined with troops and every ranking officer and official in the city walked behind the coffins. As the train pulled out a 101 gun salute was fired, and guards of honour were mounted at the principal stations through which it passed; the *Viribus Unitis* was flanked by a squadron of warships as she sailed up the Adriatic; in Trieste sailors lined the route from the harbour.

The army and the navy had escorted the Archduke and his wife on the first stage of their last journey home with all the honour due to his rank. To Prince Montenuovo the Court Chamberlain, who was responsible for the ceremonial arrangements in Vienna, rigid adherence to protocol, not the final honours to which the heir to the throne and Inspector General of the armed forces was entitled, was the primary consideration. Franz Ferdinand, aware that as his morganatic wife, Sophie could not be buried in the Imperial vault beneath the church of the Capuchins, had built a family vault at Artstetten, his castle near the Danube in the heartland of Habsburg Austria, and stipulated in his will that they were both to be laid to rest there. But for him there must be a lying-in-state and a service in Vienna, and at this since she was a nobody in protocol terms, the presence of Sophie's coffin was in Montenuovo's view inadmissible. Morsey indicates that the Prince first planned that it should be "left at the station", but was forced to abandon this when Archduke Karl, Franz Ferdinand's nephew and the new heir, prevailed on the Emperor to decree that there should be a joint service.

Foreign royalties were requested not to come to Vienna for the funeral; it was said that the Emperor's health was too frail to stand the strain of receiving them, which may have been true. Since the coffins could not be separated, Montenuovo decided that they should be kept out of sight as much as possible, that there should be no military parade, and ceremonial should be cut to the bone. On his orders the train from Trieste did not arrive at the Südbahnhof in Vienna until 10 p.m. Archduke Karl was on the platform to meet it, together with some Court officials and high ranking officers; it was not a large assembly. The coffins were carried to two court hearses each drawn by six black horses and, preceded in accordance with tradition by two lackeys with lanterns, flanked by a small escort of life guards with halberds and household cavalry with drawn swords, taken to the chapel of the Hofburg.

On the following morning the chapel was opened to the public at 8 a.m., but closed again at midday although a very large number of people who had queued for several hours were still waiting to be admitted. The service, at which the coffins of Franz Ferdinand and Sophie, on two high catafalques draped in black at the foot of which was a wreath of white roses from "Sophie, Max, Ernst" – their children – were blessed by the Cardinal Archbishop of Vienna, was attended by the Emperor (who throughout it remained impassive) and the Imperial Family, the diplomatic corps, Ministers and generals. It was held at 4 p.m., lasted barely half an hour, and as soon as it was over the doors of the chapel were again shut.

At 10 p.m. the hearses bearing the coffins left the Hofburg for the West-bahnhof, from where they were to be taken by train to Pöchlarn and ferried across the Danube to Artstetten. They again had a minimal escort and there was no military parade. But the Minister of War had compelled Montenuovo reluctantly to agree that commanding officers of units in the Vienna garrison might turn out their troops to line the route, and this they did. In addition, over a hundred members of the great aristocratic families who for generations had served the Habsburgs, demonstrated their resentment of the Court Chamberlain's staging of a "third-class funeral" by joining the cortège at the outer gateway of the Hofburg and walked bareheaded behind the hearses on their long journey to the station. Members of the Imperial Family too left no doubt of what they thought of Montenuovo's shabby ceremonial arrangements; a phalanx of Archdukes headed by Karl assembled on the platform and saw the train off.

So far as Montenuovo was concerned from then onwards the coffins of Franz Ferdinand and Sophie ceased to exist; it was for the funeral directors of the city of Vienna and the Archduke's entourage to get them to Artstetten. His timing of the departure of the train meant that they had to be ferried over the Danube in the pitch dark and (which admittedly he could not have foreseen) in the middle of a tremendous thunderstorm. The terrified horses drawing the hearses lashed out, one of the coffins nearly tipped into the river, and because torrential rain had made the steep country road on the far side in some places nearly impassable, they did not reach Artstetten until four in the morning.

Next day there was a simple service for Franz Ferdinand and Sophie in the village church. Their children were there, Maria Theresia his "dearest Mama", Karl, his wife, and other relatives, friends, members of their entourage. No ministers were present; they were attending the official requiem mass in Vienna. Morsey was sure the Archduke would have wished that

> only those came to Artstetten who honoured and loved him. When he was borne on his last journey from the church to the vault by non-commissioned officers of his two regiments, he was accompanied by those who knew only too well what Austria had lost in him, and there were many of them.

(ii)

IT was now July 4th; six days had passed since the assassination. Prince Clary's outstanding memory of that time was "of the confusion in which most people were". This was true not only of the Prince's friends and acquaintances, but also of those who had to decide how the Monarchy should react to the murder of the heir to the throne. It began to escalate on the afternoon of the 29th when a telegram arrived from Potiorek reporting that Princip and Čabrinović had revealed when interrogated that they had planned the murder together in Belgrade, where they had been in contact with *komitádjis* (one of whom was called Ciganović), who gave them weapons and money. Within hours Potiorek followed this up with a further telegram saying he was convinced that the origins of the plot were to be found in Serbia.

During the next twenty-four hours Conrad, the Chief of Staff, and Count Tisza, the Minister President of Hungary, both went to see the Foreign Minister. Conrad urged immediate mobilisation, arguing that if Austria did not now assert herself and knock out Serbia, her prestige in the Balkans would be gone for good and her continued existence as a Great Power imperilled. Tisza flatly opposed this, saying that to use Franz Ferdinand's assassination as an excuse for a final reckoning with Serbia would be an appalling blunder. There was no conclusive proof of official Serbian involvement in it, and so no grounds for going to war with her; to do so would only result in a general conflagration. Berchtold told Conrad that immediate mobilisation was out of the question. To Tisza he said that lack of action would be interpreted by Serbia as a sign of weakness. To both he stressed that before anything was done it was essential to make sure of German support, and a great deal would depend on the degree of proof of Serbian guilt produced by the investigation into the crime which was now in progress in Sarajevo.

When Berchtold saw the Emperor, whom he found outwardly calm, they agreed that a policy of patience with Serbia had not paid off and that action (what this should be they did not discuss) must be taken as soon as the results of the Sarajevo investigation were known. He then drafted a personal letter from Franz Joseph to Wilhelm II which the Emperor approved and signed. It said that investigations to date showed that the crime

> is not the deed of a single individual, but the result of a well organised plot whose threads lead back to Belgrade . . .. After the recent terrible events in Bosnia you too will be convinced that there is no longer any prospect of bridging the gulf between us and Serbia, and that the peaceful policy of all European monarchs will be threatened so long as this criminal agitation in Belgrade remains unpunished.

All the monarchs of Europe, the Czar included, were shocked by Franz Ferdinand's assassination, but none more than the Kaiser who had so recently been staying at Konopischt. He was yachting at Kiel when the news reached him, ordered the regatta to be abandoned and returned at once to Berlin. In the past he had repeatedly urged Vienna to show restraint towards Serbia and applauded the Archduke's opposition to a pre-emptive attack on her. Now he veered to the other extreme and on July 5th, after reading Franz Joseph's letter which was handed to him by the Austrian Ambassador in Berlin, at once told Szögyeny to inform the Emperor that even "in the event of action against Serbia giving rise to serious European complications", the Monarchy could rely on the full support of Germany. If military action was to be taken it should be soon, and if Russia entered a war at the side of Serbia, Germany would be at the side of the Monarchy.

This sweeping assurance was given over lunch. Wilhelm added a caveat that he must of course consult his Chancellor von Bethmann-Hollweg, but had no doubt he would endorse it. In the afternoon he saw Bethmann-Hollweg, who without considering what might be involved, said of course Germany must support Austria to the limit, and they agreed the text of a telegram replying to Franz Joseph's letter. The Kaiser also saw representatives of the army and navy whom he informed of his discussion with Szögyeny, adding that there was no need for their superiors – von Moltke the Chief of Staff, Waldersee his deputy, and Admiral von Tirpitz – all of whom were away on leave, to come back to Berlin. In the evening, convinced that no crisis was imminent, he returned to his yacht and departed on a cruise along the coast of Scandinavia.

On the following morning the telegram was sent to Vienna. It was not as forthright as Wilhelm's declaration to Szögyeny in that it made no mention of a war involving Russia, but the assurances it contained were clear enough. It said that the Kaiser was "not blind" to the danger threatening Austria and so the Triple Alliance from Russian and Serbian Pan-Slav agitation, and while he could not adopt any position on the differences between Austria and Serbia, for they were outside his competence, Franz Joseph could be certain that, true to his treaty obligations and their long friendship, he would stand firm by Austria's side. Twenty-four hours after this promise of unconditional support – it was to go down to history as "the blank cheque" – arrived from Berlin Franz Joseph returned to Bad Ischl, having rejected yet another plea from Conrad for mobilisation against Serbia. Barely recovered from his serious illness in May, viewing the future with the fatalistic resignation of the very old, he left Berchtold and the rest of his Ministers to work out what should be done next.

Berlin's response was entirely satisfactory, but unfortunately the same could not be said of the results to date of the investigation in Sarajevo. This was being conducted by Leon Pfeffer, the judge appointed to interrogate Čabrinović and Princip after they were arrested on June 28th. His past career was undistinguished – in 1909 there had been a suggestion that he should be dismissed for inefficiency – and he was not a senior member of the Bosnian judiciary. It soon became clear that he was not competent to handle this crucial investigation: he was making no attempt when questioning the accused to challenge their statements, nor to subject them to anything approaching a hostile interrogation. But for some reason nobody thought of replacing him by a more experienced and forceful member of the legal profession and Pfeffer, at times seemingly almost bending over backwards to be "amiable", was left to carry on.

Ilić, because Princip said he had lodged in his mother's house, had been arrested on the evening of June 28th and Grabež, suspected of being the man whom Čabrinović said had accompanied him and Princip on their journey from Belgrade, two days later. Pfeffer dismissed Ilić as small fry and concentrated on the other three, but apart from establishing that Grabež was the third man, made no headway with any of them. When, however, on July 4th he interrogated Ilić for the first time the latter volunteered a great deal of information – the names of the Sarajevo trio of assassins whom he had recruited, his journey to Tuzla to collect the pistols and bombs from Miško Jovanović, their distribution to the assassins and where they had all been stationed on the Appel Quay. He also said that in Belgrade Ciganović, who was a Bosnian employed by the Serbian State Railway, had put Princip and his two associates in touch with a Serbian army officer, Major Tankosić, who instructed them how to carry out the assassination.

Ilić's statement revealed that in Bosnia many more people had been involved in the murder of Franz Ferdinand than anyone had realised. Above all, what he said about Tankosić seemed at last to provide a lead which might make it possible to establish the complicity of the Serbian government. But on this by July 7th Pfeffer had made no progress. Princip, Čabrinović and Grabež stubbornly maintained that, contrary to what Ilić had said, only one of them had seen Tankosić, and one occasion only, when all he had done was to order Ciganović to teach them to shoot.

Nine days had now elapsed since the Archduke's assassination. On the instructions of Pašić the Serbian Prime Minister (whom Berchtold regarded as the epitome of Balkan deviousness), Serbian diplomats in every European capital were asserting that, as Pašić said in an interview with a Hungarian journalist, it was "absurd" to think that Serbia had anything to do with it; it had been carried out by Austrian citizens, "demented children" for whom Belgrade was not responsible. A growing body of opinion in Vienna was convinced that the threads led back to Belgrade, and that an end must be put to Serbia's intolerable behaviour. Berlin was pressing for action; something must be done, and fast.

Berchtold later wrote that the shadow of the Archduke loomed over all the deliberations of those fateful days, and that he constantly saw before him that commanding figure with those piercing blue eyes. Unfortunately he no longer heard Franz Ferdinand reiterating that war with Serbia must be avoided, because it would lead to war with Russia and that would be the end of the Monarchy. Presiding over a meeting of the Council of Ministers he said that Austria "should get ahead of her enemies by a timely reckoning with Serbia"; Germany had assured "unconditional support" in the event of a "warlike complication". The Council agreed that rapid action was essential, but after a lengthy discussion decided, largely on Tisza's insistence, that Austria should not immediately prepare to attack Serbia, but should send a Note to Belgrade. If Serbia agreed to comply with the demands set out in it she would have been compelled to swallow a severe diplomatic defeat; if she refused to do so, mobilisation would start forthwith. Two days later Berchtold trekked to Bad Ischl (several hours train journey from Vienna), and told the Emperor of this decision. Franz Joseph, saying that it was a question of bringing Serbia under "practical control", agreed that a Note should be sent. He seemed to be unable, or unwilling, to envisage that it might result in war.

In the Ballhausplatz work on the preparation of the Note had begun. It was not progressing well. Berchtold was adamant that under no circumstances must there be a repetition of the Friedjung debacle; therefore the demands which it contained must be based on unassailable evidence. But Potiorek's daily summaries of what Pfeffer was managing to elicit were confusing, and next to nothing could be done in Belgrade to check the statements of the assassins about their contacts there. The Legation pointed out that Aehrenthal's order that it should have nothing to do with agents was still in force and the Consulate staff was new; even such information as it might be possible to obtain could not be guaranteed to be correct. The Foreign Minister therefore decided that someone from the Ballhausplatz must be sent to Sarajevo, to go through the record of the investigation proceedings, and examine all other information on file there about Serbian subversive activities and Greater Serbia propaganda, with the object of establishing precisely what this revealed about the extent of the involvement of the Serbian Government in the Archduke's assassination.

Sektionsrat von Wiesner was selected to go to Sarajevo. A lawyer who had joined the Ministry of Foreign Affairs in 1911, he was not a South Slav expert, but at the beginning of July had been assigned the task of assembling firm documentary evidence of Belgrade's subversive and propaganda activities which could be used as additional justification for action against Serbia. When it became apparent that adequate material either did not exist or could not be found in the archives of the Ministries in Vienna and the General Staff Intelligence Bureau, the provincial Governments in Dalmatia, Trieste and Croatia were ordered to forward all their relevant files to the Ballhausplatz. Wiesner found himself wading through a sea of paper – agents' reports of doubtful reliability, newspaper cuttings, propaganda brochures, some of them in languages which he could not read – a mass of information which as a result of years of bureaucratic and intelligence ineptitude was neither assessed nor co-ordinated. In the Ballhausplatz archives for example, in addition to the file of press cuttings on the Black Hand, there were a number of references to it in despatches from Belgrade, and a recent report from the Consular representative in Nish quoting a Serbian officer as saying that the Black Hand had been responsible for Franz Ferdinand's assassination. But this information was not cross-referred, no overall assessment of it had been made, and it is doubtful if Wiesner saw it. If he did, he did not appreciate its possible significance any more than anyone else in Vienna, where it was generally believed that the Narodna Odbrana was the principal Serbian subversive organisation.

Wiesner arrived in Sarajevo on the morning of July 11th with instructions to report his findings on the 13th. He conferred with Potiorek, Pfeffer and a dozen other officials, went through and discussed a great deal of material which they produced, elucidating obscure points, filling in gaps "as far as possible" and, working late into the night, read the record of the results of the investigation to date. At midday on the 13th he telegraphed Vienna. He began by saying that there was no evidence to support the assertion of responsible officials in Sarajevo that the Greater Serbia propaganda campaign was conducted by the Serbian Government, but there was information, if scanty, which showed that it was being carried out by organisations in Serbia with the knowledge of that Government. He had been shown "valuable and useful" material on the Narodna Odbrana which had not been assessed; this must be done urgently.

187

Turning to the crucial question of the information produced by the investigation of Franz Ferdinand's assassination, he then stated unequivocally

> There is no evidence to show or even suspect that the Serbian Government was involved in the organisation of the attack or the provision of the weapons for it. On the contrary there is far more to indicate that this is to be regarded as out of the question.

After summing up the salient points in the statements of Princip and his associates about the assistance which they had received in Serbia, Wiesner said that they provided justification for the presentation of three demands to Belgrade. These were that the participation of their officials in smuggling individuals and goods into Bosnia must be stopped at once; that the gendarmerie and customs officers at Sabač and Loznica who had assisted the assassins to cross the frontier should be dismissed, and that Ciganović and Tankosić should be arrested and tried. That was all.

Within hours of the arrival of Wiesner's telegram Berchtold conferred with the Minister Presidents of Austria and Hungary. Its conclusions did not affect their decision to send a Note to Belgrade, and they now agreed that it should be accompanied by an ultimatum to the Serbian Government stating that all the demands which it contained must be accepted, unconditionally, within 48 hours. In a memorandum informing Franz Joseph of this (which the Emperor marked for file without comment), Berchtold said that the content of the Note would be such that it was likely the Serbs would reject it; war was therefore probable.

Members of the diplomatic corps in Vienna were now beginning to suspect that Austria was proposing to send a stiff list of demands to Belgrade, but the possibility that these could lead to war did not occur to them. To foster the impression that no kind of military action was contemplated, Berchtold told Conrad and the Minister of War to absent themselves from the capital, ostensibly on leave, and officials were instructed to be conciliatory when talking about Serbia, and to avoid discussing the implications of Sarajevo with foreign diplomats. The Foreign Minister did not inform the Germans of the contents of the Note, telling them only that it would not be delivered until the 25th, in order to ensure that the Czar had no opportunity of discussing it with Poincaré, the President of Russia's ally France, who would be in St Petersburg on a State Visit from July 20th–23rd.

At a secret meeting in Berchtold's house on the 19th the Council of Ministers approved the final text of the Note and decided, as a result of pressure from Berlin, to put forward its delivery to the Serbian Government to 6 p.m. on the 23rd, about four hours before Poincaré was due to leave St Petersburg. It was despatched by courier to Giesl the Minister in Belgrade with instructions to this effect, and copies of it were sent to Austrian envoys in the principal European capitals, who were told to hand it to the governments to which they were accredited on the morning of the 24th, informing them that as a result of the assassination organised by Belgrade of the Archduke, of the involvement and the assistance of the Narodna Odbrana in which there was no doubt, the patience of the Government of His Imperial and Royal Majesty Emperor Franz Joseph with Serbia was exhausted. The outlook of Ministers, the Ballhausplatz, senior officers and officials, politicians, by now resembled that of the proverbial hen whose field of vision is confined to the chalk line to which its beak is affixed. Their thinking had narrowed to one conviction – regardless of the consequences there must be a decisive reckoning with Serbia. They realised that Russia was likely to support Belgrade, but to what this might entail the majority of them closed their minds.

In St Petersburg on the 20th the Czar gave a banquet for Poincaré at Peterhof, Catherine the Great's favourite palace. Paléologue, the French Ambassador, thought that the magnificence of the setting, the brilliance of the uniforms, the dazzling display of jewellery worn by the women, "a fantastic shower of diamonds, pearls, rubies, sapphires, emeralds, topaz, beryls – a blaze of fire and flame", made it "a spectacle which no court in the world can rival". During the evening and on the following morning Nicholas and the President discussed a variety of problems, and ended by reviewing the Austro-Serbian dispute, which they agreed was becoming worrying because of the "mysterious attitude" of Austria. When Szápáry, the Austrian Ambassador, was presented to him at a reception in the Winter Palace, Poincaré asked how the judicial inquiry into the Archduke's assassination was progressing, saying he was anxious about its results; the Friedjung inquiry he recollected had not improved Austro-Serbian relations; Serbia had many friends in Russia, Russia had an ally – France – there could be serious complications. Szápáry replied that it was proceeding, but volunteered no further information. The French President deduced from this as he told the Czar, that "some Austro-German manoeuvre" was being planned against Serbia. Nicholas agreed that their Governments must be prepared to take firm united diplomatic action to frustrate this. By the time Poincaré left for France on the evening of the 23rd there was some increasing disquiet – but no more than that – in St Petersburg about Austria's intentions.

(iii)

ON the morning of the 23rd the Austrian Minister in Belgrade notified the Ministry of Foreign Affairs that he would have an important communication to make to the Serbian Government at 6 p.m. Pašić was away electioneering in the provinces and Giesl was received by Paču, the Minister deputising for him. He handed the latter the Note, saying that he had instructions to leave Belgrade if he did not receive a satisfactory reply to it within 48 hours. When Paču protested that this time limit was too short in view of the Minister President's absence from the capital, he retorted that in the age of railways, telegrams and

189

telephones, Pašić could soon be back in Belgrade, deposited the Note on Paču's desk and marched out, leaving the Minister to study it.

The Note accused the Serbian Government of having permitted criminal and terrorist propaganda, intrigues, and machinations against the Monarchy, and said that it must publish an official condemnation of these activities, suppress them, and punish with the utmost rigour all those engaged in them. Specifically it must dissolve the Narodna Odbrana and all similar anti-Austrian societies, dismiss teachers, army officers and officials named by the Austrian Government as spreading subversive propaganda, and explain the hostile utterances of senior Serbian officials after "the crime of June 28th". With regard to that crime, the Note included the demands which Wiesner suggested were justifiable – the prohibition of the co-operation of Serbian officials in any form of smuggling on the Bosnian frontier, the dismissal of those officials who had assisted the assassins to cross that frontier, and the arrest of Tankosić and Ciganović. It also, however, included two additional and more drastic demands – the acceptance of the collaboration within Serbia of Austrian Government representatives in the suppression of subversive movements directed against the territorial integrity of the Monarchy (Article 5), and the participation of Austrian officials in the investigation relating to the judicial proceedings against accessories on Serbian territory to the plot to assassinate the Archduke, i.e. Tankosić and Ciganović (Article 6). Finally the Serbian Government was required to notify the Austrian Government without delay of the execution of all these measures, and to reply to the Note at the latest by 6 p.m. on Saturday July 25th.

Paču and his colleagues were horrified. They sent an urgent message to Pašić to return to Belgrade, and a plea for help to St Petersburg which reached Sazonov, the Russian Foreign Minister, in the early hours of the morning. The Prince Regent telegraphed the Czar saying that Serbia could not defend herself, and implored him to come to her aid.

Pašić got back to Belgrade at 5 a.m., and at 10 the Serbian Council of Ministers met. A telegram arrived from the Ambassador in St Petersburg saying that Sazonov had told him Serbia could count on Russian help, but he did not know what form it would take – the Czar had to decide this and France must be consulted. In Vienna the first reports of reactions to the Note were received by the Ballhausplatz. The Austrian Ambassador in London telegraphed that the British Foreign Secretary considered it to be "the most formidable instrument which one sovereign State had ever addressed to another". From St Petersburg Szápáry reported Sazonov as saying that Austria was merely using the Archduke's assassination as an excuse to attack Serbia; after the Friedjung affair nobody would believe her accusations. In the evening a telegram arrived from Giesl to say that the Serbian Ministers had not reached a decision.

On the next day, July 25th, when the Ministers met again, the heat in Belgrade was suffocating. To Giesl time barely seemed to move at all. Rumour succeeded rumour. It was said in the morning that an unconditional acceptance of the Note was imminent; then in the early afternoon that "the situation was deteriorating". In fact by then the Serbian reply had been drafted. It was conciliatory, accepted, if in some instances with reservations, all the Austrian demands except Article 6, the participation of their officials to the investigation of individuals in Serbia involved in the plot to assassinate the Archduke. To this, it said, the Serbian Government could not agree because it would be a violation of the Serbian constitution. The reply had to be translated from Serbo-Croat into French, which took some time. While it was being typed the typewriter broke down; Pašić finally handed it to Giesl at the Legation two minutes before the ultimatum was due to expire. The Minister said he must compare it with his instructions and would then give an immediate answer. Pašić had barely returned to the Ministry of Foreign Affairs when this arrived. It said the reply was unsatisfactory and broke off diplomatic relations. The Minister and his staff left Belgrade by train at 6.30, and a quarter of an hour later crossed the frontier into the Monarchy.

All day Franz Joseph in Bad Ischl had been waiting anxiously for news. When, at 7.15 p.m. on a peaceful summer evening, he was told that Giesl had left Belgrade, he sank into a chair and sat for a moment rigid and speechless. Then he said, as if to himself, "A break in diplomatic relations does not necessarily mean war". But Serbia had begun to mobilise. A telegram arrived from Szögyenyi saying Berlin urged that, because delay entailed the grave risk that other Powers would interfere, Vienna should attack at once and confront the world with a *fait accompli*. Conrad at last got the Emperor to sign the mobilisation order, and on July 28th the Monarchy declared war on Serbia.

England had proposed an international conference to try and resolve the Austro-Serbian dispute. This foundered because Germany was not prepared to co-operate. The Monarchy's declaration of war now put paid to any further similar diplomatic initiative. A European conflagration could still be averted if the Germans and Russians both ignored their promises of support to Austria and Serbia, stood aside and left them to fight it out. But Russia, the self-appointed champion of the Slavs, her position and prestige in the Balkans at stake, could not afford to let Serbia be annihilated. Germany, confronted by the hostile combination of Russia and France, and the probability that England would side with them, could not risk the defeat by Russia of the Monarchy, her only reliable ally – Berlin had written off Italy as, at long last, had Vienna. And both the Kaiser, the Czar, and their Governments were under pressure for a decision from their Chiefs of Staff, each of whom in the event of war had to get an enormous number of men into position, and knew that to obtain a head-start on their opponents was vital.

Both rulers, however, laboured under the delusion that they could influence one another and so the course of events. On a number of occasions over the years there had been exchanges of telegrams and letters between them (usually initiated by the Kaiser), in which they addressed one another by the familiar second person "*Du*" and signed themselves "Willi" and "Niki". After the Serbian Government rejected the Austrian Note the Kaiser (at last on his way back to Berlin from his yachting holiday), telegraphed asking dear Niki in view of their warm friendship to stand out against public opinion and take no action, pledging himself to use his influence to get Vienna to arrive at a peaceful understanding with Russia. The Czar ignored this, and on the 28th, the day the Monarchy declared war on Serbia, signed two orders, one for mobilisation against Austria only, the other for general mobilisation. He then havered, and telegraphed the Kaiser saying that unjust war had been forced on a weak country and he would soon be compelled to react to this unless, as he implored, Willi could stop his ally from going too far. Willi replied that it was not an unjust war, and urged Niki to ensure that Russia did not get involved in it. But by then (the evening of the 29th) Sazonov having told him that diplomacy was now useless, the Czar had ordered general mobilisation to begin. Next day the Kaiser sent a telegram to Niki saying that if there was war he would be entirely to blame for it, and at midnight on the 31st Berlin dispatched an ultimatum demanding that the Russian army and fleet be demobilised.

On August 1st France ordered general mobilisation. Zimmerman, the Under Secretary at the German Foreign Office, said to the British Ambassador that the situation was the fault of "this damned system of alliances . . . the curse of modern times". St Petersburg remained silent. Tension mounted: Bethmann-Hollweg issued a statement ending, "If the iron dice roll, God help us". At 6 p.m., the ultimatum having expired, Germany declared war on Russia and began to mobilise. 48 hours later she declared war on France and her troops advanced into Belgium. This violation of Belgian neutrality caused England to declare war on Germany on August 4th; on the 6th Austria declared war on Russia. The iron dice had begun to roll; how they would turn up nobody knew.

Ten days after that declaration of war on Serbia which Franz Ferdinand would have done everything in his power to prevent, what came to be known as the Great War had begun. The Monarchy was committed to fighting on two fronts – in the Balkans and against the Russians in Galicia. Everything which the Archduke had feared had happened.

(iv)

IN Sarajevo, the outbreak of war notwithstanding, the investigation into the assassination plot continued. With the exception of Mehmetbašić, who had escaped to Montenegro, all the assassins had been arrested, together with all those who had helped Princip and Grabež to transport the pistols and bombs across Bosnia, and several people who had known about the plot but said nothing to the police. Pfeffer plodded on, but failed to elicit any further evidence of Serbian involvement in it.

The investigation ended on September 21st. The "Trial of Gavrilo Princip and his associates for high treason", to which the public was admitted, began on October 12th, at which time Serbian advance patrols were within 20 miles of Sarajevo. There were twenty-five accused, of whom the youngest was aged sixteen and eleven were under twenty. All of them pleaded guilty except Princip who said, "I am not a criminal because I have killed a man who has done wrong; I think I have done right".

During the trial Grabež said he had been convinced that Franz Ferdinand must be eliminated because all the wrong from which Bosnia was suffering emanated from him; the fact that he was Inspector General of the army made him the enemy of the Slavs; while he was alive the South Slavs would never gain political liberty. Nevertheless had he known that a European war would result from it, he would never have taken part in the assassination. Čabrinović said much the same. He had read somewhere that Franz Ferdinand intended to attach Serbia to the Monarchy, and believed he was preparing for war against Serbia and Russia. He had "heard it said" that he was an enemy of the Slavs. But it had never occurred to him that the Archduke's assassination would have "serious consequences", and he too would never have taken part in it had he thought it would lead to a European war.

That this war had resulted from his murder of the Archduke seemed to be of no consequence to Princip. He stated that, apart from the fact that he had not meant to kill Sophie – his second bullet was intended for Potiorek – he regretted nothing. As the son of a peasant he knew the peasants' miseries and was determined to avenge them. When, after Harrach's deposition with its account of Franz Ferdinand's last words to Sophie had been read to the Court, one of the lawyers asked him whether he was not moved by it, he replied, according to one source, "Do you think I am an animal?", but apart from this throughout the trial said nothing to suggest that he thought of the Archduke as other than a quarry which must be destroyed. Asked on the final day if he wished to exercise his right to make a statement, after calmly reiterating that he, Čabrinović and Grabež alone were responsible for planning and carrying out the assassination, his final words to the Court were, "We have loved the people. I have nothing to say in my defence".

The Court's verdict was announced three days after the trial ended. All the five youths who had taken part in the assassination were found guilty of treason and murder, but under Austrian law could not be condemned to death because they had not reached the age of twenty at the time of the crime. Princip, Čabrinović and Grabež were therefore sentenced to the maximum term of imprisonment, 20 years, Vaso Čubrilović and Popović to 16 and 13 years respectively. Ilić was sentenced to death. So were Veljko Čubrilović (Vaso's elder brother) and Miško Jovanović, both of whom had played a leading part in helping the assassins to transport the arms across Bosnia, together with two of the peasants who had been involved in this; the sentences of the latter were, however, later commuted to life imprisonment. Of the remaining accused five, found guilty of being accessories to either treason or murder, received prison sentences ranging from 3 to 10 years; the rest were acquitted.

Princip, Čabrinović and Grabež were sent to Theresienstadt in Bohemia, a fortress which for some years had been used as a military prison. All three probably had latent tuberculosis – it was widespread in Bosnia – and in Theresienstadt all three died of it, Čabrinović and Grabež in 1916, Princip slowly and painfully in April 1918. By then the countless dead on the battlefields which stretched across Europe included several hundred thousand of those people his love for whom, as he declared at the trial, had led him to decide that the Archduke must be killed – the South Slav peasantry.

*　　*　　*

Because, as Paléologue said, "the part played by reason in the government of nations is so small", the bullet with which Princip killed the Archduke proved to be the opening shot in the final round of the contest between Habsburg and Slav, the victory of the former in the first of which had established them as a ruling dynasty, and which Franz Ferdinand had warned must not take place because it would be "the end of the story". That end came in 1918 when the Monarchy disintegrated, Karl his nephew who had succeeded Franz Joseph as Emperor two years earlier, was forced into exile, and the curtain fell on the role played for over six centuries on the European stage by the House of Habsburg.

Sources

THE sources of quotations cited in the text are indicated in the Reference Notes preceding the bibliography.

Much of this book is based on printed works. Of the biographies of Franz Ferdinand, the most useful for its theme are Leopold Chlumecky's *Erzherzog Franz Ferdinands Wirken und Wollen* (Verlag für Kulturpolitik, Berlin, 1929), and Rudolf Kiszling's *Erzherzog Franz Ferdinand von Österreich-Este* (Hermann Böhlaus Nachf., 1953). Chlumecky was in close touch with the Belvedere, knowledgeable about the South Slav problem, and a personal friend of Brosch. Kiszling had access to the *Nachlass Erzherzog Franz Ferdinand*, the vast collection of papers from the Archduke's personal archives (as opposed to the archives of his Military Chancellery), which was deposited by his son, the late Duke Maximilian of Hohenberg, in the Vienna Haus-Hof- und Staatsarchiv after the Second World War, as did Professor Robert A. Kann, whose *Franz Ferdinand Studien* (Verlag für Geschichte und Politik, Vienna, 1976), an updated version of a series of articles which he wrote on the Archduke, are indispensable to any study of him. With the exception of a few drafts, this *Nachlass* does not, however, contain any letters written by Franz Ferdinand. There are a number of them in other sections of the Staatsarchiv, and his correspondence with Max Vladimir Beck is amongst the latter's papers in the Österreichisches Verwaltungsarchiv. Extracts from it are quoted by Dr Allmayer-Beck in his biography of his grandfather, *Ministerpräsident Baron Beck* (Oldenbourg Verlag, 1956).

The account of Franz Joseph, his attitude to the problems of the latter part of his reign, and to Franz Ferdinand, owes much to the documents quoted by Count Corti in *Der Alte Kaiser* (Styria Verlag, 1955), the third volume of his biography of the Emperor.

The literature on Franz Ferdinand's assassination, the events leading up to it, the inception and planning of the conspiracy, indeed every aspect of the Sarajevo affair, is immense, much of it controversial, and some of it doubtfully accurate. Many writers are partisan; eyewitness accounts of the assassination differ in detail. The would-be objective historian is therefore confronted with a labyrinth of information, through which he must grope his way as best he can. The works referring to it listed in the bibliography are confined to those which I found most useful when endeavouring to do this. Amongst them two were particularly illuminating – Vladimir Dedijer's *The Road to Sarajevo* (Macgibbon and Kee, 1967), which contains a study in depth, based on Serbo-Croat sources, of Princip, his associates and contemporaries and their mentality, and Friedrich Würthle's *Die Spur führt nach Belgrad* (Molden Verlag, 1975) in which there is an analysis, from the Austrian point of view but based on a variety of sources, of relations between Vienna and Belgrade.

The principal object of my examination of material in the Austrian State Archives was to gain an idea of how much information about feeling amongst the South Slavs in the Monarchy, the situation in Bosnia and Hercegovina, Serbian subversive propaganda and activities, was likely to have been available to Franz Ferdinand. In the course of this I found and quote from some documents in the Kriegsarchiv which, so far as I am aware, have not previously been cited.

All the biographies of the Archduke and over half the other printed works listed in the bibliography are in German. The reader unfamiliar with this language interested in learning more about developments in the Monarchy and its leading personalities during the period covered by this book will, however, find a full and eminently readable account of them in Edward Crankshaw's *The Fall of the House of Habsburg* (Penguin, 1983).

Reference Notes

Abbreviations

BN   Brosch Nachlass, Kriegsarchiv, Vienna.
FF   Franz Ferdinand.
HHSA   Haus-Hof-und Staatsarchiv, Vienna.
KA   Kriegsarchiv, Vienna.
NEFF   Nachlass Erzherzog Franz Ferdinand, Haus-Hof-und Staatsarchiv, Vienna.
MKEFF Militärkanzlei Erzherzog Franz Ferdinands, Kriegsarchiv, Vienna.
ÖUA   *Österreich-Ungarns Aussenpolitik von der Bosnischen Krise 1908 bis zum Kriegsausbruch 1914*. An eight-volume selection of documents, numbered serially, from the archives of the Ministry of Foreign Affairs, Vienna.

To reduce bulk, sources for quotations and material from printed works (other than the ÖUA), are generally confined to the author's name – under which full details of the book from which it is derived will be found in the bibliography – and the relevant page number. Quotations from Sosnosky and Kiszling are from their biographies of Franz Ferdinand unless otherwise stated.

For the same reason, details of the source of quotations from, or references to, ÖUA documents, are confined to the serial number of the document, and the number of the volume in which it appears.

Prologue: **The House of Habsburg**
The personalities of successive generations of Habsburgs are vividly described in Crankshaw, *The Habsburgs*. Accounts of the reigns of some of them are given in Kann, *A History of the Habsburg Empire, 1526-1918*; Macartney, *The Habsburg Empire, 1790-1918*; A. J. P. Taylor, *The Habsburg Monarchy, 1809-1918*. Hantsch's *Die Geschichte Österreichs* covers the whole history of the dynasty. Habsburg patronage of artists is described in Trevor-Roper, *Princes and Artists*.
page
2 'So Prague is lost': qtd. Crankshaw, *Maria Theresa*, 92.
3 19th-century restructuring of Vienna: Hennings, *Die Ringstrasse*.

Part One
Archduke Franz Ferdinand

Chapter 1: An Archduke of no interest
page
8 'A treadmill': qtd. Eisenmenger (the Archduke's personal physician), 210 f.
8 'I had to write to the Emperor': qtd. Krug von Nidda, 8 f.
10 'Learnt everything and knew nothing': qtd. Eisenmenger, 210 f.
13 'I doubt if one could enjoy oneself more in Paradise': qtd. Tissot, 136.
14 'If you are careful for a while': Rudolf to FF, 28, 11.1886. NEFF.
14 Albrecht's admonitions to FF, 10.2 & 3.8, 1887: NEFF.
16 'I do pity you': Rudolf to FF, 27.9.1888: NEFF.
15 Mayerling and its aftermath: Cassels, 195 ff.

Chapter 2: Uncle and Nephew
page
18 'Arrogance, vanity and sanctimoniousness': qtd. Corti, *Herrscher*, 449.
19 'Reins of government': qtd. Redlich, *Emperor*, 91.
20 FF's impression of German army: Kiszling, 23 f.
21 'Fortitude and courage': qtd. Cassels, 201.
21 'When you were younger': NEFF.
22 'I shall never be told officially': qtd. Kiszling, 19 f.
23 'In the entire regiment not a word of German': qtd. Glaise-Horstenau, *Weggefährte*, 476.
25 FF's request for a command in Bohemia: qtd. Glaise-Horstenau, *Weggefährte*, 425 f.
27 FF's views on future of the Monarchy: Margutti, 129 ff.

Chapter 3: Illness
Much of the material in this chapter comes from Eisenmenger, who was with Franz Ferdinand throughout his illness.
page
28 'You now have only one duty': qtd. Corti/Sokol, 197.
29 'I am sorry to be unable to send you a good report': qtd. Fugger, 118.
29 'Iron will power and moral determination': Eisenmenger, 28.
29 'It is unendurable': qtd. Eisenmenger, 33.
30 *Ausgleich*, 'the ultimate catastrophe': qtd. Kann, *FF Studien*, 116 f.
30 'These people know very well what I think about them': qtd. Corti/Sokol, 200 f.
30 'I think it incomprehensible and possible only in Hungary': qtd. Kann, *FF Studien*, 118 f.
31 FF's behaviour on arrival in Egypt: Eisenmenger, 45 ff.
31 FF's appeal to his stepmother: qtd. Sosnosky, 18.
32 'I am feeling quite miserable': qtd. Fugger, 218.
32 'Thank God, I shall be able to embrace you in a few days': qtd. Sosnosky, 18 f.
32 'It is not very pleasant to be regarded on all sides as written off': qtd. Allmayer-Beck, 32.
32 'I can rebuild houses and roads': qtd. Eisenmenger, 129.

33 'Your Imperial Highness is the man of the future': 'You understand so well': qtd. Allmayer-Beck, 18.
34 'This terrible hole, Ajaccio': qtd. Fugger, 222.
34 'In view of the manner, however, in which I am treated': qtd. Fugger, 223 f.
35 'It is very difficult to swallow some things': qtd. Fugger, 225.
35 'I too have long felt the need of discussing with you', Emperor to FF, 7.4.1897: qtd. Weissensteiner, 112.
36 'My health, thank God, is very good': qtd. Eisenmenger, 193 f.
36 Emperor's appointment of FF as an inspecting General under his direct orders: Egger, 144.

Chapter 4: Marriage
The pressure on Franz Ferdinand to give up Sophie Chotek, and the negotiations to resolve the constitutional problems raised by his determination to marry her are described in Kiszling, *Erzherzog Franz Ferdinand*, and Allmayer-Beck. Much of the account of the happiness of the Archduke's marriage and his delight in his family, is derived from descriptions by his daughter, Countess Sophie Nostitz-Rieneck, to the author of her childhood.
page
38 'Nothing has been spared me in this world': qtd. Kiszling, 60.
38 'I must now redouble my efforts to be of help to His Majesty': qtd. Fugger, 227.
38 'If some member of our family is attracted to someone'; 'It must be wonderful to marry a woman whom one loves': qtd. Kiszling, 38 f.
39 'You too urge me to marry'; FF to Countess Nora Fugger, 16.10.1898: qtd. Hennings, 273 f.
40 'Busabella': Glaise-Horstenau, *General in Zwielicht*, 336.
41 FF's fears about passing on tuberculosis to wife and children: Eisenmenger, 197.
43 Family Dinner, Jan. 1 1900: Corti/Sokol, 252.
43 'I have once again summoned up courage to approach your Majesty': HHSA, qtd. Corti/Sokol, 253 ff.
44 'A question of my life, my existence, my future': qtd. Sieghart, 53 ff.
44 'Please exert your skill to help me': qtd. Allmayer-Beck, 47.
45 'This fraught episode is now over': qtd. Allmayer-Beck, 51-52.
45 Act of renunciation: NEFF, qtd. Sosnosky, 34 f.
46 'Deeply moved, flushed and with tears in his eyes': Allmayer-Beck, 53.
47 'On the most beautiful day of our lives': qtd. Kiszling, 46 f.
47 'We shall be grateful to you until the end of our days': qtd. Sosnosky, 35 f.
47 'You have no idea, dearest Mama, how happy I am with my family': qtd. Sosnosky, 36 f.
49 FF's guardianship of nephews: Kann, *FF Studien*, 141.
49 Continuing happiness with Sophie: Funder, 189, Sosnosky, 37.
50 Worries about a recurrence of tuberculosis: Eisenmenger, 201.
51 'It's easy for you': Bardolff, 112.
51 Attitude to shooting of British aristocracy: see Ruffer.

Chapter 5: Frustration
page

53 'She was natural and modest': qtd. Corti/Sokol, 263.

53 'Your wife belongs to our family': qtd. Kiszling, 167 f.

54 FF's chiselled character: Czernin, 62 f.

54 'For seven hundred years people have been coming to us Habsburgs'; 'When I meet anyone for the first time': qtd. Krug von Nidda, 111.

55 FF's nervousness before audiences with the Emperor: Nikitsch-Boulles, 49.

56 FF's exclusion from affairs of state: Chlumecky, 222.

57 Max Vladimir Beck's summary of the problems of government in the Austrian half of the Monarchy: Allmayer-Beck, 127.

57 'The most cool-headed become ecstatic': qtd. Polzer-Hoditz, 45.

58 FF's attitude to the Hungarians: assessment of this in Kann, *FF Studien*, 100 ff.

58 Emperor to FF Feb. 1903 on problem of dealing with the Hungarians: qtd. Corti/Sokol, 281.

58 'Because of the advanced age of our King': qtd. Kiszling, 81-2.

58 'Experience has shown that in view of the attitude of the Hungarians, a policy of concession does not work': qtd. Corti/Sokol, 297.

58 'I pray God my remaining strength may not fail me': NEFF.

59 'The so-called decent Hungarian simply does not exist': qtd. Kiszling, 82 f.

59 'I must somehow learn this infernal language': KA, *Remy Nachlass*, B/1087/10.

Part Two
The Monarchy and the South Slavs

Chapter 6: The emergent South Slav threat
page

63 Cultural heritage of Slovenes, Croats and Serbs: Vucinich.

64 1868 *Ausgleich* agreement between Croatia and Hungary: Kann, *Multinational Empire*, I, 113.

66 'With the Serbs we can do a great deal': Kiszling, *Kroaten*, 78.

66 Governor of Krain's report May 1903: *Donaumonarchie und die Südslawische Frage*, 74.

66 'There is not a name in that heroic muster roll': Sir Arthur Evans, qtd. Dedijer, 259.

67 'The conception of Serb unity is rooted in revolution': qtd. Uebersberger, 5.

68 'Overblown, over made up, plump, stupid and middle class': Musulin, 11.

Chapter 7: Bosnia and Hercegovina: the world of Gavrilo Princip
The material in this chapter about Princip's childhood and school days comes from Vladimir Dedijer's *The Road to Sarajevo* (Macgibbon and Kee, 1967).
page

70 'The primitive but loyal province': qtd. Cassels, 24.

70 'If for example Bosnia becomes independent': Hübner Diary, 10.4.1876, qtd. Corti, 440 f.

71 'Our most helpful and powerful allies in Europe are the Slavs': qtd. Cowles, 37.

72 'The joining of the two provinces to the Monarchy': qtd. Mitis, 156.

72 'Worse off than many a serf in our darkest ages': Sir Arthur Evans, *Through Bosnia and Hercegovina on Foot*, 331, qtd. Dedijer, 32.

73 Memorandum from Mr Widowitch: Dedijer, 64.

74 Baernreither's impressions of Bosnia and Hercegovina in 1892: Baernreither, 12 ff.

75 'Krajina's like a blood-soaked rag': qtd. Dedijer, 26.

76 Princip's memory of the *selos*: Doboslav Jevdjević, *Sarajevski* Atintatori, Zagreb, 1934, qtd. Dedijer, 190.

76 'Serbia knows of its great mission to fulfil its destiny': qtd. Würthle, 105.

77 'Either we shall make Serbia one vast graveyard': qtd. Fay I, 114.

77 Duty of Serbs of Bosnia Hercegovina 'to identify themselves with the fate of Serbia': qtd. Conrad I, 567.

78 'Born to provoke a feeling of uneasiness': *Ogledi i pisma*, 181 f., qtd. Dedijer, 181 f.

78 'A tendency to feel the sufferings': T. Ujević, *Vladimir Gaćinović. Jugoslavenska Njiva*, Nov. 1921, qtd. Dedijer, 177.

Chapter 8: The Annexation of Bosnia and Hercegovina
page

80 'He is prepared to listen': qtd. from Brosch's appraisal of FF dated October 1913 in Chlumecky, 355 ff.

80 Brosch's expansion of FF's Military Chancellery: Egger, 147 ff.

81 'We govern Dalmatia without any real affection': Baernreither, 11.

82 'Not to give an inch': qtd. Kiszling, 91.

82 'We have not only two Parliaments, but two Emperors': Koerber, qtd. Kiszling, 96 f.

83 'I have not taken the fortress at the first assault': Conrad I, 36.

83 'A formal correct and courteous reply': Conrad I, 39.

83 'Sad turbot eyes': Nicolson, 412.

83 'Frightful characteristic of overlooking facts': Hantsch, *Berchtold*, I, 136.

85 'The relationship of Serbia to the Monarchy fundamentally depends on Russia': Musulin, 117.

85 Aehrenthal's conversation with the Czar and instructions to Berchtold: Uebersberger, 12 ff.

86 Aehrenthal's speech to the Delegations Jan. 1908: qtd. Baernreither, 36 f.

86 Ministerial conference in St Petersburg Feb. 1908: Fay I, 368 ff.

87 Conrad's memorandum on Bosnia and Hercegovina: Conrad I, 567 ff.

89 'Before anything else I want to tell you how glad I am that you have fully recovered': qtd. Conrad I, 564.

89 'I tell Your Imperial Highness everything I am permitted to': Conrad I, 157.

89 'I have no love for the Italians': qtd. Corti/Sokol, 315.

89 'For ultimately the will of the Emperor is decisive': Conrad I, 575.

90 FF's letter to Aehrenthal on the proposed annexation: qtd. Chlumecky, 98 f.

91 Aehrenthal's account to Berchtold of discussion with Izvolsky at Buchlau: Hantsch, *Berchtold*, II, 120.

Chapter 9: The Post-annexation Crisis

page

93 Slogan of the Narodna Odbrana: qtd. ÖUA VII, No. 8461.

93 'Anyone who spends one night in Sarajevo': Ivo Andrić. *Story from 1920*. Nemisi, Zagreb, 1920, qtd. Dedijer, 215.

94 Sarajevo schoolboys protest: Dedijer, 208.

94 Baernreither's impressions of situation in Bosnia summer 1908: Baernreither, 19 ff., 51.

95 Russian reactions to the annexation: Uebersberger, 31; Hantsch, *Berchtold*, I, 132.

96 'The diplomatic and military views of the situation are diametrically opposed': Bolfras, qtd. Conrad I, 121.

96 FF's conditions for assuming supreme command: Chlumecky, 329 f.

96 'Please restrain Conrad': qtd. Chlumecky, 99.

96 FF's intention of visiting Bosnia: Chlumecky, 322.

96 Situation in Bosnia: Appel, Sarajevo to Brosch 27.11.1908: BN.

97 'I am greatly concerned': qtd. Chlumecky, 182.

97 FF's letters to Brosch from St Moritz: qtd. Chlumecky, 36, 249 f., 323 f., 326.

98 'The Slav danger has revealed itself': qtd. Kann, *FF Studien*, 58 f.

99 'All eyes were fixed on the heir to the throne': Chlumecky, 106 f.

99 'I still do not believe there will be a war with Serbia': qtd. Chlumecky, 100.

99 Argument in Salzburg FF – Brosch: Funder, 393 f.

100 'If I was Commander-in-Chief': Kiszling, 137.

100 'It is better to be safe than sorry': Conrad I, 151.

Chapter 10: A Man called Stefanović

The account of the Friedjung case is based on Friedrich Würthle's *Die Spur führt nach Belgrad*, Part V (Vienna, 1978).

page

102 Summary of Stefanović information sent by Conrad to Brosch: MKEFF P/45, 1909.

102 'There are now only four days'; 'All would be well if I had at least a note': qtd. Würthle, 149 f.

103 Friedjung's opening speech: qtd. Würthle, 149 f.

104 'Stefanović is at present living undisturbed in Belgrade': qtd. Würthle, 161.

106 'Unfortunately intelligence work': Conrad I, 82 f.

106 'A bitter blow': Conrad I, 451.

107 'Hampered every form of intelligence activity': Urbanski, *Beitrag*, 83.

107 Agents' reports of Serbian plans to exploit situation in annexed provinces: MKEFF P/34 res. 1909; Pc/2 res. 1910.

108 Bombelles to FF on situation in Croatia: MKEFF Pw/1912.

Chapter 11: "The Smell of Blood"

page

110 Reports plots to assassinate Emperor during Bosnian visit: MKEFF Pc/5 and 10 res. 1910.

111 Aehrenthal's reaction to above reports: HHSA. Politisches Archiv XI. Interna. Liasse XLVII/7, Box 226.

112 Appel to Brosch, Sarajevo 5.6.1910 on Emperor's visit: BN.
113 Reports on Žerajić's attempt to assassinate the Governor of Bosnia: MKEFF MF/94 res. 1910.
114 Statements Žerajić's friends: qtd. Dedijer, 241 f.
115 'A man of action, of strength': qtd. Fay II, 97 ff.
116 'The smell of blood': Borivoje Jevtić. *Sarajevsk Attentat. Politika,* 28.6.1926, qtd. Dedijer, 238.
116 Influence Žerajić's assassination attempt on Princip: Dedijer, 249 f.

Chapter 12: "History moves too slowly: it needs a push"
(i) Serbia
page
117 'Today we too light a candle': Fay II, 96 f.
118 Military Intelligence Bureau's assessment for FF of Vasić: MKEFF Pd/8 res. 1910.
119 Vasić's account of execution of forgeries: qtd. Würthle, 165.
120 'Our diplomatic service in the Balkans requires thorough reorganisation': Baern-reither, 109.
120 Baernreither's impressions of Belgrade summer 1911: Baernreither, 120-22.
121 The Black Hand: Bogićević, 681 ff.
122 'Combining the self-effacing loyalty of the Jesuits': Schmitt, *July* 1914, 170.
122 'As all fanatics': Slobodan Jovanović. *Moji Savromenici,* 36 ff.: qtd. Dedijer, 374-75.
123 'He speaks, offers encouragement and disappears again': qtd. Remak, 36.
123 Black Hand's newspaper *Pijemont*: Dedijer, 376.

(ii) The Monarchy
page
125 Continued dispute Conrad-Aehrenthal about intelligence operations: Conrad II, 272.
126 Minister of War presses Aehrenthal for funds for intelligence: MKEFF Ms/206, 1911.
126 'It is no concern of mine': Conrad II, 177.
126 'It is high time that all concerned should be left in no doubt': MKEFF Ms/206, 1911.
127 'Losing no opportunity of behaving as if he was Commander-in-Chief': qtd. Corti/Sokol, 361.
127 'This Count and master of diplomacy': qtd. Chlumecky, 113.
127 'My policy deals with the present': Baernreither, 131.
127 'It is not surprising': MKEFF Ms/206, 1911.
127 'A typical Aehrenthal note': MKEFF Ms/206, 1911.
127 'Brosch's request to return to regimental duties 13.2.1911: NEFF, Box 11.
128 'I cannot tell you often enough how much I value': qtd. Chlumecky, 37 f.
128 'Who can guarantee': NEFF, Box. 11.
129 Bosnia and Hercegovina, 'politically unconsolidated': MKEFF Pc/5.
129 Potiorek's shortcomings: Auffenberg, 145.
129 FF advised against visiting Bosnia 1911: Funder, 446 f.

Chapter 13: South Slav imbroglio
page

131 'The tense atmosphere in the Balkans': MKEFF Pb/12 1912.

132 Princip goes to Belgrade: Dedijer, 195.

132 'In Croatia we must answer': qtd. Dedijer, 266.

132 Jukić's attempted assassination of the Governor of Croatia: Dedijer, 263, 266, 270.

133 'I only too often lacked': qtd. Kann, *FF Studien*, 213.

134 'My spare time gets less': qtd. Chlumecky, 39.

134 Unrest amongst South Slav schoolboys and students: MKEFF Ps/37, 1912.

135 'The Emperor hates the Croats': Chlumecky, 202.

135 'I believe I can best make Your Majesty aware of the situation in Croatia': MKEFF Pu/25 1912.

135 Lack of intelligence about Serbia and Russia October 1912: MKEFF 194/7 Mo/49 1912.

136 'Let these ruffians bash in one another's skulls': qtd. Kann, *FF Studien*, 216.

136 'The prestige of the Monarchy in Serbia has never been lower': MKEFF Hand-register 1913, 177.

137 'The atmosphere was like a funeral': qtd. Chlumecky, 138.

137 'I cannot describe how exasperated people here are': qtd. Würthle, 96.

138 'Even assuming that nobody hinders us'; 'If we move against Serbia': qtd. Kiszling, 193, 197.

138 Serbia 'well used to war': ÖUA VII, No. 8707.

139 'So arrogant and haughty': ÖUA VII, No. 8799.

139 'After Turkey it will be the turn of the Monarchy': ÖUA VII, No. 9005.

139 'Militarist-police regime' in Bosnia and Hercegovina summer 1913: Baernreither, 244 f.

139 Potiorek's aloofness: Appel to Brosch, Sarajevo 29.10.1913. BN, B232:11.

Part Three
Encounter at Sarajevo

Unless otherwise noted, the accounts in Chapters 14 (ii), 15 (i), 16 (ii) and 17 of the inception of the plot to murder Franz Ferdinand, the preparations for the assassination and its execution, are based on statements made by Princip and his associates during the investigation into the plot and at their trial, as recorded in *Prozess in Sarajevo*, Part VII of the *Franz Ferdinand Nachlass* in the Haus-Hof-und Staats Archiv Vienna, and Mousset, *Un Drame historique, l'Attentat de Sarajevo, documents inédites et texte intégral des sténogrammes du procès* (Paris, 1930).

Chapter 14: Decision making
(i) Vienna and Sarajevo
page

143 'That an imperial prince should at least visit Bosnia': Conrad I, 702.

143 'The power of the dynasty and the Monarchy': MKEFF 8-26.

144 FF's tentative programme for Bosnian visit: MKEFF No. 1235 43-12/2.

144 Potiorek undertakes full responsibility for security arrangements: MKEFF 15-2/5.

144 FF finally decides programme: MKEFF No. 1961.

144 Ministry of War's report on the Black Hand: Würthle, 179.

(ii) Belgrade
page
145 Reports on the Black Hand: Conrad III, 475; ÖUA VII, No. 9260.

145 'The Serbs already see themselves at the gates of Vienna': ÖUA VII No. 9360.

147 Tankosić 'an evil impression': Pharos, 24.

148 'If it is asserted': V. Bogićević. Sarajevski Atentat. Drž. Arhiv. Nrbib, Sarajevo, 1954, 348: qtd. Dedijer, 345.

149 Apis's 1917 'confession': Gavrilović, 410 f.

149 'Must be treated with reserve': Schmitt, *Comment on New Evidence*: 413 f.

149 Apis's 1915 version of role in assassination inception: Popović, 1114.

Chapter 15: The Assassins and their Target
(i)
page
156 'Convinced that I had only until June 28th to live': Cvetko Popović. *Prilog Istoryi Sarajevstrog Atenta. Politika*, April 3, 1928: qtd. Dedijer, 305.

(ii)
page
157 Criticism of FF: Redlich, Tagebuch, 180.

157 'In spite of his complex personality': Hantsch, *Berchtold*, II, 556.

157 Redl case: bibliography in Asprey.

158 FF's sanity: Eisenmenger, 247.

159 'A most charming woman': Portland, 283.

159 'One aim in life was peace': Portland, 327.

159 'I am *schwarz-gelb* and a Catholic Austrian': War with Russia 'unthinkable': Morsey, *Memoir* 16, 42 f.

159 FF at Konopischt: Clary, 156.

160 Security arrangements at Ilidže: MKEFF 15-2/5 – 47.

161 'If the heir to the throne goes to Bosnia': qtd. Corti/Sokol, 408.

162 'But of course we are going to Cividale!': Sosnosky, 197 f.

162 'We are all constantly in danger of death': Kiszling, 291.

163 Programme for Sophie's part in Bosnian visit: MKEFF 15-2/5 – 31, 39, 47.

164 'I want to thank you and your wife': qtd. Weissensteiner, 12.

164 'I am about to go with Sophie for a short visit to Bosnia': qtd. Weissensteiner, 13.

Chapter 16: On Stage in Sarajevo
(i)
page
165 'If things go on as they are with us': Baernreither, 303.

165 'You see what we are in for': Morsey, *Konopischt und Sarajevo*, 490 f.

166 Made him feel as though he was in a vault: Nikitsch-Boulles, 212.

166 FF's reunion with Sophie. At 5.20 a.m. before leaving the *Viribus Unitis* for Mostar he telegraphed her: 'Good morning. I feel splendid. Weather beautiful.

Hope you have arrived safely and not too tired. Looking forward immensely to seeing you again. All my love. Franzi': Aichelburg, *Sarajevo*, 19, photograph of original telegram in the Erzherzog Franz Ferdinand Museum, Artstetten.
167 Sophie's visit to Sarajevo: Morsey, *Konopischt und Sarajevo*, 490 f.
(ii)
page
168 FF's telegram to the Emperor at end of manoeuvres: qtd. Weissensteiner, 21.
170 Princip's behaviour on evening of June 27th: Jevtić, 684.
170 'Dear Dr Sunarić, you have been quite wrong': Funder, 483 f.

Chapter 17: Sunday June 28th 1914
page
173 'Mama and I are very well': Morsey, *Memoir*, 66.
174 'Rather strangely dressed': qtd. Sosnosky, 216 f.
176 'It is horribly particoloured': West I, 337.
176 'To hell with your speech': Kiszling, 298.
176 'Our hearts are filled with joy': MKEFF 5030/14, 15-2/5-45.
177 'An expression of pleasure': qtd. Remak, 131.
177 'We are going to have some more of this today': Harrach's statement qtd. Sosnosky, 220.
177 'Avoiding the town to punish it': Conrad IV, 20, quoting Bardolff's account of the assassination.
178 'As long as the Archduke appears in public today I am not leaving him': Morsey, *Memoir*, 70.
178 'Without looking round or listening': Morsey, *Memoir*, 71.
178 'Because I was convinced': Harrach's statement, qtd. Sosnosky, 220.
179 'As the car quickly reversed': Harrach's statement, qtd. Sosnosky, 220.
180 Assertion that FF because of injuries would have been unable to speak: Holler, 293.
180 Janaczek's view of FF's feelings for his children: Morsey, *Memoir*, 71.

Epilogue: **"The End of the Story"**
page
182 'Left at the station': Morsey, *Memoir*, 82.
183 'Only those came to Artstetten': Morsey, *Memoir*, 87.
183 'The confusion in which most people were': Clary, 158.
183 Potiorek's telegrams, 29.6.1914. ÖUA VIII, Nos. 9947, 9948.
184 'Not the deed of a single individual': ÖUA VIII, No. 9984.
185 The 'blank cheque': ÖUA VIII, No. 10058; Fay II, 214 f.
186 'Demented children': Würthle, 243.
186 'A timely reckoning with Serbia': Fay II, 224 ff.
186 'Practical control': Hantsch, *Berchtold* II, 558.
186 Difficulty of obtaining information in Belgrade: ÖUA VIII, No. 10074.
187 Information about the Black Hand in Ballhausplatz archives: Bittner, 55 ff.; ÖUA VIII, No. 10084.
188 Wiesner's report from Sarajevo, 13.7.1914: ÖUA VIII, Nos. 10252, 10253.

188 Final decision on Note to Belgrade: ÖUA VIII, Nos. 10272, 10393, 10395, 10400.
189 Czar's banquet for Poincaré; Paléologue, 6.
189 Poincaré's warning to Austrian Ambassador St Petersburg: Paléologue, 10 f.
189 Note handed to Serbian Government 23.7.1914: ÖUA VIII, No. 10526.
190 Content of Austrian Note to Serbia: ÖUA VIII, No. 10395.
190 Russian reactions to Note: Würthle, 195; ÖUA VIII, Nos. 10616, 10617, 10619.
190 'The most formidable instrument': ÖUA VIII, No. 10537.
191 Serbian reply to Note: ÖUA VIII, No. 10648.
191 'A break in diplomatic relations does not necessarily mean war': Margutti, 218.
191 25.7.1914, Berlin urges immediate attack on Serbia: ÖUA VIII, No. 10656.
192 'Willi' 'Niki' interchange of telegrams, 26.7.-30.7.1914: Russian Orange Book, 66, 83, 84, 106.
192 'This damned system of alliances': qtd. Fay I, 35.
192 'If the iron dice roll': qtd. Tuchman, 80.
193 'I am not a criminal': Mousset, 113.
193 'Do you think I am an animal?': Pharos, 158.
193 'We have loved the people': Mousset, 671.
194 'The part played by reason in the government of nations is so small': Paléologue, 40.
194 'The end of the story': FF to Brosch, 20.10.1908, qtd. Chlumecky, 99.

Selected Bibliography

Printed Sources

AICHELBURG, Wladimir. *Erzherzog Franz Ferdinand und Artstetten.* Verlag Orac, Vienna, 1983.

AICHELBURG, Wladimir. *Sarajevo, 28 Juni 1914.* Verlag Orac, Vienna, 1984.

ALBERTINI, Luigi. *The Origins of World War I.* Oxford University Press, 1952-1957, 3 vols.

ALLMAYER-BECK, Johann Christoph. *Ministerpräsident Baron Beck.* Oldenbourg Verlag, Munich, 1956.

ASPREY, Robert. *The Panther's Feast.* Putnam, New York, 1959.

AUFFENBERG-KOMAROW, Moritz. *Aus Österreichs Höhe und Niedergang.* Drei Marken Verlag, Munich, 1921.

BAEDEKER'S *Austria-Hungary.* 1911 Edn.

BAERNREITHER, Josef Maria. *Fragments of a Political Diary.* Ed. Josef Redlich. Macmillan, London, 1930.

BARDOLFF, Carl Freiherr von. *Soldat im alten Österreich.* Eugen Diederischer Verlag, Jena, 1938.

BARDOLFF, Carl Freiherr von. *Franz Ferdinand. Ein Beitrag des Wesens der am 28 Juni 1914 in Sarajevo ermordeten Thronfolgers Österreich-Ungarn. Kriegsschuldfrage,* Berlin, vol. V, 1925.

BENEDIKT, Heinrich. *Monarchie der Gegensätze.* Ullstein Verlag, Vienna, 1947.

BENEDIKT, Heinrich. *Die Monarchie des Hauses Österreich.* Oldenbourg Verlag, Munich, 1968.

BITTNER, Ludwig. *"Die Schwarze Hand". Material aus dem Wiener Pressarchiv. Berliner Monatshefte,* vol. X, 1932.

BOGIĆEVIĆ, Milan. *Die serbische Gesellschaft, "Vereinigung oder Tod" genannt die "Schwarze Hand". Kriegsschuldfrage,* vol. IV, 1926.

BRIDGE, F. R. *From Sadowa to Sarajevo. The Foreign Policy of Austria-Hungary 1866-1914.* Routledge and Kegan Paul, London and Boston, 1972.

BROOK-SHEPHERD, Gordon. *The Last Habsburg.* Weidenfeld and Nicolson, London, 1968.

CASSELS, Lavender. *Clash of Generations.* John Murray, London, 1973.

CHLUMECKY, Leopold von. *Erzherzog Franz Ferdinands Wirken und Wollen.* Verlag für Kulturpolitik, Berlin, 1929.

CLARY, Prince. *A European Past.* Weidenfeld and Nicolson, London, 1978.

CONRAD von HÖTZENDORF, Franz. *Aus Meiner Dienstzeit 1906-1918.* Rikola Verlag, Vienna, 1921-1923, 5 vols.

CORTI, Egon Caesar, Count. *Mensch und Herrscher.* Styria Verlag, Graz, Vienna, 1952.

CORTI, Egon Caesar, Count and SOKOL, Hans. *Der Alte Kaiser.* Styria Verlag, Graz, Vienna, 1955.
COWLES, Virginia. *The Russian Dagger.* Collins, London, 1969.
CRANKSHAW, Edward. *The Fall of the House of Habsburg.* Penguin, New York, 1983.
CRANKSHAW, Edward. *Maria Theresa.* Longman, London, 1969.
CRANKSHAW, Edward. *The Habsburgs.* Weidenfeld and Nicolson, London, 1971.
CZERNIN, Ottokar. *Im Weltkriege.* Ullstein Verlag, Berlin, Vienna, 1919.
DEDIJER, Vladimir. *The Road to Sarajevo.* Macgibbon and Kee, 1967.
Die Donaumonarchie und die Südslawische Frage von 1848 bis 1918. Papers read at the first meeting of Austrian and Yugoslav historians. Verlag der Österreichischen Akademie der Wissenschaft, Vienna, 1978.
DJORDJEVIĆ, Dimitrije. *The Serbs as an Integrating and Disintegrating Factor.* Austrian History Yearbook, 1967, vol. III(2).
EGGER, Rainer. *Die Militärkanzlei des Erzherzog Thronfolgers Franz Ferdinand und Ihre Archiv im Kriegsarchiv Wien. Mitteilungen des Österreichischen Kriegsarchivs,* vol. XXVIII, 1975.
EISENMENGER, Victor. *Archduke Franz Ferdinand.* Selwyn and Blount, London, 1931.
Erinnerungen an Franz Joseph I. Ed. Eduard von Steinitz. Verlag für Kulturpolitik, Berlin, 1931.
FAY, Sydney B. *The Origins of the World War.* Macmillan, New York, 1932, 2 vols.
FRANZ FERDINAND, Archduke. *Tagebuch meiner Reise um die Welt 1892–1893.* Vienna, 1896.
FUGGER, Countess Nora. *The Glory of the Habsburgs.* Harrap, London, 1932.
FUNDER, Friedrich. *Vom Gestern ins Heute.* Herold Verlag, Vienna, 1952.
GAVRILOVIĆ, Stoyan. *New Evidence on the Sarajevo Assassination.* Journal of Modern History, vol. XXVII, 1955.
GLAISE-HORSTENAU, Edmund von. *Franz Josephs Weggfährte. Das Leben des Generalstabschef Grafen Beck.* Amalthea Verlag, Zürich, Leipzig, Vienna, 1930.
GLAISE-HORSTENAU, Edmund von. *General im Zwielicht.* Memoirs ed. Dr Peter Broucek. Hermann Böhlaus Nachf., Vienna, Graz, Cologne, 1980, vol. 1.
HANTSCH, Hugo. *Die Geschichte Österreichs.* Styria Verlag, Graz, Vienna, Cologne, 2nd edn., 1955, 2 vols.
HANTSCH, Hugo. *Leopold Graf Berchtold.* Styria Verlag, Graz, Vienna, Cologne, 1968. 2 vols.
HENNINGS, Fred. *Die Ringstrasse.* Amalthea Verlag, Vienna, 1977.
HOLLER, Gerd. *Franz Ferdinand von Österreich-Este.* Verlag Carl Ueberreuter, Vienna, Heidelberg, 1982.

JEVTIĆ, Borovoje. *Weitere Ausschnitte zum Attentat von Sarajevo. Kriegs-schuldfrage*, Berlin, vol. III, 1925.

KANN, Robert A. *The Multinational Empire*. Columbia University Press, New York, 1950. 2 vols.

KANN, Robert A. *A History of the Habsburg Empire, 1526-1918*. University of California Press, 1974.

KANN, Robert A. *Franz Ferdinand Studien*. Verlag für Geschichte und Politik, Vienna, 1976.

KISZLING, Rudolf. *Erzherzog Franz Ferdinand von Österreich-Este*. Hermann Böhlaus Nachf., Graz, Cologne, 1953.

KISZLING, Rudolf. *Die Kroaten*. Hermann Böhlaus Nachf., Graz, Cologne, 1956.

KRUG von NIDDA, Roland. *Franz Ferdinand*. Amalthea Verlag, Vienna, Munich, Zürich, 1964.

MACARTNEY, C. A. *The Habsburg Empire, 1790-1918*. Weidenfeld and Nicolson, London, 1969.

MARGUTTI, Albert Freiherr von. *Vom alten Kaiser*. Leonhardt Verlag, Leipzig, Vienna, 1921.

MAY, Arthur J. *The Habsburg Monarchy, 1867-1914*. Harvard University Press, 1951.

MITIS, Oskar Freiherr von. *Das Leben des Kronprinzen Rudolf*. Insel Verlag, Leipzig, 1928.

MORSEY, Andreas Freiherr von. *Konopischt und Sarajevo. Berliner Monatshefte*, vol. XII, 1934.

MOUSSET, Albert. *Un Drame historique, l'Attentat de Sarajevo, documents inédites et texte intégral des sténogrammes du procès*. Payot, Paris, 1930.

MUSULIN, Alexander Freiherr von. *Das Haus am Ballplatz*. Verlag für Kulturpolitik, Munich, 1924.

NICOLSON, Harold. *Sir Arthur Nicolson Bt., 1st Lord Carnock*. London, 1930.

NIKITSCH-BOULLES, Paul. *Vor der Sturm*. Verlag für Kulturpolitik, Berlin, 1925.

Österreich-Ungarns Aussenpolitik von der Bosnischen Krise 1908 bis zum Kriegsausbruch 1914. Documents from the archives of the Ministry of Foreign Affairs. Ed. Ludwig Bittner, Alfred Pribam, Heinrich von Srbik and Hans Uebersberger. Österreichischer Bundesverlag für Wissenschaft, Vienna, 1930. 8 vols.

PALEOLOGUE, Maurice. *An Ambassador's Memoirs, 1914-1917*. Octogon, New York, 1971.

PHAROS, Professor. *Der Prozess gegen die Attentäter von Sarajevo*. Berlin, 1918.

POLZER-HODITZ, Arthur Graf. *The Emperor Karl*. Putnam, London, 1930.

POPOVIĆ, Cedomir A. *Das Sarajevoer Attentat und die Organisation "Vereinigung oder Tod"*. Berliner Monatshefte, vol. X, 1932.

PORTLAND, Duke of. *Memoirs*. Faber, London, 1937.

REDLICH, Josef. *Emperor Franz Joseph of Austria*. Macmillan, London, 1929.

REDLICH, Josef. *Schicksalsjahre Österreichs 1908-1919. Das politische Tagebuch Josef Redlichs*. Ed. Fritz Fellner. Verlag Hermann Böhlaus Nachf., Graz, Cologne, 1953-54. 2 vols.

REMAK, Joachim. *Sarajevo*. Weidenfeld and Nicolson, London, 1959.

RONGE, Max. *Kriegs und Industriespionage*. Amalthea Verlag, Vienna, 1930.

RUFFER, Jonathan. *The Big Shots. Edwardian Shooting Parties*. London, Debrett's Peerage.

Russian Orange Book. Documents relating to the outbreak of the war published by the Russian Foreign Office 1914. Reprinted Berlin, 1925.

SCHMITT, Bernadotte E. *The Annexation of Bosnia 1908-9.* Cambridge, 1937.

SCHMITT, Bernadotte E. *July 1914: Thirty Years After*. Journal of Modern History, vol. XVI.

SCHMITT, Bernadotte E. *Comment on New Evidence on the Sarajevo Assassination*. Journal of Modern History, vol. XXVII, 1955.

SETON-WATSON, R. W. *Sarajevo*. Hutchinson, London, 1926.

SIEGHART, Rudolf. *Die Letzte Jahrzehnte einer Grossmacht*. Ullstein Verlag, Berlin, 1932.

SITTE, Martha. *Alexander von Brosch. Dissertation*, Vienna, 1961.

SOSNOSKY, Theodor von. *Die Balkanpolitik Österreich-Ungarns seit 1866*. Deutsche Verlags Anstalt, Stuttgart, Berlin, 1913, vol. 1.

SOSNOSKY, Theodor von. *Franz Ferdinand*. Oldenbourg Verlag, Vienna, Munich, 1929.

TAYLOR, A. J. P. *The Habsburg Monarchy, 1809-1918*. Hamish Hamilton, London, new edn. 1955.

TISSOT, Victor. *Vienne et la Vie Viennoise*. E. Dentre, Paris, 23rd edn. 1881.

TREVOR-ROPER, Hugh. *Princes and Artists*. Thames and Hudson, London, 1976.

TUCHMAN, Barbara. *August 1914*. Constable, London, 1962.

UEBERSBERGER, Hans. *Österreich zwischen Russland und Serbien*. Verlag Hermann Böhlaus Nachf. Graz, Cologne, 1958.

URBANSKI von OSTRYMIECZ, August. *Mein Beitrag zur Kriegsschuldfrage. Kriegsschuldfrage*, Berlin, vol. IV, 1926.

URBANSKI von OSTRYMIECZ, August. *Conrad von Hötzendorf und die Reise des Thronfolgers nach Sarajevo. Berliner Monatshefte*, vol. VII, 1929.

VUCINICH, Wayne S. *The Serbs in Austrian History*. Austrian History Yearbook, vol. III (2), 1967.

WANDRUSZKA, Adam. *Das Haus Habsburg*. Friedrich Vorwerk Verlag, Stuttgart, 1956.

WEISSENSTEINER, Friedrich. *Franz Ferdinand*. Osterreichischer Bundes-verlag, Vienna, 1983.

WEST, Rebecca. *Black Lamb and Grey Falcon*. Viking, New York, 1943. 2 vols.

WIESNER, Friedrich von. *Der verfalschte und der echte Text des "Dokument Wiesners"*. *Kriegsschuldfrage*, Berlin, vol. III, 1925.

WÜRTHLE, Friedrich. *Die Spur führt nach Belgrad. Sarajevo 1914*. Molden Verlag, Vienna, Munich, paperback edn. 1978; first published 1975.

WÜRTHLE, Friedrich. *Dokumente zum Sarajevo Prozess. Mitteilungen des Österreichischen Staatsarchiv Ergänzungsband IX*, 1978.

Manuscript Sources

Haus-Hof-Und Staatsarchiv Vienna:
Franz Ferdinand Nachlass
Part II
Letters to Franz Ferdinand from Franz Joseph, Archduke Albrecht, and Crown Prince Rudolf.
Letters from Brosch (Box 11).
Part VII
Prozess in Sarajevo. (Statements of the accused and some other material from the investigation and trial of Princip and his associates.)

Kriegsarchiv Vienna:
Archives of Franz Ferdinand's Military Chancellery
P/45 1909, Pol/8 res. 1910 – Friedjung case and the Stefanović forgeries.
Pc/5 and 10 – Plots to assassinate Franz Joseph during his visit to Bosnia.
MF/94 res. 1910 – Reports on Žerajić's attempt to assassinate the Governor of Bosnia.
Pc/5 1910 – Situation in Bosnia and Hercegovina.
MS/206 1911 – Dispute over the procurement of intelligence between Conrad and Aehrenthal.
P/34 res. 1909, Pc/2 res. 1910, 191-196 Balkankrise – Military intelligence reports on Serbia.
MO/49 1912 – Intelligence deficiencies.
Ps/37 1912 – South Slav student unrest.
Pw/1912, Pu/25 1912 – Situation in Croatia.
43 – 19/2, 1691, 15-2/3-7, 15-2/5-37, 39, 45, 47 – Arrangements for Franz Ferdinand's visit to Bosnia.
Brosch Nachlass B232
Remy Nachlass B/1087

Morsey Memoir
Typescript in possession of Countess Nostitz-Rieneck and other members of the Archduke's family.

Index

Adriatic, 27, 84, 120, 125, 136
Aegean Sea, 71
Aehrenthal, Baron (later Count) Alois
  von, 82–6, 89, 97–8, 111, 117,
  124–5, 127, 133, 135–6;
  and the annexation of Bosnia
  Hercegovina, 88–91, 94–5,
  99–100, 108;
  disagreements with Conrad, 88, 95,
  99–100, 105–8, 125–6;
  and the Friedjung libel case, 101–7
Agram, Croatia, 64–5;
  treason trial in, 97, 101–2, 104–5,
  107
Albania, 72, 125, 136–7
Albrecht, Archduke, 14–15, 20, 23
Alexander II, Czar of Russia, 71
Alexander III, Czar of Russia, 24
Andrassy, Count Julius, 71, 73
Apis, see Dragutin Dimitrijević
Appel, General Michael von (quoted),
  96–7, 112, 139–40
Appel Quay, Sarajevo, 169, 173,
  178–9
Army and navy of the Monarchy, 24,
  27, 58–9, 63, 84, 124–5, 129, 133
Artstetten, 8, 12, 182–3
Asquith, Herbert, 159
Attems, Count, 134–5
Auffenberg, General Moritz von, 125,
  129
Ausgleich, the, 10, 18–19, 30, 82, 86
Austria, general, 1–2, 9;
  nationality problems in, 57–9, 63–5
Austrian intelligence and counter-
  espionage operations, 105–111,
  118, 125–7, 129, 135–8, 157–8,
  161–2, 187
Austro-German alliance, 1, 18, 94,
  184–6, 188, 191
Austro-Hungarian Compromise
  (1867), see Ausgleich.
Austro-Russian relations, 71, 85–6,
  90–1, 95, 107, 135, 188–9, 191

Austro-Serbian relations,
  before annexation of Bosnia
  Hercegovina, 76–7, 81, 84–6;
  after annexation, 92–5, 99–100,
  105–8, 111, 117–21, 127, 136–9,
  145;
  after Franz Ferdinand's
  assassination, 183–4, 186–92;
  ultimatum to Serbia, 188–91;
  outbreak of war, 191

Baernreither, Josef (quoted), 73–5, 81,
  94, 119–21, 139, 165
Bakunin, Mikhail Alexandrovitch, 78
Balkan War 1912–13, 135–8
Bardolff, Colonel Karl, 127–8, 133–6,
  144, 158, 160–1, 163, 165, 171,
  173, 175, 178
Beck-Rzikowsky, Feldzeugmeister,
  Count Friedrich 25, 56, 83–4
Beck, Max Vladimir, 9–10, 24, 26,
  32–4, 38, 42–7, 50–1, 57–8, 82
Becker, Dr von, 31
Belgrade, development of as Serbian
  capital, 68, 120
Belvedere Palace, see Franz
  Ferdinand, Archduke
Berchtold, Count Leopold von, 83, 85,
  91, 133, 136, 157–8, 162, 164;
  action after assassination, 183–8
Berlin, Congress and Treaty of,
  (1878), 72, 90, 94
Bethmann-Hollweg, Theobald von,
  184, 192
Bilinski, Leon von, 160–2
Bismarck-Schönhausen, Prince Otto
  von, 72
Black Hand, the, 121–24, 132–3,
  144–5, 187
  see also Pijemont
Blühnbach, 46
Bohemia, 1, 2, 25–7, 93
Bolfras, Baron Arthur, 36, 56, 95–6

Bombelles, Count Marko, 108
Boos-Waldeck, Count Alexander, 175
Bosna Brod, Bosnia, 111, 114
Bosnia and Hercegovina, 70, 72, 84,
  131;
  Austrian occupation of, 1878–1908,
  72–8;
  Serbian propaganda and subversive
  activities in, 76–7, 87–8, 121,
  137, 140;
  annexation of, 1908, 88–91, 93–4;
  situation in after annexation, 96–7,
  108, 110, 114–116, 128–9, 131,
  137–8, 139–40
Brioni, 46
Brosch von Aarenau, Major
  Alexander, 79–80, 82, 96, 97, 99,
  102–3, 108, 112, 127–9, 133, 139
Bucharest, Peace of, 138
Buchlau Castle, 91, 95
Budweis, 25–6
Bulgaria, 70–2, 98, 135, 138
Bülow, Prince Heinrich von, 94

Čabrinović, Nedeljko, 145–6
  joins plot against Archduke, 146–9;
  journey Belgrade-Sarajevo, 150–1,
  153–4, 160–1;
  waits in Sarajevo, 154–6, 161,
  169–70;
  throws bomb, 172–5;
  statements at investigation and
  trial, 183, 185–6, 193;
  imprisonment and death, 193–4
Capuchins, Church of the, (Vienna),
  16, 182
Carol, King of Roumania, 84–5
Chernishevksy, Nikolai Gavrilovitch,
  78
Chlumetz Castle, inherited by Franz
  Ferdinand, 15
Chotek von Chotkowa und Wognin,
  Countess Sophie, see Sophie,

Princess, later Duchess, of
Hohenberg
Ciganović, Milan, 147–8, 150, 185–6,
188, 190
Cilli, 65
Clary, Prince *(quoted)*, 159–60, 183
Collas, Count Carlo, 161
Conrad von Hötzendorf, Franz, 82–5,
89, 97, 102, 124, 127, 137–8,
157–8, 162, 167–8;
and Bosnia Hercegovina, 87–8, 95,
143;
and Serbia, 84–5, 95–6, 99–100,
126, 137, 183, 185;
disagreements of with Aehrenthal,
88, 95, 99–100, 105–6, 108,
125–6, 136;
after assassination, 183–5, 188, 191
Croatia and the Croats, 63–65;
discontent in, 66, 68–9, 81, 87, 97,
108–9, 128, 131–2, 135, 137;
schoolboys strike 1912, 131–2, 134;
see also Friedjung libel case, South
Slavs, attempts to assassinate
Governor, 132, 140;
Čubrilović, Vaso, 154–5, 169, 170,
173–4, 193
Čubrilović, Veljko, 151–3, 193
Curzon, Lord, 159
Cuvaj, Baron Slavko von, 131, 133,
135, 140
Cvitas, Wilhelm, 104
Czechs, the, 21, 98;
demonstrate in favour of Serbia
1908, 97

Dalmatia, 63, 70–1, 74–5, 81, 135;
discontent in, 66, 68, 81;
schoolboys' unrest in, 131, 134–5;
See also South Slavs
Degenfeld, Count, 8
Disraeli, Benjamin, 71
Doboj, Bosnia, 155
Dragutin Dimitrijević, Colonel, alias
Apis, 122–23, 132–3, 145, 148
Dreikaiserbund, the, 71
Drina, river, 96–7, 150–1

Eckartsau, 26, 33
Eisenmenger, Dr Victor, 28–9, 31–4,
36, 38, 41, 50, 158
Elisabeth, Empress, 20–1, 25, 32–3,
35, 38–9, 48
Enns, 12, 14
Essad Effendi, 96
Eugen, Archduke, 31
Eugen of Savoy, Prince, 46

Fehim Čurčić Effendi, 173–4, 176–7
Ferdinand I, Emperor of Austria, 10
Ferdinand II, Emperor of Austria, 15,
46
Ferdinand, King of Bulgaria, 99

Ferdinand Karl, Archduke, (Franz
Ferdinand's brother), 42
Fiume, 27;
declaration at, 1905, 68–9
Forgách, Count Johann, 101–2,
104–5, 111, 117–20
France, 1, 18, 188–90
Franz Ferdinand, Archduke, 3, 12–13,
15–17, 25, 50, 79–80, 89–90,
98–9, 112, 116, 133–4, 157–60,
164;
birth and upbringing, 7–11;
character, 8–9, 22–4, 33, 36, 51–2,
54–5, 79–80, 82, 99, 127, 134,
157–60, 162–3, 177;
and the army and navy, 12, 15,
22–7, 29, 36–7, 56, 58, 63,
79–80, 83, 88–9, 96–100, 124–5,
127, 133, 136–8, 143, 158,
167–8;
and Crown Prince Rudolf, 13–14,
16, 48;
Archduke Albrecht's admonitions
to, 14–15, 20;
relations of with Emperor Franz
Joseph, 12, 20–2, 24–5, 27, 33,
35–8, 40–8, 55–9, 82–3, 96, 125,
137, 157;
attitude towards the Hungarians,
22–4, 26–7, 30–1, 58–9, 81–2,
97–9, 108–9, 124, 127–8, 135;
view of Russia, 24, 33, 35, 82, 138,
159, 186;
illness, 25, 28–36;
marriage, 38–50;
and the South Slavs and Serbia, 79,
81–2, 90, 96–8, 102–3, 108, 118,
128, 134–9, 186;
opposition to war, 88–9, 96, 99,
126, 136, 138, 159, 186, 192, 194;
visit to Bosnia of, 140, 143–4, 146,
148–9, 155–7, 160–171;
plot to assassinate him, 146–9,
168–70, 173–4;
assassination of, 173–180;
funeral, 181–3
Franz Joseph I, Emperor of Austria,
1, 7, 9, 16, 20–1, 34, 38, 56, 124,
157, 160;
attitude to the Imperial family, 7,
10–14, 20;
as ruler and statesman, 9–10,
18–21, 55, 58–9, 63–4, 70–2, 82,
88–9, 91, 95, 100, 105–6, 109,
124–6, 137;
and Franz Ferdinand, 12, 20–2,
24–5, 27, 33, 35–7, 40–7, 53,
55–6, 58–9, 82–3, 89, 125, 137,
143, 163;
and the South Slavs, 81, 135;
visit to Bosnia, 1910, 110–12,
114–15;
after Franz Ferdinand's
assassination, 181–2, 184–6, 188,
191, 194

Franz Joseph Strasse, Sarajevo, 176,
178–9
Franz, Otto, 102
Friedjung libel case, 101–4;
repercussions of, 105, 107, 117–19,
139, 186, 189, 190
Friedrich, Archduke, 39, 42
Funder, Dr Friedrich, 102

Gaćinović, Vladimir, 78, 115–16, 123,
139
Galicia, 135–6, 192
Gellinek, Colonel Otto, 102, 145
George V, King, 159
Gerde, Dr Edmund, 161, 168, 173–4,
177–8
Giesl, Baron Vladimir, 188–91
Goluchowski, Count Agenor, 33–5, 42
Grabež, Trifko, 145–6;
joins plot to kill Archduke, 147–9;
transports weapons over the
frontier, 150–4, 160–1;
waits near Sarajevo, 154–6, 169,
170;
fails to shoot, 172, 174–6, 178;
statements of at investigation and
trial, 185–6, 193;
imprisonment and death, 193–4
Grahovo valley, Bosnia, 75, 78
Grbić, Sergeant, 150–1
Grdjić, Vasily, 114
Great War, outbreak of, 191–2
Greece, 125, 135, 138
Grey, Sir Edward, 159, 190
Guslas, 66, 77

Habsburg *Familien Fond*, 11
Habsburg Family Law, 10–11
Habsburg, House of, 1–3, 194
Habsburg, Count Rudolf, 1
Habsburgs, family traits of, 2, 8, 54,
96
Hadžiće, Bosnia, 138, 154
Harrach, Count Franz, 173, 175,
177–80, 193
Hartwig, Nikolaj, 107, 139
Hofball, 12–13
Hohenberg, Prince Ernst, (Franz
Ferdinand's son), 47–8, 182–3
Hohenberg, Prince Max, later Duke
of, (Franz Ferdinand's son)
47–8, 182–3
Hohenberg, Princess Sophie, later
Duchess of, wife of Franz
Ferdinand;
see Sophie, Princess, later Duchess,
of Hohenberg
Hohenberg, Princess Sophie, later
Countess Nostitz (Franz
Ferdinand's daughter), 47–8,
163, 173, 182–3
Hungary and the Hungarians, 1, 10,
18–19, 57–9, 63, 97, 124;

treatment of minority nationalities, 57, 64–6, 81, 85, 97, 108

Ilić, Danilo, 78, 116, 139;
 role in Franz Ferdinand's assassination, 147, 154–6, 168–70, 174;
 statements of at investigation, 185–6;
 sentence, 193
Ilić, Stoja, (Danilo's mother), 78
Ilidže spa, Bosnia, 112, 144, 155, 160, 163, 166–70, 173, 178
Isabella, Archduchess, 39–42
Italy, 1, 9, 84–5, 107, 125, 191
Izvolsky, Alexander, 86, 90, 92, 95, 100

Janaczek, Franz, 29, 33–4, 163, 165, 180
Jovanović, Miško, 148, 152–3, 155, 186, 193
"Jugoslavia" (South Slav youth organisation), 134
Jukić, Luka, 132–4

Kaiserin Elisabeth, (cruiser), 25
Kalláy, Count Benjamin von, 73–4
Karadjordjević Petar, King of Serbia, 68, 121
Karl, Archduke, (Franz Ferdinand's nephew), 43, 49, 50, 163, 182–3, 194
Karl Ludwig, Archduke (Franz Ferdinand's father), 7–11, 15–16, 25, 32–3
Kerović, Mitar, 152
Kinsky, Prince, 2
Klopp, Onno, 9, 16
Koerber, Dr Ernst von, 42, 44
Königgrätz, battle of, 9–10, 18, 20
Konopischt Castle, 15;
 Franz Ferdinand's restoration of, 15–16, 32–3, 36, 49, 51;
 garden, 49;
 Wilhelm II's visit June 1914, 164
Kosovo, battle of, 64, 66, 144
Kossuth, Ludwig, 9
Krain, 66
Krajina, Bosnia, 75
Kropotkin, Prince Pyotr Alexeyevich, 78, 113, 174

Lanjus, Countess Wilma, 166, 175
Lansdowne, Lord, 25
Lazar, Tsar of Serbia, 64, 67
Leopold I, Emperor of Austria, 2
Lölling, 33
Louis XIV, King of France, 2
Loyka, 179
Loznica, Serbia, 150

Macedonia, 72, 120, 133, 136–8
Magyar Hirlap, (Budapest), 30
Magyars, see Hungary and the Hungarians
Mandić, 96
Margarethe, Archduchess, (Franz Ferdinand's sister), 25
Margutti, Albert von, 27
Maria Christina, Archduchess, 39
Maria Josefa, Archduchess, 15, 24
Maria Theresa, Empress, 2, 7, 10, 51
Maria Theresia, Archduchess, (Franz Ferdinand's stepmother), 7, 31–2, 34, 42–3, 46–7, 182–3
Marković, Professor Božidar, 103
Marković, Svetozar, 67
Marschall, Gottfried, 9, 42, 49
Masaryk, Thomas Garrigue, 101–2, 105, 117–19
Mašin, Draga, 68
Mayerling, 16, 21, 22
Mazzini, Giuseppe, 78
Mehmetbasić, Muhamed, 154, 169, 170, 173–4, 192
Mensdorff, Count Albert, 158
Metković, Hercegovina, 163
Merizzi, Colonel Erik, 171, 175, 178
Miljačka river, Sarajevo, 113, 169, 173–74
Milović, Jakov, 151–2
Miramar, 46, 157
Modena Este, Duke of, 15, 50
Moltke, General Helmuth von, 184
Montenegro, 68, 70, 125–6, 135, 136
Montenuovo, Prince Alfred, 181–3
Morsey, Baron Andreas von (quoted), 159–60, 165–7, 173, 175, 177–8, 180, 183
Mostar, Hercegovina, 74, 112–15, 139, 163, 166
Musulin, Baron Alexander von, (quoted), 68, 85

Narodna Odbrana, 92–3, 121–3, 147, 151, 153, 187, 189
Neue Freie Presse (Vienna), 101
Nicholas, King of Montenegro, 68
Nicholas II, Czar of Russia, 33, 85, 92, 95, 188–9, 192
"Niki", see Nicholas II
Nostitz, Countess, see Hohenberg, Princess Sophie, (Franz Ferdinand's daughter)
Novi Bazar, Sanjak of, 72, 86–7

Obilić, Miloš, 66
Obrenović, Alexander, King of Serbia, 68, 121
Ödenburg, 22–6
Octacbina, (Banjaluka), 87
Otranto, Straits of, 125
Otto, Archduke, (Franz Ferdinand's

brother), 8, 13, 24, 32, 33–5, 42, 44, 49
Ottomans, see Turkey and the Turks

Paar, Count Eduard, 56
Paču, 189–90
Pale, Bosnia, 154, 156, 169
Paléologue, Maurice (quoted), 189, 194
Pašić, Nikola, 67–8, 76, 92, 101, 104, 136, 186, 189–91
Persenbeug, 8
Peter the Great, Czar of Russia, 71
Pfeffer, Leon, 185–87, 192
Piedmont, 78
Pijemont, (Belgrade), 123, 132, 139
 see Black Hand
Plönnies, Colonel Hermann von, 15
Poincaré, Raymond, 188–9
Politika, (Belgrade), 117–18
Popović, Cedomir (quoted), 149
Popović, Cvetko, 154–6, 169, 170, 174
Popović, Captain Rade, 148, 150
Portland, Duke and Duchess of, 158–9
Potiorek, Feldzeugmeister Oskar, 129, 131, 134–5, 139–40, 146, 154;
 and Franz Ferdinand's visit to Bosnia, 129, 140, 143–44, 160–61, 163, 166–8, 170–1, 173, 176–79;
 after the assassination, 183, 186–7, 193
Priboj, Bosnia, 151–2
Princip, Gavrilo;
 family background and education, 75–6, 78, 116, 131–2;
 influences on, 76, 78, 116, 131–2, 138–9;
 visits to Serbia, 131–3, 138, 145–6;
 plots in Belgrade to kill Franz Ferdinand, 146–9;
 transports weapons over the frontier, 150–54, 160
 waits in Sarajevo, 154–7, 161, 168–71;
 shoots Franz Ferdinand and Sophie, 172–3, 175–6, 178–80;
 statements of at investigation and trial, 183, 185–6, 193;
 imprisonment and death, 193–4
Princip, Jovo, (Gavrilo's brother), 77–8
Princip, Nana, (Gavrilo's mother), 75
Princip, Petar, (Gavrilo's father), 75, 77–8
Prosvjeta, 77
Prvanović, Captain Jovan, 150

Redl, Colonel Alfred, 157–8
Reichspost, (Vienna), 102
Reichstadt Castle, 46
Ringstrasse, Vienna, 3, 7
Ripon, Lord, 51

Roberts, Lord, 159
Roumania, 72, 84–5, 138
Rudolf, Crown Prince, 11, 13–14, 16, 18, 20–1, 36, 38, 48, 72
Rumerskirch, Baron Carl, 165, 173, 175
Russia, 71–2, 85–7, 92, 95, 99–100, 120, 131, 135–6, 188–9, 191; see also Austro-Russian relations

Šabac, Serbia, 148, 150
Salonica, 86
San Stefano, Peace of, 71–2
Sarajevo, appearance and layout of, 72, 74, 113, 174, 176, 178–9; preparations in for Franz Ferdinand's visit, 160–1, 168–9; see also France Ferdinand, Archduke, visit to Bosnia, assassination of
Save river, 148
Sazonov, Sergei, 190, 192
Schillers delicatessen shop, Sarajevo, 176, 179
Schönbrunn Palace, 51, 124
Schönaich, Feldzeugmeister Franz, 99, 124–5
Schwarzenberg, Prince Karl, 30
Semiz tavern, Sarajevo, 170
Serbia, 67–8, 70, 85, 135, 136–9, 166; past history of, 64, 66–7; and the South Slavs, 66–70, 76–8, 81, 107–8, 120–1, 130, 137, 140; reactions in to annexation of Bosnia Hercegovina, 92–3, 108, 120 see also Serbs, Slovenski Jug, Narodna Odbrana, Black Hand, Austro-Serbian relations
Serbs, 63–7, 70, 139, 145–6; see also South Slavs
Sieghart, Rudolf, 44
Slijepčević, Pero, 114–15
Slovenes, 63–7; see also South Slavs
Slovenski Jug, 68, 101–4, 111, 118
Solferino, battle of, 9–10, 18
Sophie, Princess later Duchess of Hohenberg, wife of Franz Ferdinand, 39–40, 49–50, 53, 97–8, 112, 128, 133, 144, 158–9, 164;

marriage to Franz Ferdinand, 39–50; accompanies husband to Bosnia, 163–8, 170; assassination of, 173, 175–180, 193; funeral, 181–3
Sopron, see Ödenburg
South Slavs, 71, 86, 107–9, 130, 135, 137; schoolboys and students demonstrations, 131, 133 see also Croatia, Slovenes, Serbs, Bosnia and Hercegovina, Serbia
Spalajković, Dr Miroslav, 101, 104, 117
Srboban, Chicago 162
Srpska Riječ, (Sarajevo), 74, 114
Starović, Jovan, 115
Stefanović, Milan, 101–6, 109, 117–19 see also Vladimir Sergian Vasić
Sunarić, Dr Josif, 129, 161, 170
Supilo, Franjo, 101
Swietochowski, Viktor, 102, 104, 118–19
Szápáry, Count Friedrich, 189–90
Szécsen, Count Nikolaus, 30
Szögyeny-Marich, Count Ladislaus, 184–5, 191

Taafe, Count, 21
Tankosić, Major Vojin, 93, 133, 138, 147–9, 185–6, 188, 190
Tarčin, Bosnia, 167
Theresienstadt prison, 194
Three Emperor's League, see Dreikaiserbund
Thun-Hohenstein, Count Jaroslav, 40
Tirpitz, Admiral von, 185
Tisza, Count Stephan, 183–4, 186
Trieste, 25, 27, 163
Triple Alliance, the, 84
Triple Entente, 95
Trotsky, Leon (quoted), 78
Turkey and the Turks, 1, 10, 64, 66–7, 70–2, 86, 88, 125, 131, 138; and Bosnia Hercegovina, 70, 72–3, 88
Tuzla, Bosnia, 116, 148, 150–3, 155

Urbanski von Ostrymiecz, Baron August, 107

Valerie, Archduchess, 33
Varešanin, Feldzeugmeister Marijan, 90, 110, 112–14, 117, 129
Vasić, Vladimir Sergian, 117–19 see also Stefanović, Milan
Vetsera, Mary, 16
Victoria, Queen, 36, 71
Vidović, Vaso, 73
Vienna, 19th century restructuring of, 3; reaction in after Franz Ferdinand's assassination, 181–3, 186, 189
Vienna, Court of, 12–13
Viribus Unitis (battleship), 163, 181
Vivodan, 66
Vlajnić patisserie, Sarajevo, 170

Waldersee, General Count von, 184
Wales, Prince of, (later King Edward VII), 51
Wallenstein, 15
Walsingham, Lord, 51
Wartholz, Villa, 8
Widerhofer, Dr Hermann, 28
Widowitch, Mr, 73
Wiesner, Sektionsrat Friedrich von, 187–8
Wilhelm I, Emperor of Germany, 18
Wilhelm II, Emperor of Germany, 16, 20, 98–9, 158, 164, 192; reactions after Franz Ferdinand's assassination, 184–5
"Willi', see Wilhelm II

Zadar, see Zara
Zagreb, see Agram
Zara, Dalmatia, 68–9
Žerajić, Bogdan, 113–17, 123, 132–3
Zhelyabov (quoted), 124
Zimmermann, Arthur (quoted), 192
Zvornik, Bosnia, 151